Mary Vowell Adams:
RELUCTANT PIONEER

IN MEMORY
OF
ELSIE ALLEN
2000

An emigrant camp on the Overland Trail. — OREGON HISTORICAL SOCIETY

Mary
Vowell
Adams:

RELUCTANT PIONEER

One Woman, Without Rights, Caught in
the Wave of an Historic Migration

by

Beatrice L. Bliss

MEREDITH L. BLISS
FOREST GROVE, OREGON

Acknowledgments

Grateful acknowledgment is due the following for their help in re-creating the story of Mary Vowell Adams: Pauline Lockhart McMahon, Constance French Hodder, Margaret Legge Griffith (Mrs. Wallace), Jennette Meredith Brown (Mrs. Rodney), Oregon State Archivist David Duniway, Alice Rowe (Mrs. Clifford), Neta W. Barr (Mrs. Charles), J. Willard Church, Leonard Wiley, John R. Leach, Columbia River Pilots President D. E. Hughes, CLEAR-WATER RECORD Editor Donald L. Russell, Ox-trainer John Treadwell and his assistants on WAY WEST location, Auditor for Washington County, Iowa, Walter W. Schroeder, Auditor for Van Buren County, Iowa, Clyde J. Roberts, Mrs. M. C. Wheelwright, Mrs. V.W. Hamner, Beverly Weatherly, Daniel Burroughs, the staff of the Oregon Historical Society, and all the kind people in churches, schools, and museums from Iowa to Oregon who answered my questing letters. To Pacific University I am indebted for the use of microfilm and their microfilm reader. To Emma Jane Brattain's procuring a copy for me of a list of the members of the wagon train to which both the Brattains and the Adamses belonged at the beginning of their long trek to Oregon. Her friendship, and that of many others was a special bonus for writing *Reluctant Pioneer*. Of the "others," there were those who frequently decked Mary's grave with flowers. Finally, to son Bill, 1941 - 1974.

© Copyright 1972, 1992 by Beatrice L. Bliss
Second edition, September, 1992
Printed in the United States of America
All rights reserved.

Library of Congress Catalog Card No. 70-188685
ISBN 09622738-4-8

MEREDITH L. BLISS
P.O. BOX 492
FOREST GROVE, OR 97116-0492

Table of Contents

To My Husband

I

In Dreams Begun

MARY SCOWLED AT THE CLOUD boiling ominously in the already gray sky of February. Her hands gripped the edge of the steps on which she sat.

"Why can't they just go on to Oregon without trying to take the whole country with them?" The cloud, looming there in her sky, was just like the Reverend Delazon Smith. Its shadowy rolling edges even looked to her the way his brown hair brushed loosely back from his imperious face. She had once thought that face handsome!

Back in July he had been appointed to their little church in southern Iowa. What a stir he had made! A former ambassador to some country in South America, a newspaper editor, now converted to Methodism. Those deep-set, fierce eyes, under striking brows, the luxuriant roll of dark hair, the big words, the impassioned gestures — all made Delazon Smith a commanding figure among them.

Even before Thanksgiving, he had started calling Oregon Emigration meetings as if they were part of his Conference assignment. Duty, Opportunity — he used both words as slogans to stir the men. And now they were drawing up wagon train rules and electing company officers.

Mary braced herself against the step. As if she didn't know already how little her resistance would accomplish!

Charles had said, "I am the one who must decide. Reverend Smith has laid it all out clear. It's the Promised Land. We must go and save Oregon for our country. I know it won't be easy for you — or any of us, for that matter — but God is on our side.

"You just do your part as helpmate and I'll get us through."

But Charles couldn't go unless he sold the farm. It would take all he could hope to get for it to stock a wagon for their family of seven, and the baby to be born somewhere along the trail.

"O God," she whispered, "please let me stay."

Over yonder lay the fields which Charles had cleared of hazelbrush. The oxen had earned their keep on that job. The fencerails, all of them, Charles had split from trees felled in the clearing, and the house, too, was off the place, with enough hickory and ash left standing for all the yokes and wagons they would ever need here.

Past the road where sumac had flamed last fall, springtime would bring Dutchman's Breeches and Bluebells and the Dog-toothed Violets that Mary had loved to gather — yes, and Jack-in-the-Pulpits, and Buttercups to hold under the children's chins. "Let's see whether you like butter," she would ask, and then point to the yellow reflection on the kissable throat.

It would be fun to picnic along the Skunk River, where Indian arrowheads were so thick they might have been seeded. The big ones, large enough to lie across the palm of your hand, had a lovely feel along the broad, smooth side.

If only at dusk this summer she could sit on this step and watch the children catch fireflies. "God, please ... please."

Mary looked up, almost hoping to see a sign or hear a voice. But there was only the billowing black cloud, chilling the air and reminding her to get back to the bedroom and finish sorting out the baby things.

"All right for you, God." The hand in her apron pocket clenched, touching the note that she had found in the little sweater this afternoon.

At first it had looked strange to her and then she had stood there turning it over in her hand as she tried to place it in her mind. Remembering, she had found herself blushing.

There they were, the words that had made her tuck the note away in the wrappings of that little gift Nancy had made for her before John Henry was born. "So Charles did tame you," the note taunted.

The remembered sound of Nancy's chuckle had echoed through the silent room as Mary visioned those black-fringed hazel eyes, measuring her with infuriating candor. And the hair, a mass of sunny ringlets that always made Mary more than ever aware of the thin, drab wispiness of her own.

Mary had tried not to be jealous — had tried not to care.

"I guess twelve years of marriage and child-bearing would just about take the spirit out of anybody!" she found herself talking back at Nancy, with a toss of her head.

Heavens, how long had it been? "I guess they wouldn't call me 'Spunky' any more."

She backed away from the bureau and scanned herself from across the room.

She was still fairly small and neat — considering. She never had had any color. The faded brown hair, parted in the middle, was drawn up in braids around the crown of her head. The added height helped balance the squaring effect of her deep-set eyes under the wide brow, and the firm, short little jaw. Mary pulled herself up a bit, realizing as she did so that anyone who looked twice would know that she was pregnant.

Nancy hadn't been the only one who had taunted her with Charles's boast that he would tame her. Just about everyone had plagued her with it all that summer, mostly for the fun of seeing her flare up.

By August baiting her had lost out to love and romance. Charles's high-handed way that had at first invoked resistance also attracted. They married September 13, 1838, in Greencastle, Indiana — Charles Adams of Kentucky and Mary Vowell of Tennessee.

Mary came back to the mirror to study herself at close range. A serious, intent face looked back attentively.

"Charles is a good husband and a good father. Lots of men are about as paternal as tomcats. Why can't you accept what you must?"

"I'd like to settle down long enough for the vines to come up over the porch. I'd like to fix what we have and be able to enjoy it for a while. I want to have this baby in a civilized place. I want Millie and Margaret and Mamie and Pauline to have music lessons. I don't want to emigrate to Oregon."

"Are you sure that is all?"

"That will do. I don't want to cast reflections on ...."

Was Nancy still in Greencastle? Would she be there when

just about everyone was moving West?

Mary shivered, remembering the nightmares she had been having.

Once she had been captured and bound with leather thongs that cut her wrists. Indian braves danced about her making horrible cries and menacing gestures. The biggest and fiercest danced closer and closer, brandishing a huge arrowhead as if to spear her with it. He came so close she could see the streaks of brown in the *chert*, flintrock. Finally, with a loud cry, he held it over her head. She writhed in agony of fear as she watched his hand descending ....

Once they were fording a river and she suddenly realized that they were caught in quicksand. With evil, sucking noises the water came up, up ....

Another night she found herself alone in the midst of a vast plain. Coming toward her was an onrushing herd of buffalo whose hoofbeats shook the earth. With their great heads lowered, they came straight toward her, their malevolent eyes fixed, their nostrils dilated ....

Once the wagon started to tip. As she reached out to hold back the children she found herself pitched over a high, rocky cliff, falling ....

After these dreams she could open her eyes or put out her hand to feel Charles beside her and so push away the nightmare.

But one dream was different. There was nothing really horrible about it, and yet nothing would dispel the sense of reality.

There stood Charles, halfway up the aisle after class meeting, shaking hands with a precision that suggested he might be counting the number of shakes he gave each one.

Mary was standing back where she could keep an eye on Mamie, playing in the sandtable by the wall, and on Margaret, silently "playing" the organ, her feet dangling high above the pedals.

With Charles were the Carters and others. Little Father Light, at the end of the near row, stood with his thin gray face lifted toward Charles so that when he could get a word in edgewise his little gray goatee jiggled as it jutted over his Adam's apple. The goatee must have been intended to give it decent cover.

Embarrassed by the exposure, Mary started to look away.

Then she heard Mrs. Carter say it, not loudly, but distinctly, "Dear Charles."

Surely the whole group heard, yet they gave no sign — no pause in the conversation, no change of expression.

She just had to head Mrs. Carter off before she said something that the others could not miss hearing or understanding. Father Light was standing directly in her way, with his hand on the back of the seat in front of him, yet somehow she did not disturb him as she quickly slipped herself between Charles and Mrs. Carter.

Taking a firm stance she turned to Mrs. Carter and in a tone that was as light but firm as she could manage, she said, "Sister Carter, don't forget that Charles is my husband."

Mrs. Carter couldn't — or wouldn't — hear her. She kept right on talking to the others. Charles had not noticed her either.

She plucked his sleeve.

He ignored her.

She spoke again.

They all ignored her. In fact, they acted as if she were not there at all.

But of course it was just a dream. Illogical. But unshakable, too.

Could it be some kind of mystical revelation. like Joseph's dream? Or was it petty jealousy, surfacing in sleep?

She shivered again. The cloud no longer looked like anything but a big rain cloud. Its shadow lay over her whole garden plot.

The teakettle was spluttering in the kitchen. She must hurry and scald out the chamber pots if they were to dry before she had to take them in.

She headed for the warm kitchen, letting the screen door come against her heel as she went in.

"Yes," she told herself, picking up the hot pad and moving the dancing kettle off the heat, "the dream is a sign, all right — of my own pettiness. I'm ashamed of myself, begrudging Charles a little appreciation from Sister Carter. She hasn't heard his class meeting stories as many times as I have."

She took a firm grip on the kettle handle and returned to the

5

yard with the swaying, steaming load. There she braced herself beside the four white porcelain chamber pots, gingerly tipped the kettle, circled a thin stream of hot water around the inside of each, and finally emptied the last drops upon the upturned lids. She had laid them on the planks that led to the outhouse. Then she emptied each steaming chamber to let dry.

With all the fuss over Charles as class leader, with all his duties of visiting the membership, with all that importance, she had not once been consciously jealous, she consoled herself.

Tears were running down her cheeks now. What a state she had worked herself into, and there was a wagon stopping out front. It was idiotic, crying over a silly dream. She touched her eyes with the edge of her apron and rubbed her cheeks to make them pink while she hurried through the house to the front door.

"Think about the devil ..." It was the Carters' wagon out there, and "Doc" Carter was at the door. "Thank goodness he isn't a mind reader."

"Doc" Carter, always neat, was in clean workclothes. The boyish high color on his cheeks and the glint on his light brown hair enhanced the fresh look of him, especially now as he smiled. A dimple played at odds against the austerity that his aquiline nose would otherwise suggest.

"Sister Adams," he drew a letter from the inside pocket of his jacket, "I know Brother Adams isn't home. I'll just leave this for you to give to him."

He handed her the letter. As she looked up she saw a kindness in his eyes that made her wonder whether he had noticed the redness of her own.

When he had gone, she put the letter on the clock shelf against the pendulum door and darted into the downstairs bedroom to look into the bureau mirror. No sign of redness around her eyes, but her cheeks were pink and her hair not too disheveled, glory be! As she smoothed here and tucked in there, she realized that she did not look into the mirror often enough these days. Really, it isn't vanity to keep one's appearance presentable.

Strange — she'd never thought of it before, but perhaps Sister Carter just looked more impressed by Charles than she really was because she wasn't used to looking up at a man. It could be that Charles's edge in height gave him more of an appearance of authority. Yes. Sister Carter might very well be impressed with Charles, or she might just look impressed.

Brother Carter was a kind and gentle man. Certainly not much of a talker, but a nice man. He hadn't looked especially sympathetic or curious — just pleasant.

Reassured by the mirror, Mary felt suddenly almost gay — more energetic than she had for days — as she began the ritual of returning the chamber-pots to their respective commodes.

As if following the lilt of some inaudible music, she went back through the house and out into the back yard, with light, quick steps. Carefully lifting the crocheted lid-silencers off the clothesline in a practiced gesture which let them hang loosely over the extended fingers of her right hand, she dipped in a slow, swooping motion, like a bird in lazy flight, as with her left hand she flipped the porcelain tops over and dropped the covers off her fingers, one on each, so that now with freed hands, she could fit the crocheted covers over the righted lids and settle the lids, now muted with the lace, onto the pots, without that familiar, embarrassing sound.

Then, standing between two and carefully straightening her spine, she squared her shoulders manfully, let her knees buckle until her fingers found the bail on each, centered on the wooden handles, and, with a firm grasp on each of the fresh and shining white porcelain majesties, she straightened. Like Hebe, or maybe Justice, she moved with stately precision up the steps and onto the porch. There, standing before the screen door, she set the right one down at the left side; then opening the screen door with her nearer right hand, and, using her shoulder, elbow, and rear (in that order) to hold the door open, she retrieved the pot in one continuous motion which ended with the door coming to a close against her retarded heel. Then she sailed through the kitchen, up the stairs, and into each bedroom, straight to the commodes with their doors still slightly ajar to air them while their appointments were elsewhere.

As she came back by her bed, with her foot she pushed the trundle clear under, then, going to the window. she pulled out the peg and carefully let the window down. On the way back by the bed she straightened the rag rug again. It was getting too thin to lie smoothly any more, she noted.

A breeze, gusting now, promised snow or rain before long. Maybe she shouldn't wait for Millie to fill the big kettle from the well. She would do that and let Millie finish the lamps. Meanwhile, the fire would just barely hold until John Henry could fill the wood box.

The house had been quiet all afternoon. She would enjoy the bustle of the children coming in from school and all the preparation for supper. They were good children, almost too good. John Henry seemed more like a man than a boy already. And Millie, she half-guiltily congratulated herself, was her mother all over again. If Millie married well, that primness of hers could be quite regal. At any rate, she could be a humble, good wife and enjoy matching wits with fortune to make ends meet, too proud to pretend, and glad for what she had.

Mary had a lot to be thankful for — a good husband, healthy children, and a place with the righteous in the community. Yes, a lot to be thankful for, she repeated firmly, proud of herself that she had the good sense to be grateful. Not many men would take three little girls for a trip to town, even if they were "corralled" in the wagon, and Margaret was almost as good as Millie in caring for Pauline and Mamie.

She stopped down-stairs. "Humble-proud, that's what I am, and it's likely that Millie will be, too," she thought. She was in such a study that her lips tightened in a straight line, but the corners twitched up when she heard the familiar sound of the children coming home from school, like little hoof-beats pounding around the house and up the back steps as they raced each other into the house.

John Henry and Millie scrambled onto the porch. Now they were inside, shoving their lunchpails up onto the shelf over the dry sink. Then they tumbled into the sitting room before she had moved more than a step or two.

"Mama," chattered Millie, breathlessly, "are we going to Oregon, too?"

For Mary, it seemed as if the floor shook and the walls

echoed. She caught hold of the back of the rocking chair and felt it give with her grip. For a minute she could hardly breathe. She hung on for dear life, and that was what it was, for the child within her jumped.

Surely the children must have noticed, but if they did they gave no sign. She formed the word with her lips, but there was no sound. If only she could say "No," but she didn't.

"As far as I know," she said carefully, "nothing has been decided."

Millie turned upon John Henry triumphantly, pivoting and stamping her foot, assuming a ludicrously defiant stance for her size. "You see? I told you so." Her grey-blue eyes were flashing.

Millie slipped into the mannerisms of others as easily as most folks put on coats. "I wonder who she's mimicking now? Someone John Henry likes?" Mary looked at John Henry for a clue.

He was not impressed. He loftily ignored Millie and looked almost, but not quite, vindictively at his mother. "You mean you don't want to go and are holding us back."

Around the edges of her dismay at his steely-eyed assessment, she wondered whether he guessed how much she was holding back. And how could a boy of twelve be so much like his father!

He wheeled back to the kitchen to hang up his cap and jacket. There was no way of knowing from the flat tone of his statement whether it was recrimination or what. Of course he wanted to go. It was all anybody ever talked about, it seemed; especially the men and boys, with bravado and eagerness.

Mary opened her mouth but no sound came out. Her face must have looked stricken, for Millie flew to her, arms wide. "Oh, Mamma, I don't want to go if you don't want to," she assured.

Millie must have heard her and Charles talking last night after they had gone to bed. Millie slept in the trundle and must have been awake later than they had supposed. Her tone certainly suggested that she had heard them. Too bad Millie didn't go to sleep as soon as her head hit the pillow as John Henry did!

Mary wondered how much more Millie had heard and whether the child had understood what Charles would not when she had tried to tell him without actually putting it in words. Mil-

9

lie sensed things. No need to let the child worry any more than Mary could help.

Mary gave her a quick hug, which she tried to make gay and reassuring, then gently smoothed the soft brown hair away from the center part and over the squared lines of the brow, under which the deep-set blue eyes looked up at her with a maturity that awed her.

It seemed like a long time since early December when Charles had gone to the Oregon Emigrant meeting in Birmingham, "just to find out about things," and she had watched the Oregon fever mount, knowing that he would want to strike out again westward and that all she could hope for was postponement. Just one more year and then she wouldn't mind so much — if another baby wasn't on the way again.

Last night she had tried to tell him in such a way that he would feel what she felt. Pure foolishness on her part! She had found herself saying over and over, "But I can't see any end to it." And he kept reminding her about all the other people who could, people who had courage and faith enough to "go and possess the land."

Old Father Light and his wife were going. Then he'd name the others, one by one, as if the names were irrefutable arguments. He called the roll, an emphatic silence after each name.

"But, Charles, I just can't see the end of it," she found herself repeating lamely, as to herself she counted desperately, February, March, April, May — four months. Four back would be January, December, November, October. Would the baby be born in early or late June?

When she realized that she had been counting to herself with the slow measured tones of Charles's words, he was saying something, but she wasn't sure what. All she got was the last about "living by faith."

"But having a baby on the way . . ."

"Birth is a perfectly natural process."

"So is death."

"You are afraid, aren't you." He became possessive and almost tender and strong. "Have faith, Mary."

She didn't know how far into the night they had talked, supposing Millicent, in the trundle bed, was fast asleep.

He was so sure that he could realize enough from "The place" to cover provisions for the wagon, supplies at the forts along the way, with enough left over to carry them well into their first winter, which, "in Oregon, would be mild," he reminded her.

Slowly, methodically, he built his argument for pulling up stakes and getting in on the great Oregon Opportunity. Inexorably he dislodged her grip on everything she laid a hand to that might hold them to "The place." He pointed to the unknown Oregon country — so frightening to her — as the land of promise and fulfillment of every good thing. A Methodist community already planted by the waters of the Willamette, rich land needing only the clearing to yield more lumber than they would need for buildings and fences galore, leaving soil deep and rich for planting, a wholesome climate so mild a man could work outdoors practically the whole year around, with early planting and long harvest seasons. What more could hardworking, God-fearing folk want?

Embarrassed as she was to mention it another time, she tried, without much hope, another tack. "It doesn't seem right for folks like us to have a baby along the way — like gypsies."

"We'll just let nature take its course, as God wills, and don't forget, there'll be just as good doctoring in the wagon train as there is at home. Doc Carter is thinking more about going all the time."

"Charles," she pleaded desperately, "you don't understand. Having a baby in a wagon, and keeping going day after day with the cooking and all ...."

"Oh," he said loftily, "when you see how many good people are going, you won't want to hold your family back from this God-given opportunity."

She couldn't ignore the implied reprimand for the folly of her fears, and she knew she was pounding on a door that was already locked and barred. All she could do was to repeat inanely, "If I could only see the end of it ...."

"Everything in God's good time; there will be a time for seeing. The time for talking is past. You'll have to trust your husband, woman," he said.

Millie is too young to be burdened with worrying, Mary thought, though worry well she might. The next three years would make all the difference in her young life. Three years after this and she'd be going into her fifteenth year. She didn't want Millicent growing up like poor white trash in that distant Oregon country where Mary and Charles would be just another immigrant family to most people, even though their position would probably be fairly well established among the Methodists there. Charles's long service as class leader in the church ought to be worth something to folks out there.

"Well, Millicent," she shrugged, and even forced a laugh, "I guess we won't be going before supper. Please change your dress and fill the big kettle for me. If you can get the carrots and potatoes ready, we will have an early meal. Then we will be through early enough for you to do some sums before class meeting."

By the time they were ready for work in the kitchen, John Henry had changed his clothes and was out chopping the stovewood.

Automatically, Mary picked up a hot pad, opened the firebox door, and put in enough quick wood on the coals to have a good, hot fire going and the teakettle purring hot again in a hurry. Well, anyway, the children knew, and that was some sort of relief. Whatever hung in the air these days was understood, at least. Mary wasn't much for subterfuges, except those necessary and proper.

John Henry chopped steadily. Soon he brought in his first load and carefully lowered it in the woodbox behind the stove. He lowered it quietly, almost gently. It was an unmistakable statement of feeling so clear that she said, for the wood as well as the gentleness of manner, "Thank you, John Henry!"

Always glad to do what I can for you, Mrs. Adams," he said,this time speaking so flatly that she could make as much or as little of it as she wanted. Was the "Mrs. Adams" his reminder of her duty, or was it another of his almost-not-at-all funny jokes! It seemed as if she were always trying to interpret what John Henry said. If she only knew how much of him was her and how much of him was Charles, she might be able to tell what he meant at least part of the time.

Classmeeting night was always rushed because Charles liked to be there early. In the hustle and bustle of getting the meal, she didn't see him take down the letter from the clockshelf. In fact, she had forgotten all about it. The lamp was pulled down over the table and the clock was out of the circle of its light.

She was flushed but ready when Charles and John Henry brought the buggy around. Her coat already wouldn't button easily, not even with the buttons set back, but the long fichu obscured the fact, and her hat was rather pert when she got it at the right angle. Her appearance was quite tolerable, she told herself, as she drew on her gloves. But getting into the buggy, she was awkward enough to destroy any pride she might have taken in her appearance. She was always afraid of pulling the cord around the baby's neck as she had been warned jerking stomach muscles might do. By the time she was settled in the back seat with Millie, she was acutely uncomfortable, her heart pounding ridiculously, her cheeks hot enough to fry a hoecake.

A ghastly thought curdled. If getting into the buggy was difficult now, how in the world would she ever get in and out of a Conestoga three or four times a day in another three months! In her thoughts she posed this awkward question to Charles, but his back showed no evidence of hearing anyone's thoughts but his own as he drove along, going over "the lesson" on the way.

The children, understanding this preparatory contemplation, offered no disturbing chatter. Mary joggled along with her own noisy silence, an uncomfortable turmoil, physical and spiritual, playing a kind of tag for her conscious consideration. Before she was married, riding horseback had been a delight, but now, even riding in a buggy upset her. "Always is when I am pregnant," she thought. She tried to remember when she had not been pregnant, but she could not evoke the feeling of being just herself. It seemed so long ago it must have been someone else. She had been Polly Vowell who was someone else. Charles had insisted on calling her Mary because his sister was Polly. Mary Adams was a wife and mother of five. She wondered whether Charles was someone different — not just older and more encumbered by having become a husband and father. Rebelliously, she doubted it. Yes, riding cer-

13

tainly didn't put her into a very receptive mood for classmeeting.

Father Light's buggy was the only one hitched there ahead of them at the meeting house. He had lit some lamps and had a fire going in the great stove.

Charles never failed to comment appreciatively on these preparations, and Father Light always responded that it was the least he could do. It was a ritual as good as any other for maintaining the amenities.

"I always say (sniff, sniff) that if Brother Adams can lead the meeting (sniff, sniff) for our spiritual nurture and comfort, I can get the lamps lit and the fire started to warm the cockles of our hearts," he would say. The parallelism sounded Biblical to him and he glowed with the pleasure of pronouncing it once more before each class meeting.

Mary always wondered what she would say if the children asked what cockles were. "With cockle shells and silver bells and pretty maidens all in a row," her only other experience with the word, was not very helpful.

Father Light went back to his self-appointed task of setting out the songbooks. When he had finished that, he offered to shake hands with each as he greeted them, sniffing with a kind of nervous cheer. Mary invariably thought of dogs sniffing, but she could not think of a single way in which his sniffing could be likened to a dog's. She had scolded herself more than once for having made such a demeaning comparison for such a nice old man — forty years old if he was a day — but the dog comparison always popped into her mind when she heard him sniff.

The sniffing was so much a part of his personality she would have missed it if it had been suddenly and miraculously cured. The sniffing and the over-all grey cast to his skin and hair were the sign of his long servitude at the flouring mill. All the millers sniffed and looked flour-y. His neat, clean, blue worsted suit, the hard, white collar, and the little jutting goatee — all seemed to be overcast with the same dusty look that the mill wore.

If he went to Oregon and worked out in that healthful air instead of in a flouring mill, would he, she wondered, get over that sniffing? And if he quit sniffing, would she feel differently toward him?

The first time she had ever noticed him was when he arose to lead in prayer. His appearance so amused her when she covertly glanced up that she had feared some other "peeker" might catch the irrepressible expression of amusement on her face.

He was such an inconsequential-looking little man as he arose to lead in prayer, he reminded her of a little rooster in the wind. He stretched his neck and shut his eyes, the flour-colored goatee jutted forward, leaving the adam's apple exposed in profile to deepen the impression of a little roaster getting ready to crow.

Since that first amused glimpse, her impression of the little man had not really changed — had only grown more definite. Her amused compassion combined with condescending appreciation: amusement at his almost childlike animation and excitability; compassion for his diminutiveness which obviously frustrated him constantly; appreciation for his keen mind and bubbling good spirit; and respect for his indomitable drive overrode any noticeable concern for the ludicrousness of his appearance. Even now there was a knowing twinkle in his eye, reflecting the anticipated amusement in the eyes of his beholders.

Suddenly she realized something she must have known all along. He actually capitalized on his lack of physical presence. He disarmed them all. By their generous act of condescension, he was in reality, a central figure and exerted from that vantage some power. He was amusing, he was good, and he was nobody's fool.

As he looked up at Charles while they were shaking hands, Charles laid his hand on Mr. Light's shoulder, very much as he might have done with one of the boys. Mr. Light twinkled up at him from under his bushy grey eyebrows. At that moment Mary would have given a great deal to know what Mr. Light was thinking of her husband.

At the same moment the question formed in her mind, Mary knew she wanted him to think well of Charles, not for Father Light's sake, but for Charles's. She could not explain why. She had steadfastly held that Charles was superior because he was too serious and good to be playful. She certainly wasn't going to start questioning it now.

Mrs. Light buzzed up with her usual fussing, scolding manner, not because she was scolding or even felt like scolding, really;

it was just her way of gaining a conversational foothold by getting attention without having anything to say and without any particular physical presence. Mary marveled at the effect that habitually pursing her lips had created around her little dismayed "O" of a mouth. Little lines, darkened by down, radiated in ridges from the thin, almost colorless circle of her lips. Under raised eyebrows, dark eyes stared out from amazing circles of heavy brown lashes. Hers was an exclamatory kind of face.

Just as her husband accepted the role of excitable naivete, Mrs. Light adopted that of the excitable, ineffective scold. She accentuated the roundness of her little button nose by the curve of hair on either side of the center part as it arched around her ears into a little, light round bun in the middle of the back of her head, which Mary found herself noticing as Mrs. Light buzzed off to fuss over some of the others as they came in.

For the life of her, Mary couldn't remember what Mrs. Light had been talking about. Vaguely she hoped her response had been adequate. Not that Mrs. Light would have noticed!

When Father Light started ringing the last bell, by pulling the long rope that dangled in the little vestibule, the folks quickly settled into their accustomed places. Altogether, they made up a better than average meeting crowd. Almost twenty tonight.

Most families brought lamps in with them, so that as the assemblage grew, the number of lamps in the holders around the walls increased. By meeting time one could read in almost any part of the room.

Mary had not realized how tired she was until she sat down. Even the cold hard seat felt comfortable to her back. In the reality that seemed so different from the mood of the dream that had haunted her all day, she found relief.

Oddly, the Carters had not arrived. Each time the stir of latecomers attracted her attention, she was sure it would be they. "Well," she thought to herself, finally, "if they aren't even going to be here tonight, as a dreamer I am not much of a prophet."

Charles had been greeting folks as they came in at the door, swapping talk. Now he was coming up front. He was stopping by her row.

What in the world could he want? The children were behaving well enough, playing their favorite waiting-for-meeting-to-begin game of trying to get as many hymn titles as possible into one sentence. They weren't hurting the books at all, even though they were rustling the pages. Charles surely wasn't going to tell them to stop now. He knew that they would stop just as soon as he started the meeting.

No, it wasn't the children. He was looking at her intently and he bent over so far the watch fob his father had given him swung out abruptly. Whatever was the matter? He looked somewhat embarrassed. She distinctly remembered putting out a nice, clean, white handkerchief for him. Could he have forgotten it himself? He was reaching into his coat pocket.

"Mary," he whispered, "I haven't any hymns picked out. Find two to start us off with and then look up the number for 'Shall We Gather At The River' to close. Put them down on the back of this."

He handed her an envelope. It looked like the same one Doc Carter had left that afternoon. It seemed odd that Charles had found it and made no comment. Seeing it made her start guiltily for having forgotten to see to it that he got it.

When she had confirmed the page numbers for "Sweet Hour of Prayer," "Just As I Am," and then, dutifully, "Shall We Gather At The River," she raised the envelope as the signal which Charles, now up front, had been looking for.

The Kanes were just coming in. They came past and on up the aisle to the place that was always saved for them on account of Mrs. Kane's being deaf.

Charles moved to greet them and picked up the envelope quite unobtrusively.

As the Kanes passed by, John Henry hissed, "They're going to Oregon if they can sell their farm, Ma."

How well she knew! Charles had made quite a to-do of comparing their two farms and how much Brother Kane expected to get for his — "three times what he paid for it. That is the regular asking for improvements like ours. As long as a man can realize that kind of profit on his improvements, it seems plain ridiculous not to make it while he can."

Was he right? Was she, then, wrong to want to cling to what

was theirs now, what was a part of them?

A baby born on the way would have very little chance, and if the baby died, couldn't they really be nearly murderers? Why hadn't she thought of bringing that up to Charles?

A surge of triumph flushed her at the thought, as if she had already presented this dissuader and it had carried weight with him. Her fancied triumph was cut short almost immediately by Charles's announcing the first hymn and with much ado, Mrs. Light's flurrying to the organ. Once settled just right on the stool, she pushed up the lid, pulled out the stops, and sat there, alternately rubbing her hands and rearranging the hymnals on the rack.

Afterwards, Mary never was able to recall more than a kaleidoscope of impressions of the meeting from that point. The waves of heat from the stove, the shifting light from the lamps, the prayers, the scripture, the lesson discussion — nothing that of itself might not have been spoken and considered by a classmeeting anywhere in the country, and yet everything that was spoken glistened with a special meaning, filling her with panic.

How could the old familiar story of the Israelites push her to the very precipice of fear, she tried to ask herself, but while she sat there with her gloved hands folded in her lap, she fought an inner battle against hysteria. Mrs. Kane's elongated jet-laden earlobes hung, as usual, directly in her line of vision. Mr. Light's goatee jutted nervously, as usual, across the aisle to her left. Mrs. Light's head bobbed in self-conscious agreement. It was a nightmare of reality.

"By faith ... in the desert ... cloud by day and fire by night ... Promised Land ..." the words ricocheted through the plain little meeting house. The double intent of his words was committing them all to the Westward migration.

Suddenly there was a flutter within her so intense that she raised her hymnal on edge in her lap and laid her arm along the top edge so that she could keep her coat from revealing the stir. Poor baby, upset by her emotional tempest. She vowed henceforth to be calm. She must not mark the baby if she could possibly help it. She had seen a badly marked baby.

Her little figure stiffened as she resolved to accept the coming difficulties with whatever Christian fortitude she could muster. She had a life to protect, and it was not her own. Immediately she realized that she had crossed a kind of spiritual threshold for, suddenly, as if a physical presence, a benediction of peace, released the tension of anxiety. "I can and I will," she promised the presence with new-found grace.

Charles was pulling out Brother Carter's envelope, but instead of referring to the page number on the back, he opened it. "I want to read you a message from Brother and Sister Carter," he said. Then he read, "Dear Friends, perhaps you have not missed us." Here everyone smiled. Of course they had all noted the Carters' absence. "We have had a death in the family. When we can, we will join the earliest train of good people emigrating to Oregon in the spring."

Old Father Jacobs spoke up. "'Pears like there won't hardly be nobody left here. Everbody's a-gittin' the fever. If the plague don't git us, Oregon will!"

The Rev. Delazon Smith and a beautiful Oregon scene sketched in 1849 by an unidentified artist with the U.S. Army's Cross Rifle Regiment showing a landing place near the Cascades of the Columbia River.

– OREGON HISTORICAL SOCIETY

– OREGON HISTORICAL SOCIETY

II

The Rising Tide

ALL METHODISM WAS against her, it seemed. The very next Sunday afternoon the Lights drove up with a book. Father Light was carrying it carefully in order not to lose the little strips of paper which were sticking their little white tongues out at her from the many pages where he had evidently inserted them for markers. Mary was not in any mood to spend the afternoon listening to even a nice old man do selected readings. When he, with overtones of a trumpet flourish, read the title, she felt desperately trapped. And she was. There was no believable excuse that she could offer to avoid listening to the Light readings from the new book EXPLORING: EXPEDITION TO OREGON, by the Reverend Gustavus Hines.

Grimly she watched his progress from marker to marker, getting — as she told herself — "some small secret spiteful satisfaction" in counting the times he drawled the word "beautiful," which the reverend author used with rapturous abandon.

She thought the afternoon would never end, as the kindly little old man laboriously picked his way from passage to passage of Oregon propaganda:

> From a personal experience of more than five years, and from extensive observation in reference to this particular, the writer is prepared to express the opinion that the climate of Oregon, not excepting the Wallamette (sic) Valley, is generally favorable to health ... True, the Indians are generally diseased, and are fast dying off ... the result of their connection with diseased and dissipated foreigners ... the ague and fever, which attacks many whites ... is easily controlled, and finally leaves the person with a vigorous, unimpaired constitution, and seldom recurs to them the second season. The persons in this country who appear to be the most healthy are those who have been here the greatest length of time.
>
> ... unquestionable that the Wallamette valley is ... the garden of the country, so far as the fertility of its soil is concerned

> ... it requires less labor in this country to raise one bushel or a thousand bushels of wheat, than it does on any part of the Genesee flats.... it does not require half an eye to see that Oregon can and will compete with any other portion of the world, in supplying the islands of the Pacific, the Russian settlements, and every other flour market contiguous, with their bread stuffs, which usually bear, in these portions of the world, a handsome price.
>
> And, indeed, there are few countries, perhaps none, in which a poor man, when once he has surmounted the difficulty in getting here, in which he can get a better living, and get it easier than in this

Here Charles hitched his chair back and teetered his pleasure.

> ... One mile above the Clackamas is the Wallamette Falls ... This is a most beautiful cataract, and the hydraulic privileges which it affords, and which are beginning to be extensively used, are almost boundless ...
>
> Two miles above the falls you come to the mouth of the Tuality ... This river rises in the high lands towards the coast in a number of little streams which water the beautiful and somewhat extensive plains, which are called "The Tuality Plains"

and then he read about Mill Creek:

> ... which comes into the Wallamette from the south-east. It is a small stream, but its flowing through a beautiful, excellent and central portion of the valley, and affording some very fine water-privileges, it is regarded as being a very important branch of the Wallamette.

"Do you hear that, Mary?" Charles chortled, bringing his chair down with a bang and slapping his knee.

"Yes, I heard it," she answered smoothly, getting up quickly to forestall any more. "Excuse me while I make some tea."

The kitchen never looked better to her than at that moment. "I'd rather stay poor and stay here," she told the woodbox. "It's enough to make a person quit the church — almost."

It was only a few days into March when Charles brought the list of rules and regulations of the Van Buren County, Oregon Emigrant Party Number One, and insisted upon reading aloud to her all thirty-six rules, especially the last one, which allowed any good moral persons to join by signing the rules.

Mary had to admit that they sounded pretty good, with rules

against swearing, obscene talk, intemperance, and abuse of teams, as well as card-playing and gambling. Elections were provided for, and all males and females over 15 could vote. There was even a rule for cleanliness and one saying that each family should keep to themselves as a unit, respecting the rights of others. It would take a two-thirds vote of acceptance by the whole company for later joiners to get in. Yes, it was a good set of rules, as far as she could for see, with a plan for just about everything, and Doctor William Miller was going to be Captain. Members had to provide the necessary money before April 1 so that a delegate could go to St. Louis to lay in provisions.

A little sunshine, about the same time, broke the back of winter, as far as the Oregon enthusiasts were concerned. Actually, it had been a frightfully cold winter that hung on. The wind could roar, the sleet claw at the windows, and the ice in the water troughs have to be chopped. Whatever happened served to create some favorable reference to Oregon.

For instance, when the WESTERN ADVOCATE for February 25 finally came, there was Mrs. Miller's letter. (The Millers had gone to Oregon from the North Indiana Conference just last spring.) Charles read it aloud as soon as he had time to open it. He did not like to have anyone open the paper before he had read it. He liked to choose edifying bits to read aloud, and he was assured of a receptive audience.

Charles particularly savored this section of Mrs. Miller's letter:

> Oregon is indeed a delightful country, affording every variety in scenery — dense forests of lofty pine, the extensive plains beautifully diversified by groves and streaks of fir- timber and underbrush and hemmed in by beautiful rises and swells of land, which rise one above the other, away above and beyond till they almost reach the size of mountains, and from whose sides spring forth little streams, and course their way down into the plains, and can be traced by the far-off observer only by the foliage of the underbrush and those streaks of fir-timber which guide them on and on, perhaps to assist some great river in accumulating waters. But then Oregon is a part of the frame of the one mighty creation whose beauty, grandeur, and magnificence we behold and admire at every turn of the head. Oregon is not a fairy land, only fitted for the rovings of the fancy and imagination. It is not a land whose inhabitants are freed from

every calamity ... although it is more healthy than in many parts of the world.

From that time on, all was but interlude until the coming of spring. Before they knew it, the grass would be up on the plains and wagon trains would be starting for Oregon. The rush would be on. First trains would get the first choice of the forage, which would be fresh and tender almost all the way across the plains.

Preparations could hardly be made too far in advance. Whoever was planning to go divided his possessions into three parts: what he would take, what he would leave, and what he might take. The first part ruthlessly determined the other two.

The Adamses, like just about everyone else in the country, it seemed, had the "Report of the Committee" on the wall beside the calendar. It was signed by Delazon Smith, William Miller, and Ephraim Stout, the committee "to whom had been entrusted the business of preparing and publishing a 'model, judicious outfit'."

REPORT

An out-fit for a journey from Iowa to Oregon, by the over-land route.

There are different modes of traveling adopted by different classes of emigrants. One class pack through; another drive mules, another horses, and another oxen and cows. Packing is the most expeditious; and either horses or mules — other things being equal, — will go through a little sooner, — but not more surely and safely — than oxen. But, under the supposition that all the members of the company now formed, intend to drive oxen and cows, the committee will confine themselves to a corresponding calculation. Each man should have from 3 to 5 yoke of oxen, or from 2 to 3 yoke of oxen and from 2 to 3 cows, to each wagon, according to the load.

Every man should aim to get light, firm, sound wagons. In the selection of wagons extremes should be avoided. There is danger of getting wagons so light and frail as not to be able to carry the load safely over bad roads, and still greater danger of breaking down the team with unnecessarily heavy clumsy wagons.

Every man should lay in provisions enough to last him THROUGH, and have some to spare in case of emergency.

In preparing the load, great care should be taken to leave out and behind every pound's weight not absolutely necessary for the journey; so that all may start with as light a load as possible under the circumstances.

After entering the plains, companies, of twenty wagons each, are large enough for convenience and expedition.

All wagons should be provided with bows and covers. Each family ought to be provided with a tent, sufficiently large to accommodate its members.

When practicable, every owner of a team would do well to provide himself with horse or pony. And no family should be destitute of at least one cow.

Every man should start, from the Missouri River, with 200 pounds of flour and 100 pounds of bacon, to every one capable of eating a man's rations.

The committee deem it sufficient to enumerate the following articles, leaving each individual and family, to determine for themselves, by reference to the amount which they usually consume at home, in health, during a period of four or five months, when engaged in manual labor: —*viz*—

Coffee, tea, and tobacco (for those who use those articles), sugar, spices, dried fruit, lard, honey, Indian meal (a small quantity), hard bread or crackers (a small quantity), rice, beans, salt, soap, oil, or candles, salaratus (a small quantity) and molasses. A small quantity of butter may be taken by those who desire that luxury and who cannot depend upon their cows on the road.

It would be well to take a small quantity of dried corn.

Each family will provide themselves with such medicines as they may choose.

Those who choose to do so, will find a small sheet iron cook stove, with corresponding furniture, very convenient, especially in wet weather, as they can then cook in a wagon or under a tent without difficulty. Each man should provide himself with a lanthern *(sic)*, matches and match safe.

All are recommended to leave their trunks behind them: — use sacks as substitutes. Feather beds may be taken according to the taste or necessities of persons. A buffalo robe however, is an excellent substitute; and so is a light matrass *(sic)*. If, in addition to what has gone before, many should wish to have a few luxuries — such as sweet meats, &c., which our wives and mothers know so well how to prepare, they will, of course, gratify themselves.

Each man should possess a hand hatchet, a rifle, an axe and a large knife. The company should possess saws, spades, shovels, hoes, drawing knives, augers, chizels *(sic)*, &c., &c. There should be, also, in the company, a rope, long enough to reach across a moderate sized river. There should also be a large spy-glass. And

25

every family should be provided with a water can capable of holding from 4 to 8 gallons of water — according to the size of the family.

Every person will prepare clothing to their own taste. Every one, however, should be provided so as to meet the extremes of heat and cold; and no one should start with less than two pair of boots.

The place for rendezvous, and the general starting point will be Council Bluffs. Each member of the company will make his way to that point, by the route and in any manner which may suit his convenience. The estimates of the committee have had special reference to Missouri River, as a starting point.

Each team should be supplied with one or more extra ox yokes, &c., to be used in case of breakage, &c. Cooking utensils, and table dishes, should be as few and simple as practicable. Boxes, bucket, tubs, etc., should be dispensed with as far as possible. What are absolutely necessary only, should be taken, and these of the lightest and most convenient kind.

All of which is respectfully submitted.

DELAZON SMITH
WM. MILLER
EPHRAIM STOUT
Committee

Mary never did know whether Charles had made up his mind irrevocably before February 28 or not, but she did suspect that he would never change his mind after she circled "Hints on Domestic Happiness," when she finally got a chance to see that ADVOCATE for herself. Although he did not acknowledge noticing it in so many words, she could not have misunderstood had she tried when that night he chose St. Paul's First Epistle to Timothy for their evening devotions. The children listened, solemn-eyed, as he read with considerable emphasis, "But I suffer not a woman to teach, nor to usurp authority over the man, but to be in silence."

After that, Mary knew she didn't have a chance. Anything she said would just go against her. She did, however, indulge herself in some rather rebellious thoughts about the Apostle Paul himself, but those did not give her as much satisfaction as holding more positive thoughts about the Woman's Rights convention, which had been held at Worcester, Massachusettes in the fall. Yet, in the final analysis, she was a bit uneasy about that too. Could Rights be right if they were not righteous? Saint Paul just had to be righteous! When she reached that point in her thinking she wondered whether she was being wicked and deserving of punishment for having such radical thoughts.

But the modern authority, sanctified by being printed in the ADVOCATE, surely was not heretical, and she wished she could discuss this deep intuitive fear of hers. What would *he* say to that, he who had written, "The intuitive judgments of women are often more to be relied upon than the conclusions which *we* reach by an elaborate process of reasoning," and "that they are very apt to be sound on the practical matters of domestic life, nothing but prejudice or self-conceit can prevent us from acknowledging." Indeed, she went around for days, in the depths of her wicked thoughts, jabbing Charles with Dr. Boardman's saying "the man who thinks it beneath his dignity to take counsel with an intelligent wife, stands in his own light, and betrays that lack of judgment which he tacitly attributes to her." But Mary did not get much comfort from it. Resistance was utterly useless and she might as well save her strength.

Finally, Charles offered magnanimously, "We won't try to start before the first of May. That way you can get a little done each day." She couldn't see whether the rhyme was supposed to be funny or not.

He brought a map to the kitchen table where she was working and spread it out.

"We'll get to the Missouri in two weeks," he said, running his finger straight across. "It shouldn't take us more than a day or two to get started from there, and we'll be on the coast of Nebraska by the middle of May."

"We won't be across the plains by the end of June?"

"Probably not."

She looked at the map with renewed foreboding. Somewhere out there in The Great American Desert her sixth child would be born.

Aloud, she said, "I just can't conceive of it."

"You already have," he answered shortly, turned on his heel and left the room, leaving no sound but the *tck, tck,* of the clock, his ill-spoken jest having embarrassed him as soon as it was out, she knew.

27

He won't forgive me for causing him to say a thing like that — not for a long time, she thought. When she had mentioned that having a baby in a wagon didn't seem quite respectable, he came back at her with something about a manger having been good enough for the Son of God. She couldn't ever be right!

If it had not been for her deep disquiet, some of Charles's tactics would have struck her as amusing. When the weather was stormy, he reminded her that the Oregon climate, by actual report, was "Mild and delightful." If the weather turned mild — which it didn't do that winter very often — he said he guessed it was like Salem, Oregon. If Mary had the croup, he quoted Brother Woodward's letter last spring about "our little Asbury" being "more healthy." If they had stew, he mentioned the onions were a great crop in Oregon. And he reminded them of the letter that they had read in the ADVOCATE just before Christmas, when the weather had been as bitter as could be, the letter from the Reverend Roberts saying "Frequently in winter the weather is warm and traveling — except in places — is delightful. On the whole, Oregon is a goodly land and pleasant." He had gone on about the beautiful scenery, rich land, and comfortable people. Some, he had said, were already wealthy.

One day Charles came across an item about a seminary for young ladies in Oregon City. "You see," he said, leaning back and tapping the print with his forefinger, "a fine school under the Methodist and Congregational churches, ready and waiting for the girls."

Before he could take another breath, the girls were dancing around his chair. in gleeful anticipation of being young ladies at a seminary out in Oregon.

Mary surmised that he had intended the comment to appease her ambitions and not as a promise to the girls, and she detected some dismay at the way the girls had caught on. She could not forego a bit of malice at his expense, "Well, girls, see that you hold him to his offer when we get there," she jibed.

As she watched his sheepish grin disappear behind the paper, she enjoyed a wicked moment of triumph. And maybe she had got even with him for making a special dream of hers impossible. She had always hoped he would see fit to send John Henry to

Greencastle for college. She had fondly imagined going back there proudly for his graduation. Many a time she had tried to imagine the fine changes, what with all the new buildings and their spires that she had read about in the ADVOCATE.

But the weeks were not all broken dreams and malice and forebodings.

Sometimes Mary almost forgot her dread when she got caught up in the general excitement. One day they all laughed until tears were running down their cheeks — even Charles! That was the day they named the lead ox team.

Charles had been looking for a strong, young team. One evening he announced that he had found a fine pair and would probably bring them in late the next afternoon, with John Henry's help.

When he did, the girls were quick to spot them coming. They all ran out to greet the vital new members of the family.

"May we name them?" Margaret had asked.

Charles had thought it over for a minute and then allowed, "I doubt that oxen care much what they are called. I see no reason why you should not, as long as they answer to 'Gee' and 'Haw'."

"Let's have 'ox' in their names," Millie proposed, looking them over rather solemnly.

"How about 'Doxology'?" Mary proposed.

The suggestion worried John Henry. "How can we find another name to match that?" he asked.

"Occident," Charles suggested.

"Socks," said Mary.

"Flocks," added Pauline.

"Box, or clocks — or tick-tocks," Margaret rattled off, and set them all going at once: fetlocks ... flintlocks ... buttocks ... building blocks ....

"Rocks-and-rills: I love the rocks and rills," cried Pauline.

"Intoxication?" from John Henry. Then, "How about Paradox?"

"That is a good one," Mary commented.

But Charles already had a better one. "Orthodox," he shouted over the hubbub. That was it they all had to admit.

The innocent unconcern of the oxen made it all the funnier.

Margaret, walking heels first on the rather muddy ground, came close and looked into their faces. "One of you is Doxology and one is Orthodox, but which is which?"

Charles had the answer. "It will have to be Orthodox-Doxology, reading from behind left to right," he said.

Breathless from laughing, they all trooped into the house together. Mary couldn't remember when they had all laughed so hard.

Thereafter, because the team was always together in the same order, they were most often called "Orthodoxology."

Everyone in the little town soon heard about the team and their amusing names. A surprising number of people drove by just to have a look at them and to be able to tell others that they had seen them. Orthodox and Doxology thus became local celebrities.

Some of those who came to stare remained to praise. Charles had made a good choice of steers, and everyone who pretended to know anything at all about cattle began to mention what a good judge of cattle he was when the topic of the celebrities came up. By such quirks of fate are reputations made!

Before long, both the Carters and the Lights asked Charles to keep an eye out for dependable oxen for them. Some others did, too. Charles had long since had such a reputation for the strictest honesty that the new reputation made him irresistible as their cattle-buyer.

Mary, eyeing the barnyard one afternoon as Charles was coming in after having brought home some more "proxpects," as Margaret liked to call them, couldn't resist; a barbed comment over her shoulder as she went through the door ahead of him. Over her shoulder she tossed it at him, "Well, now we can have our own private stampede!" Then she went on quickly into the kitchen.

"You coward," she told herself, "You're afraid to stand and fight. You just shoot and run."

The truth of the matter was that she took no little pride in Charles's new status and the excitement that it engendered. For instance, there was the afternoon that the Lights came over for Father Light to pick his team from a number of animals Charles had acquired.

Mary and Mother Light watched from the porch when he and Charles went out to the yard where the oxen were tethered.

"I really think he would as soon have had Brother Adams make the choice for him," she confided, and then, as if not wanting to pursue that topic further, she turned a maternal eye on John Henry, who was perched precariously on the top rail of the fence. "My, you must be proud of that boy. Too bad you couldn't have had another just like him."

"Maybe I will," laughed Mary, knowing full well that it wasn't likely for her luck to change after four girls.

"But you have four of the nicest little girls a person could ask for," Mother Light carefully added.

"Mary's laughing retort was out before she thought twice, as usual, "I don't know as I asked for them," she said jokingly, and immediately regretted it.

Mother Light considered the light tone with a non-committal smile and seemed to decide that the younger woman was a mite out of line. "You asked for them when you married their father," she reminded her.

This time Mary was ahead of herself only in her thoughts. Mother Light probably never dreamed that Mary was saying to herself, "I did. I surely did!"

Mother Light's eyes were on the two men. Her eyes popped and her mouth flew open. "Why, look at him sashaying up to that great beast! And I thought he was timid around those animals. You know he's never been around cattle very much, working in the mill as he has. I declare, he's scratching its neck."

Sure enough, that was exactly what Father Light was doing, and Charles was saying, "That's your ox all right. He's taking right to you. Sodom likes you. That means you'll be driving Sodom and Gomorrah to Oregon." and he laughed and laughed.

Father Light's laughter sounded feeble to Mary, perhaps because she was quite a distance away.

John Henry shook his head in wonder at the supper table that night while discussing Father Light's choice. "You never can tell about people. When I saw Father Light coming across the yard, at first I thought maybe he was afraid — him not being around cows and all very much. There was a queer look on his face, and he was walking funny, but I guess he just didn't want to get his shoes dirty and wasn't used to being around the mess oxen make. I'll put in with you if Mother Light doesn't follow him around with a broom when he comes into the house, as it is."

"That will do, John Henry," said his father quickly. Then, as if in fairness to the boy, he added. "I had much the same impression — that Father Light was indeed a bit timid about approaching the cattle, but even though he is not accustomed to barnyards like ours, he went right along with me and started talking to the oxen as if they were all but companions of the trail already. He certainly showed no fear at touching Sodom as soon as he chose him."

Mary got an interesting angle on the incident a few days later in a confidence that she never felt the slightest inclination to divulge to either Charles or John Henry. She felt the little man deserved the respect he had earned.

Perhaps Mother Light felt that she had been too short with Mary and perhaps she wanted to retrieve confidence by sharing confidence. Maybe it was just too good to keep and she trusted Mary to keep what she herself could not. Whatever the reason, Mother Light betrayed her husband's version of the story to Mary in what seemed to be his own words:

"There I was going across that yard straight for the herd of them. Well, six is a herd, isn't it? And I began to wonder how they look when they start to stampede. They were all looking right at me, watching me and maybe waiting for me to make just the right excuse for them to come at me. For a minute I wondered if I ought to tip-toe. But that didn't seem practical. A brown and white one started rolling its eyes at me, and I had to start doing something, I was that nervous, so I started talking to the critters. It was the stupidest remark — didn't even make sense, 'Which one of us boys are walking to Oregon together?' I said.

"The one that had rolled its eyes huffed right in my face. Before I knew it, I had raised my arm to protect myself. There I was with my arm in the air, like a blooming idiot. I couldn't pretend that I was waving — I was too close for that. There wasn't anything I could do but let my hand drop on that beast's great neck, and there it froze ... I was that scared.

"And then, about a million miles away, I heard Brother Adams saying that its name was Sodom and Sodom liked me.

"Right then I realized that Sodom wasn't planning to toss me on his horns. You know what he wanted? Just like a big dog, he was lowering his head so I'd scratch the right place on his neck!"

In the weeks that followed, it seemed to Mary that every time she looked over her shoulder she saw another bridge burning behind her. Since that first organizational meeting early in December at the Seceder Church in Birmingham, when Dr. Miller had been elected president and the Reverend Delazon Smith secretary, the group had published model outfitting lists, schemes for proportioning tools, and bills to the members for those publications. Their big meeting had long been set for the first Saturday in March at the Court House in Keosauqua. By the eighth of March Charles had closed the deal on the farm for five hundred ninety-four dollars.

III

What Kind of Flowers Grow In Oregon?

CHARLES AND DOC CARTER were out looking at wagons when the young couple first came to look at the place. "Me about six years ago," Mary thought, as she looked at the young wife, a baby on her hip and another swinging on her skirt. The young husband was putting down the oldest from his shoulder as Mary opened the door.

"I'm sorry my husband isn't at home," Mary apologized as she invited them into the house. She dared not quote any figures to them.

"Oh, that's just fine," the man hastened to assure her, evidently relieved at not having to discuss prices and terms until he was sure of being really interested.

The wife, fearful that her children "might get into something," thanked Mary with a rush of gratitude when she brought out some blocks and laid them on the floor for the children to play with.

The children were so easily amused that Mary offered to watch them and let the parents "look around the place" by themselves.

"Oh, thank you, Mrs. Adams," the woman responded quickly for them both, "but we wouldn't feel comfortable prowling about someone's place by ourselves. Unless it would tire you out," she added, in deference to Mary's condition.

So Mary gave them the Grand Tour of the place. Evidently they took to it right away. They started with the house and ended with the barn, after which the young woman asked to see the kitchen again, and she went inside the pantry, commenting appreciatively. The longer they lingered, the more Mary could see how pleased they were with it, and the more pleased they were with it, the more easily she saw herself becoming resigned to giving it up. She would not mind having planted vines and set out shade trees for this nice young family.

When they finally left, Mary knew that they would be back to talk to Charles.

About the best that she could hope for now was a good sturdy wagon that could carry them all safely to Oregon.

Both Doc Carter and Charles had often been told to beware of wagons that were too heavy and to be sure to get falling tongues on them if they could, to make the going over steep hollows and short inclines easier. A twenty-five-hundred-pound wagon drawn by a single yoke of oxen would do it, it was agreed, for each family.

Charles thought he could do better by getting the basic wagon parts and then fitting it out himself. He would build beds with pull-out bottoms for storage along each side. Other boxes could be fitted along the sides above the beds during the day and then be taken down and put along the middle of the wagon at night. Across the back and front Charles would put very heavily waterproofed boxes strong enough for seats. These would hold boots and tools where they would be easily accessible. The one in front was a special addition for the benefit of Mary, so that she could sit outside when the weather allowed and not be cooped up inside all the time.

The front sent was not deep and it slanted sharply back from top to bottom so that the flooring-footrest protruded only slightly beyond the front edge of the seat, but the front edge of the floor curved up smartly for some protection from mud and dust, both of which they could expect in abundance. This seat made their wagon unique and, as John Henry sagely commented "Folks will be able to tell which is us a long way off."

Planning and working on the first stages took up so much of their time and thought that they decided Noah himself had not spent more time on the Ark, which was what they began calling it, though none of them could remember which one of them had made the original suggestion.

On the outside, Charles would drive strong hooks to hold the churn, pots and skillets and kegs for water and vinegar. Extra yokes for the oxen and the grindstone would be no problem; they could be lashed to the side with extra ropes.

If Mary was told once, she was told a hundred times, it seemed, how to pack what good china and silver she could take in the tin boxes of such staples as flour and sugar.

On Saint Patrick's day, Charles drove the wagon into the yard. "A fine day — for the Irish!" Mary thought.

Charles methodically pointed out where the fittings would go — as if they hadn't planned it all so long that, they didn't know! "I am not so big a fool as to think we can store enough bedding and clothes and food in that trap to get all of us over plains and mountains and desert in any decent condition," she told herself bitterly.

Aloud, she asked tartly, "How many of us are you planning to take?"

The children all looked at her in shocked silence.

Charles was angry, but his reply sounded mild enough. "Families larger than ours have done it, and we can, too — with a little faith. What's more, we'll be pooling some things with the Carters and the Lights. That way each wagon won't need to carry all that each family needs."

"Like a hundred and forty pounds of flour for each of us, and bushels of cornmeal and dried fruit and parched corn?" Mary turned on her heel and plodded back into the house, but not before she had seen the woebegone looks on their faces.

"Well, let them face the facts," she tried to justify herself. She did not dare look back. She went on into the kitchen and took it out on the stove by savagely stoking the fire and banging the stove lids back into place.

Speaking her mind did more than clear the air. Somehow it clarified her own thinking, too. The futility of her resistance was apparent as never before. That fact accepted, she began to think more positively about the awesome amount of planning and preparation required of her in the weeks ahead. Then her disposition improved.

"Well," she said, when Charles came into the kitchen Wednesday morning, "If we're going, we need to do some planning together. For the life of me, I don't see how we can get all that we need to take into that one wagon — even with the Lights and Carters helping out."

Charles methodically settled his hat on the hook behind the door. "I've been thinking the same thing," he admitted. "Shall we ask the folks over to do some planning with us?"

"Why not ask them for Sunday dinner? If they can't come this Sunday, at least, we'll have got things started."

Charles beamed approval. "Fine. I'll drive by their places this afternoon and ask them."

"Sister Carter will probably offer to bring a pie. If she does,let her," Mary mused aloud.

"And what about Sister Light?" Charles anticipated.

"We have the meat on hand. Why don't you tell her any vegetable or maybe light bread, if she asks."

Charles retrieved his hat without stopping for whatever he had come in for. As he went out the door, Mary called after him, "Remember to tell Sister Carter that Millie and the girls will take care of the twins, and John Henry will be mighty glad to have Amos and William for company."

Even as he was going down the steps, Mary could hear him sigh. He was not fond of having extra small children "under foot."

Mary smiled to herself. It would serve him right if she had twins, too. Wouldn't Charles have a fit! Especially if they were girls! Six girls! She almost giggled aloud at the thought as she bent over to stoke the stove and get a quick oven for the batch of cookies she wanted to finish before lunchtime. She had promised Pauline and Mamie a bit of dough to roll out and bake for their own, as soon as they put away their doll things.

It was the morning of a day like most weekdays, once Monday's washing and Tuesday's ironing were over. Each day thereafter bore forward to a sweet Sabbath of hymnsinging, sermonizing, and Christian socializing.

As she worked, she thought again of the Carter twins. Outsiders invariably referred to Samantha as "the pretty one" and to Miranda as "the plain one." The babies themselves answered to "Mant" and "Rand," though clearly they themselves were not aware of which one was which. To Pauline and Mamie, they were living dolls to be played with. When Millie was on hand to over-see their care, Sister Carter relinquished them confidently, and the chubby little near-duplicates just as confidently raised their arms to the older girls' advances. They were accustomed to being lugged about by older children. Indeed, they were beginning to expect it.

On Sunday, when the adults were finally gathered around the table after dinner, Charles, having called them together, naturally assumed the informal chairmanship. carefully deferring to the other two men.

Likewise, he assumed that the wives would speak only when they were spoken to. Mary could not tell whether the other women noticed this or not. She watched their faces and soon ob-served that they had no difficulty getting attention when they wanted it. Sister Carter tended to use a gentle hand on her husband's arm. Sister Light would dramatically catch her breath. Mary enjoyed watching them operate.

Just for fun, she tried clearing her throat. She got prompt at-tention. Self-conscious once she had their attention, all she could think of was, "Is everyone warm enough?"

Charles let the murmur of assurance subside before recalling them to the business at hand. He, too, cleared his throat as he smoothed out the "model, judicious out-fit." published by The Committee.

"Perhaps we might compare our lists of necessaries. First on mine is 150 pounds of flour for each adult. Is that what you have?"

Sister Light's mouth flew open so fast Mary could hear her teeth click. "Why that would be more than a thousand pounds of flour for a family like yours!" she exclaimed.

"I figure on five barrels," he assented, — "two hundred pounds apiece."

Consternation showed on Sister' Carter's face as she turned to "Doc." Her eyes were wide and she spoke as if she simply couldn't believe it. "Then we ought to take four, shouldn't we?"

"Yes, Eleanor," he answered patiently. "If the Adamses can, I guess we can."

Before she knew that she was going to, Mary quipped, "If the

Adamses can!"

Father Light slowly wagged his head. "Five barrels of flour and one of those wagons is half full. Maybe we can get some young feller to drive a provisions wagon for us. Might come in handy."

Mary looked at Charles. She knew he had set his heart on making it with just one wagon. He was looking at "Doc" Carter. "Doc" looked agreeable.

"Of course," put in Sister Light, "we could let you use some of the space in our wagon, what with only two of us."

"Wait till you hear the rest of the list before you make your offers," Mary laughed.

Charles looked none too pleased as he turned back to his list. "The next biggest item is meat, of course. I aim to take as much as I can on the hoof, to start with, and I'm counting strong on game after that." A tentative smile hovered around his mouth as if to suggest an apology for such a devil-may-care attitude.

Doc looked pleased. "If we take another wagon we might even manage a coop of chickens and have eggs, too."

"All the comforts of home," piped Father Light.

Sister Light caught Mary's eye and winked broadly.

"What next?" Sister Carter spoke up like a good little girl in school asking the question the teacher wants asked.

"A bushel of dried fruit apiece is recommended," he answered.

"Aha," chirped Sister Light mischievously, "the wagon is full with seven bushels of dried fruit in it. You'll have to leave your family at home."

Charles looked sharply from Sister Light to Mary to see whether they might be conniving. It did sound as if she had put Sister Light up to it. Charles's suspicion made her feel so guilty that she could feel a warm blush creeping up her throat. She knew Charles would see it and be convinced of his suspicions.

"How much beans and rice, Brother Adams?" It was Sister Carter again.

"Ten pounds a person for rice," he read. "and a half bushel each of beans, cornmeal, and parched corn."

Doc was checking his notes. "That takes care of all the

foodstuffs except things like coffee, tea, molasses and sugar, salt, soda and vinegar, doesn't it?"

Charles nodded as his eyes left the list and followed across the page to his estimate. "To follow their advice, my load in foodstuffs alone would run to about twenty-four hundred pounds, and it would cost me over one hundred dollars."

Father Light whistled appreciatively.

His wife was all impudence. "No family's worth it," she announced. "Looks to me that a likely feller better show up to drive another wagon for us," her husband agreed.

Sister Carter slid her hand across the table toward Charles. "May I compare our figures?" she asked softly.

"If you can make them out." He spoke diffidently as he handed them across to her.

Mary wondered whether she knew how poor Charles's wife was at such things. Anyway, Eleanor Carter herself made a rather attractive figure as she sat there poised with her pencil, absorbed in housewifely accounting, her lips moving as she whispered softly,

"four barrels of flour, four-forty a barrel
sixty pounds of rice, seven cents a pound
one hundred seventy pounds of sugar, thirteen pounds
* for a dollar*
four pounds of tea, sixty cents a pound
ten pounds of Prime Rio coffee, ten cents a pound
seven bushel of dried fruit, two-fifty a bushel
molasses, forty cents a gallon
three and a half bushel of beans two-fifty apiece
fourteen pounds of soda, seven cents a pound ..."

Suddenly she looked up and laughed, "You haven't prices down here for cornmeal and vinegar."

Charles looked smug. "I counted the weight, but I didn't count the price because I think we can save out enough of what we'll have on hand so as not to have to buy them." He took a quick breath and leaned across the table confidentially. "I think I can clear enough from this place and all to stock the wagon and still have about four hundred fifty to start with in Oregon."

The response was so perfunctory and polite that Mary was

sure the others were counting on no less for themselves, but he continued, "I picked up a copy of the ST. JO GAZETTE not long ago that had a letter from Oregon in it. You know, we're likely to get more for our teams and wagons after we've crossed the plains with them than we paid out for them here."

Father Light made an impish face. "We'll have to get them there first!" Gnomish glee lit up his face. "Let's pretend we didn't know and be pleasantly surprised when we get there!"

Sister Carter turned to Mary as she returned Charles's notations to him. "Will you be putting up tents every night?"

As Mary hesitated, not sure just what they were planning to do and not sure whether she should admit it or not, Charles spoke for her, "I think we have it figured out so that we can sleep the whole family in the wagon whenever we need to. I'm going to set the beds up high enough to take advantage of the widest part of the wagon, where it's almost five feet across. We'll have the beds built along both sides atop storage boxes."

He had their rapt attention, and so he went on. "The beds along one side will be quite narrow, but I aim to pull up a part at night to widen it with a kind of hammock effect. We'll still have room behind and under the front seat to put some barrels there, too."

When he paused they made appropriate sounds of interest and approval.

He went on, "With duck only fifteen cents a yard, John Henry and I thought we'd take a few yards and make some little lean-to tents that he has an idea for ... He thinks we could drop strips from the sides of the wagon to make it quite comfortable underneath."

Mary had not heard this before. She began to wonder what other plans the two had been hatching together.

Doc said, "That boy has a head on him."

Charles beamed. "Now about the heavy equipment. Perhaps we can agree on the pieces that we could all count on using whenever they are needed — like an anvil for instance, or the pickax, and such ... If one of us has such things, the rest of us can count on not having to carry them."

Father Light's whiskers bobbed eagerly. "You can count on

me to carry the anvil, for one thing."

Doc smiled. "That's fine. Brother Adams and I can divide up most of the other things." Then he turned to Charles, "Don't you think one plow between us should suffice, since we'll be neighbors when we get there?"

Charles's beam was of pure brotherhood. "Why not!" he agreed, "and I can have things like the adze and pickax in the box on the front."

Now the men were really warming to it. They accounted for the grindstone, extra ropes, and just about all the equipment anyone might possibly need, it seemed to Mary.

A sense of real accomplishment and pleasant agreement settled upon the three couples. In the pauses they could hear Mamie's chuckles and the girlish voices upstairs. From outside came the boys' shouts and laughter. The three families were going to get along just fine.

For the time being, the prospect of going to Oregon began to seem like a friendly adventure, a kind of prolonged church camp meet without the shouting.

Mary had indeed given up resistance against going, but there was a stubborn streak in her that held Charles to his promise not to start before the first of May ... He, too, had his own pride. Having once given his word, he was not one to go back on it, though every day more wagons rolled through Van Buren County, having crossed the Mississippi into Iowa, where they would follow the Des Moines river for a while and then turn more directly west across the southern part of the state to Kanesville. There they would gird and group themselves for crossing the Missouri River to follow either the north or south bank of the Platte and beyond — far, far beyond — into the Oregon Country.

Day after day, she watched them lurch by in the rain and the cold. Night after night, she saw their campfires among the box elder down by the creek. She was determined not to join the motley train until the weather gave some promise of tenderer treatment to folk on the trail.

As more and more emigrants went through, it became apparent that this year's migration was going to be the big one. The noisy parade of stock would be out on the plains to get the pick of the new grass for grazing. Latecomers would get what was left, and from the size of the passing throng, there wouldn't be too much left.

On March 8, when Charles finished the sale of the place to the Sniders, he didn't get quite all the cash that he had counted on, but he was lucky at that to get nearly seven and a half an acre for their eighty acres: the Reverend Delazon Smith had converted many a solid citizen into an emigrant, and there were many places for sale at give-away prices. Actually, Charles did somewhat better than the actual sale price of $594, because he and the young Mr. Snider did some trading on provisions and equipment.

The swelling ranks of migrants trailing across the countryside worked upon their friends like a giant magnet, pulling loose the last frail roots that held them to their land. As the days became weeks, family after family pulled up and followed their pastor, who had himself set out on April 17.

Mary, for one, was glad to see him go. "It will be a pleasure," she told herself, to see the world go on turning without him. "He had the faculty of being the center of attention. There had been the big Donation Party for him in March; then he put on a big sale on his furniture and books whereby the faithful could subsidize his emigration .... She was sick and tired of hearing his name.

Speaking of folks going on, "You can hardly blame them," Charles said, "Especially when it is a matter of life and death to get a good start."

Mary noted that he evidently did not realize, even after he had said it, all that he implied. "Not that it is any news to me," she thought. "even as isolated as I am." Spring was always a busy time for everyone, anyway, and now that she was beginning to grow out of her clothes, she saw few people except close friends and neighbors.

"We'll wait for you till Doomsday," Sister Light promised, by way of consolation, one day after others were out of earshot.

Mary purred the adequate response aloud; to herself she dryly commented. "Thanks for the comforting thought!"

But Mary was not downhearted all the time. One morning she felt pretty good. As she served the breakfast bacon, she startled them all by trilling,

> "Even before the first of May,
> I am ready to say,
> 'Let us be on our way'."

"Amen," Charles answered fervently.

After breakfast, he drove off buoyantly. She had a pretty good idea of what he was up to, as she waved to him from the porch, and she knew whose remark had given him the impetus. "That's what I get for being funny!"

On May Day she found a basket of flowers on the front door knob. She did not have any illusions about their being for her. She knew they were for Millie. That didn't bother her. What did, was the idea that maybe she would never see flowers like these again.

"What kind of flowers grow in Oregon?" she asked the family. None of them knew.

"Such a far and alien country I'm headed for, I can't even picture the flowers!"

During the next five days, Charles completed the fittings in the wagon and began leaving more in the wagon at the end of each day, and either he or John Henry slept in it; each night for protection. When the girls grumbled and begrudged John Henry this privilege, Mary longed to tell them to enjoy the comforts of their home as long as they could, but she restrained herself, not wanting to spell out exactly what she meant, as she knew they would surely force her to do. Better let them enjoy the trip as long as they could and learn the worst no sooner than they had to, since it must be so. Mary had, as Charles put it "quit fussing about it." He didn't hear her gritting her teeth!

"Big as an ox and awkward as a cow on ice-and more so each day." Mary found to her surprise, just how helpful even the little ones could be. Once, to Millie, she exclaimed, "I declare, I just don't know how I'd manage without you."

Millie's eyes widened in a study of surprise, "Didn't you expect me to be helpful, Mother?"

"You, of course, but I didn't expect the little ones to line up the way they do."

"Oh, Pappa and I talked to them and explained things."

"I wish I could have been a mouse to hear what you and your

father said."

"Why, Mother." Millie was shocked at the thought of her mother eaves-dropping. "Pappa explained that the weight throws you off balance and makes you tire fast. That's why you get cross. Mamie asked why he didn't make you take a nap when you get cross the way you make her and Pauline when you say they are cross and need a nap."

"Hmmm," Mary commented.

"Then I explained about stretching and the cord."

"What do you mean?"

"Oh, you know, how if the mother stretches too hard the cord could pull around the baby's neck and maybe choke it."

"Who told you that?"

"Mrs. Light told me about it and said especially I could hang things on the clothesline for you and get things off the top shelves."

So it was, as Mary told Sister Carter later, "Wonderful, just wonderful. They are enjoying their responsibility and I appreciate them in a way I never did before. It's a very humbling experience." Then, "I guess I could use a little humility."

Sister Carter slowly leaned forward and looked earnestly into Mary's face. "Sister Adams, I have always liked your spirit. You have spunk."

IV

One With the Caravans

MARY HAD FELT, even after the day was set, that something would surely interfere. She could hardly believe it when they actually drove away. She had been so braced for a "situation" that she felt rather silly, as if she might not be having the baby after all! If anything could have detained Charles, it might have been the weather. It almost did. As if Nature were taking a hand at keeping them fearfully indoors, the skies really opened up with a tantrum the night before they were to set out. Thunder and lightning, wind and rain raged all night long. Tearing at roof tops, toppling steeples, and creating havoc. Then, at dawn, the fury of the storm was spent, and calm settled on the torn countryside, as if to say, Mary thought, "If that won't stop you, you might as well go."

That last morning they had the briefest of fires in the stove, ate on a bare table with only the dishes they would wash and take with them. They had slept in bedding that was to go on the top of the beds in the wagon.

When the kitchen was clear, the fire put out, and the bedding in place for the trip, they made one last tour of the house and barn to check for anything that they might have inadvertently left behind. Mary lingered in the house alone. The curtains were fresh and crisp at the windows to welcome the new occupants. But the floors were bare. Most of the rugs were over or under mattresses in the wagons, but all the chairs and tables, beds and dressers, were left where they always were.

In the living room she listened to the solemn — now loud ticking of the dear, old clock on its shelf as it accusingly tolled her last moments of home. It would go on faithfully for seven more days. Seven more days, minus one for Sabbath lay-over, would be about six times twenty miles away from home towards that Oregon country in which she could never "see" herself.

A kind of blind panic caused her to put her hand out. It touched the back of the rocking chair, which promptly gave with the pressure. As startled as if she had unexpectedly touched a living thing, she quickly withdrew her hand. In so doing, she increased the momentum of its rocking. Transfixed, watching it rock and wanting it to stop because it was bad enough to leave the clock ticking away its moments of abandonment, she finally stilled the rocker with a trembling hand and fled through the kitchen, without looking at any of the things that she was leaving behind there.

One day she was saying, this is the last time I will do this and this; the next, this is the first time I will be doing this and this. It was like growing up, getting married, and leaving home all rolled into one.

Outside, the sky was dark with clouds full of rain. The wind was raw and cold. Charles hung the house key under an old washpan on the back porch, according to a prearranged plan.

The girls were already huddled in the wagon. Charles helped Mary into the wagon beside them and they started off, he beside the oxen and John Henry behind, driving the cows.

Evidences of the storm were everywhere, but only the little ones discussed it. Mary was sure they were all thinking the same thing. What a miserable beginning!

THE SUN COMES OUT

By the 22nd of May, the third Saturday, they had been on the Oregon Trail forever, it seemed. The vast importance of the sky, the wet green panorama of the countryside through which they were slowly moving, the other wagons, the road beneath — all this had become their world. Only this constantly changing sameness was reality — all else a dream of past or future.

The thunderstorm which overcast their first day continued with rains or threats of rains — and precious little of respite between times. But when the sun did occasionally break through the great cloud structures, as it must in May, the children joyfully tumbled out and trooped along beside the wagons as gaily as the wet footing allowed.

For Mary, of course, there could be no such walking. Only the bumping, rolling, pitching, rocking with the mercifully slow motions of the wagon. Time went best when she sat in the front. She could not get in or out of the wagon without help, always acutely aware that her awkwardness was as irksome to the family as it was frustrating to her.

She was grateful that there were just a few of them traveling together. The sun had come out wanly just before their noonday stop. The sun was indeed welcome, but the humidity was oppressive.

"This is the last time I let you out, Millie." Charles spoke sharply. It was after the middle of the afternoon.

"Then I'll save my last time for later," she muttered, retreating into the wagon. Mary felt the little arm as it dragged slowly past her back into the shadowy depths behind.

As the sun began to settle lower in the sky, the oxen began to move ahead almost eagerly, but the children were fretful. Even with both ends open, the wagon was stuffy inside. Mary could see when she peered back at them that Margaret's curls stuck to her forehead and neck in damp ringlets as she pushed away the clothespin doll that Millie was trying to animate for her as she spoke in her version of a social grown-up's voice, "I do declare, Miss Margaret, I just had to run over to visit with you this afternoon and tell you an interesting story."

"So tell me your old story," came Margaret's petulant response, "and make it about Daniel in the lions' den. I like the part when the lions are roaring and scaring him."

Mary was glad that Charles was not paying any attention to their conversation. He did not favor the way the children were want to "embellish the Bible," which he said "made light of the Word." Mary considered whether it would ever be possible for her to make Charles understand that the children were in a sense making the stories their own with those extra details of sight and sound and that they did no wrong to the basic truth. Even though the imagination might be a dangerous faculty, if held to the discipline of truth, it surely must be kin to that of the original scribes who wrote the Bible. She was not at ease in such abstractions and knew she steered a dangerous course between Charles's established statements and her own rather timid differing. What she did, then, was to chart a careful mid-course between, trying not to discourage — only to curb and restrain the children from over-ly exuberant or boisterous dramatizations. For a few moments she lost herself in the attempt to organize and justify herself.

Presently, she sensed Charles's expansiveness as he almost playfully juggled the goad and, nodding toward the oxen, chuckled, "They know their day's work is nearly done."

Suddenly Millie's version of the dreadful roaring of the lions broke loose from the depths of the wagon.

Mary's heart congealed as Charles turned around. "I guess we'll be thrown to the lions," she thought grimly.

But Charles didn't sound so very angry as he said "Gag that lion or make him walk until we stop for the night." Then he caught Mary's eye and winked broadly to underline his own brand of humor.

"Oh, Pa, the lion just laid down and died," Margaret giggled.

Charles was looking far ahead of the two wagons, at the dis-tant line of trees, which probably marked the water where they hoped to lay-by for the Sabbath.

"We'll still make it with an hour of daylight to spare, "he said encouragingly. "We're getting better at setting up camp every night."

"What, Pa?" John Henry called back anxiously.

"Getting better at camp-setting?"

"We're really good, Pa."

"See, we're good, Mary."

"Pride goeth before a fall," she answered smoothly, rather proud of herself.

He let a comfortable silence settle between them.

The children fell asleep before long and the wagon kept up a kind of conversation of its own as it contended with the ruts and bumps.

About the same time that they saw the barn and then the house, they saw a rider coming toward them. As he came abreast, he said something to each of the drivers ahead.

When he came up to Charles, it was evidently with the same greeting, "We hear you're Methodists. You're welcome to lay-by in our grove, and we'll be glad to let you have some eggs."

He and Charles took a liking to each other right away, and

he rode along beside, with the talk coming easily.

"Ask him whether his wife might spare me a fresh bit of bread-starter?" Mary asked.

When Charles relayed the message, the man replied genially that his wife had an extra batch on hand for just that purpose, "and if you folks will give us a real Sabbath service tomorrow, it'll be the best pay we could ask for."

At that moment an ominous growl came from within the wagon. It was so realistic that the farmer looked startled.

Evidently the lions had been only playing dead!

Mary, hoping to remove the responsibility from Charles's shoulders, burst out with the explanation, "The lions have been threatening brave Daniel, who has just been thrown into their den."

Pleasure and surprise lit up the man's face. "Well, now, if that don't beat all. It does make the old stories real to the youngsters - and enjoyable, too. I like the idea of learning our lessons with a merry heart."

As he wheeled his horse away, he called back, "Roar away, old lions, you can't hurt good old Daniel."

Mary glanced at Charles and saw that the approval from this stranger had accomplished in a moment more than all his wife's arguments had ever done. Charles was positively beaming.

KEG CREEK

The neat, shady grove with the widening stream, so convenient for wading, and washing, made the prospect for a pleasant Sabbath lay-over exhilarating. By contrast with the past week, more like a picnic than an opportunity to provide for the weary days ahead. With enough wood, she could bank a good fire and let bread rise over night so that it would be all ready to bake after breakfast when they had emptied most of the hot water, and by putting the heavier washing to soak in cold water tonight and bring it to a boil in the morning, she could call the process "wringing things out" which didn't sound so much like Sabbath desecration. If the women could get the lines up tonight and be ready to hang up the heavier things right away in the morning there needn't be a big to-do over it. If the weather would hold clear, the lighter things might be slipped onto the lines Sunday night and be dry enough to take down right after breakfast Monday morning.

Mary silently thanked the good Lord for His words and example concerning the Sabbath's being made for man and not man for the Sabbath.

Her thoughts had gone so far ahead of herself that she looked down surprised to find herself rubbing her hands. They were getting rougher every day, she thought ruefully.

The animals were to be pastured quite a distance from the grove, in order to impose as little as possible on the good farmer's hospitality. As soon as the wagons were stationed for the night and the cows milked, the oxen and the cows would be driven to their pasture.

The warm sun, the friendly shelter of the grove, and the ripples of the stream sparkling in the late afternoon sun — they have affected everyone in the whole train, Mary noticed, as they passed or were passed in the process of stationing the wagons. The men were jovial and relaxed, the women smiling and eager to set up their outdoor "housekeeping" for the lay-over. The children, with a final, joyous burst of energy, supplied a chorus of happy chatter, for which the commands of the men seemed a kind of strong counterpoint.

Mary was glad to see the Carters' wagon pull in next to them. Tonight they would sing "Safely Through Another Week — God Has Brought Us on Our Way;" tomorrow, "Oh Day of Rest and Gladness — O Day of Joy and Peace."

But Mary wasn't the only one whose thoughts were on song. Pauline and Millie were slowly hopping up and down under a tree while they improvised their own hymn of thanks: "Thank you for the woods, thank you for the nice shallow stream where we can go wading, thank you for the sunshine ... thank you ...thank you ... thank you!

Amos Carter, helping his father with the team, looked over and grinned at John Henry, who was putting on a discreet display of mock distress by pretending to plug his ears with his fingers. Amos then responded by pointing his index finger at his temple as if to shoot. The sound of Charles, clearing his throat, miraculously reminded both of them, simultaneously that the oxen needed their care.

"How are you feeling?" Sister Carter called over.

"Never felt better in my life," Mary answered, stretching as much as she dared as soon as Charles had helped her down. She moved slowly, "Just stiff from sitting. How would you like to get a fire started for us both," she asked. "I believe I'd like to walk over to the house and see if we can't get a bit of that fresh bread starter."

Sister Carter surveyed her with an approving nod. "If you feel like it, it will do you good. I'll be glad to get things started here if Pauline will look after the twins."

The short walk increased her sense of well being — until she started on the path around the house, not wanting to draw the farm wife to the front door when she surely would be in the kitchen.

Suddenly she heard the old familiar sound of a stove-lid being settled into place on the kitchen stove inside the house. A wave of nostalgia, so strong that for a moment she lost all her bearings, swept over her. It was just like standing on a sandy beach when an ebbing wave seems to be taking the very beach beneath one's feet.

How awful, she thought, when the sounds of a stove lid can make me feel like a homeless beggar — but it does and I am. I am a poor, pathetic, pregnant pilgrim. I wish I were happily clattering the lids on my own stove back home.

Mary's homesickness was quickly dispelled in the sunny warmth of their welcome from the Scott family, however. One would have thought Charles was conveying a great favor to abide in their grove and make it their last camp before the crossing.

Somehow, with one accord, they all set themselves for one great happy Sabbath in the States. For that one day they resolutely put aside the final plans and preparation that must begin on Monday. For all its poignancy, that Sabbath was truly a "day of rest and gladness."

The Scotts were one of those couples who seem perfectly to complement each other with happy competence and each took an unabashed delight in bragging about the accomplishments of the other as if sharing the nicest of news. Beautiful, prematurely gray hair swirled luxuriantly up to a generous knot on the top of Mrs. Scott's head as smoothly as if it had been sculptured into place. It accentuated the cherubic pink-and-whiteness of her serene face and the ample proportions of her figure.

If I could only look forward to being like Sister Scott I'd cross two Great American Deserts, she thought, but in her heart she knew herself to be too mercurial to attain such serenity and all-embracing friendliness. Sister Carter, she had to admit, was closer in temperament to Sister Scott than she, even though Sister Carter could not fully reach that gaiety of spirit that immediately drew Mary to Sister Scott. Mary could not understand why, but she knew that in this woman's company life seemed rich and sweet and she herself felt appreciated and worthy of appreciation. I'll just have to enjoy it while I can, she thought.

She couldn't tell whether she imagined it or not, but she thought Brother Scott affected Charles in somewhat the same way. They were talking together near her. She couldn't help watching Brother Scott as he talked, even though he was talking to Charles, not her.

"Yes," he said, slipping his hands into his back pockets, creating a posture that protruded his round stomach as he allowed the genial lines of his face to wreathe the pink rotundity of his cheeks and nose. His blue eyes twinkled above the gold-rimmed spectacles, which had slipped down precariously, as if they really weren't needed. The glint of those gold frames added a hint of elegance to the effect of health, well-being, and good humor, all of which pleased Mary. The dark, curly ring of beard and sideburns set off his features quite well, she thought. She allowed herself to look at him so intently that she realized, too late, that she had attracted his attention. Charles wouldn't like that, but he did not notice as the man nodded easily, to include her, as he went on.

"Yes, Brother Simpson has been here almost two years. Volunteered to come. Right here in the midst of Mormonism, we're growin'. Right now, our two congregations, the one here and the one about twenty miles south of here in Fremont County number over two hundred, and we've got our eyes on quite a few likely ones to bring in during our revival meetings this fall."

"How about the Mormons?" Charles asked.

"Aw," came the chuckling answer, "they're not half as bad as they are cracked up to be. The Golden Rule still works pretty well."

Mary just couldn't imagine anyone willfully crossing him and disturbing the genial current of his manner. He's not raw-boned, pinched, or mealy-mouthed, she thought, grateful that this suggestion of grace could be so out here on the contentious edge of Iowa and Christendom.

"Brother Adams," he said, "Why don't you saddle up and ride on in to town in the morning and get your family places on the ELPASO? It's a fine ferry, up from St. Louis. There's an awful crowd of people ahead of you, but it would make a nice start for you if you could get crossing on it. You'll be surprised to see how emigrants are crowding in around here getting ready to head for Oregon. It almost gives me the fever." He laughed jovially, as if the idea of his pulling up stakes was unbelievable.

Mary wondered whether his wife knew how lucky she was.

A man from a camp down the road joined them just in time to hear. He introduced himself as a Virginian. "If it weren't for this slavery business I wouldn't be so eager to go. If we don't keep slaves, you know, it's rough to compete with those who do. The lines are drawing tighter all the time. There's going to be trouble, no matter what."

Charles took a long time on his trip into town. It was almost dusk before he rode in. Even in his obvious weariness, Mary could read suppressed excitement as he dismounted. He patted Ned and gave the reins to John Henry.

"We're going to have lots more company than we reckoned on the way to Oregon," he announced. "You may think you've seen lots of emigrants, but what we've seen weren't a drop in the bucket."

Dramatically, he extended his arm, with the palm of his hand down, and moved it in a level sweep parallel with the ground. "There's the Missouri," he indicated the vast stretch of it, "with hundreds and hundreds — maybe thousands — of wagons — on both sides of the river."

He paused for a moment, evidently choosing his words with

54

care. "Not all of them are — exactly, good Methodists. We won't want to rush into joining just any train. The Reverend Smith and Dr. Miller and all of those went on ahead the 14th. But," he added loyally. "the Reverend left quite a mark in Kanesville with his preaching."

He hesitated. Then, "in fact, it looks as if there won't need to be a choice directly. We can travel with our own folks and let the choosing develop as we go along." There was a defensive flicker in his eyes. He wasn't going to admit to her that he was disappointed not to find that Number One Oregon Emigrant Company waiting for him.

Besides, he had another bit of news especially for Mary. "I saw one family all ready to go, with a baby not two weeks old. Folks by the name of Criss," he added, as an authenticating footnote.

Mary got the message, all right, with small comfort. But there was something else. Mary watched the lines in his face tighten as he studied how to say it. Whatever it was, it wasn't good.

"There's been some sickness."

"Not plague?"

"Can't be sure." He lowered his voice, as if offering some confidential assurance. "I promise you we'll not get near it if we can possibly help it. By not joining a big train we can keep more to ourselves, if it should show up along the way."

Now he had a good excuse for not joining up with any other train until he was satisfied that he could not catch up with Number One Emigrant Company.

LEAVING KEG CREEK FOR COUNCIL BLUFFS

When they were finally ready to be on their way, Sister Scott reached up to Mary and slipped a small package into her hands. "Just some horehound for treats to the children," she whispered. "Sometimes, I know, it hath more charm than music to soothe their savage little breasts," and she laughed softly.

Having shaken hands with Charles and John Henry, their host joined his wife while the wagon slowly began to move. Together they kept apace for a way as he made little jokes to keep it a pleasant farewell. Finally, "Now Sister Adams, don't let me hear of you going stylish on this trip and wearing bloomers like

those women I read about in our ADVOCATE last fall. It's bad
enough for our women to take that style to Edinburgh but I just
don't fancy taking it to the Indians."

Mary laughed in spite of herself and was glad to hear that
she could make such a nice convincing sound when she was trying
so hard not to cry. She spread her lips in an exaggerated smile
that would show at a distance and waved hard.

The last distinguishable words she could hear across the
widening space between them were, "Write to us from Oregon."

Write to them from Oregon? She tried to imagine it. Sometime in the fall. Would it be mild enough still when they arrived
to sit outside — by the Willamette, maybe? On the doorstep of
their log cabin — while the baby slept? Would she head the letter
"By the Beautiful Walamet — or Willamut?" She would have to
learn how it should be spelled, for certain. To the dreary rhythm
of the jolting wagon, Mary sat and wondered, trying to force her
mind to focus on a picture of what the end of the Trail would be
like. Would they, at sunset, drive into a little town beside the Willamette from that last stretch of the Trail that had been opened by
people named Barlow, she wondered.

She shivered and wished the sun would come out now just a
little bit. Sitting still, as she had been, had chilled her to the bone.

Millie, who later became Mrs. J.W. Meredith, often said, "When I'm tired, I think I look like my mother." (From the author's collection.)

– OREGON HISTORICAL SOCIETY

An emigrant camp on the Overland Trail.

V

Kanesville — Bedlam
of Preparation

DESPITE CHARLES'S DESCRIPTION, Mary was not prepared for the sights and sounds — and smells — of the congregated caravans about Kanesville. The congestion was simply beyond belief.

Wagons, carriages, tents, oxen, mules, horses, cows, chickens and pigs, with children and dogs darting in and out, shifting clusters of men, of women, riding, standing about or sitting on ox yokes by campfires, sometimes by little castiron stoves. The confusion of sound matched the confusion of sights, but the sounds which scored most disagreeably were the hoarse shouts of men and the strident ring of anvils from every direction, in the open and in regular blacksmith shops.

If setting tires and shoeing horses made this much noise, how must it have sounded when the Crusaders and their armor were in preparation en route to wrest the Holy Land from the infidels, she wondered.

The EL PASO had stayed only five days. When Charles found they were too late to board her, he obtained passage on the Mormon ferry ten miles up — and lucky at that, even though it would carry only two wagons and not more than ten animals at a time. There were people who were attempting to ferry themselves out there on that expanse of muddy, turbulent water in flatboats. Evidently it was not uncommon for some to find the end of the Trail here at the Missouri.

At first Mary had wondered why the silly people across the river were camped there instead of getting on their way. Now she realized that they were either worn with the labor of the crossing or waiting for relatives and friends and maybe even the rest of their equipment, just as they and the Carters would set up camp and wait for the Lights and the others. The ferry would take about an hour and a half round trip, so it was a good thing they didn't need to wait for very many trips.

As they threaded their way slowly through the throngs, Mary found herself eagerly scanning faces and equipment, trying to read from their surfaces the spirit and purpose that impelled the individuals in the kaleidoscope of faces. Because she was not content simply to decide whether they were the kind bound for Oregon or for California, she became so engrossed she almost forgot to keep track of the girls' questions and comments.

Origins and affiliations were as interesting to her as destinations. She was not only sure she could tell a Roman Catholic at sight, from a Protestant and Jews, of course, but Baptists, Presbyterians, and Methodists — naturally. The Roman Catholics, she thought, had an aura of a worldly naivete; the Jews, a sharp, wily humorous cast; the Presbyterians, an objective coolness of manner. The Baptists were stockier, blunter. The Methodists? Why, warmer, nicer, of course.

It was a harmless game she played, and she guessed she was better at it than she would ever have the courage to prove. The thought betrayed itself with a mischievous expression on her rather serious little face, a face that in a more elevated social position would have been considered a bit imperious.

Well, she was in an elevated position — up on the front seat of the wagon, and now her chin was up, for when strangers' eyes met hers and then traveled over her figure to return to her eyes with the "knowing" look that acknowledged recognition of her being "in a family way," she did not respond. In a public place she instinctively kept strangers at a distance — not an icy distance, just a fastidious distance.

It was as if, when she felt strange eyes upon her, all her eager, questing antennae were suddenly withdrawn and she assumed an emotional, protective coloration.

And all the while this eager observation, withdrawal, and self-analysis was going on inside "the little woman in a family way up there on the seat of that wagon with the funny front," Charles was leading Orthodoxology among the maze of wagons, tents, men, women, children, horses, mules, oxen, cows, dogs,

59

sheep, and even pigs and chickens.

The odors made her almost ill at times — smoke, cooking, sweat, leather, and all the other animal smells. She was almost thankful that the weather was cold and wet. How awful it would be on a hot day!

The girls were chattering with excitement. One minute they were jiggling beside her and the next they were back looking out over the tailgate.

John Henry marched proudly with his father, when there was room, and dropped back and caught up again as the way allowed. He is growing up so fast it takes my breath away, she told herself.

The river was high, turbulent and soil-laden from spring rains. Mary's heart shriveled in fear, but the children were wild with the exciting prospect and exulted with every blast of the whistles. They were to camp as near as possible to the ferry, for they were scheduled to make the first trip across the next morning. After seeing the congestion at Kanesville, they found the upper crossing comparatively quiet, though it was a small city of canvas.

She was glad for the practice they had had in setting up camp, for this night they were being observed by many people who had become experts, they having been on the road for many weeks. Some had started last year and wintered over. Introductions were casual, with people drifting by their fire and off again with a freedom engendered by the open air and transitory nature of their association. With many of them, she considered herself lucky, both for the open air and the transitory nature of the association.

John Henry came along just in time to carry a box back into the wagon for her. "Just like a camp meeting, isn't it!" His voice said it as an amused exclamation, but his eyes were searching.

What he is really saying, she thought, is "Try to think of it as a camp meeting." She obligingly moved her lips into smiling position. Her lips were reasonably tractable, but inside there was a fuss going on over which she had no control. She dropped down on the yoke where she had just been cleaning up the supper dishes and waited, sitting as straight as she could. Evidently it was just the usual after-meal disturbance. At least there was no measurable interval.

While she was catching her breath, the smoke from their fire shifted and enveloped her eyes in a stinging cloud. As she coughed and gasped, she automatically tried to fan it away with her hands. Then she realized what a silly picture she must be making. She hoped no one was watching her antics.

Sure enough, there was Charles coming back from a wagon that had just come in while she was at her chores. He would frown on her undignified exhibition, if he had seen it, and he could hardly have avoided seeing her because he was coming straight toward her.

However, coming straight toward her though he was, he certainly was not seeing her. He was in quite a study; she could tell by the way his brows were wrinkled.

Mary gave the yoke a push and herself a pull to get up and smoothed her skirts down as fast as she could. "Well, what are they like?" she asked.

"Fine. God-fearing folks," he conceded slowly, and then, hesitatingly, added, "At least, that's the way they talk." He turned abruptly to wash his hands and end the discussion.

Mary was intrigued, but she knew she might just as well give up asking any more. She would just have to wait and see for herself.

She did not have to wait long. Just as she was turning the dishtowel to dry from another angle, she heard the voice and knew immediately whose it was, because the tone of that voice just had to be the reason for Charles's puzzlement. Unctuous and ingratiating it was. "Brother Adams, brought my missus around to meet Missus Adams."

Before she could lay down the drying cloth, he was close to her — too close for comfort, though he didn't smell any worse than any of the other men, and he wasn't repulsive in appearance. Not even in his manner was there any one thing she "could put her finger on," unless maybe one would say he was a little "pushy." Yes, probably "ingratiating" was the word for it.

He was raw-boned and wind-burned a grainy red except where freckles darkened the smoother exposed surfaces. But for a strong nose and square jaw, his head would have been too small to be much more than a ruddy terminus for a long neck. As she looked at him she couldn't help thinking of a turkey.

His big hands made up for what his head lacked in size, she noticed. One dangled loosely; the other, hooked by a thumb in the top of his trousers, rode easily. Then the dangling hand jerked upright from the elbow and let the thumb point back toward the drab female stumbling behind. "This y'ar is m' woman. Needs Christian companionship bad."

The female, thus gallantly introduced, almost imperceptibly raised her eyes, but the lids quickly dropped as if keeping them up would have taken more will than she could muster. "Pleased ta make yer acquaintance," she mumbled miserably.

"Here is a brow-beaten woman, if ever I saw one," thought Mary with a rush of compassion.

"Won't you sit down on this yoke by the fire with me?" she invited.

The woman darted over as if all too eager to become less noticeable.

Mary made quite a thing of redraping the dish cloth again and then dropped down beside the woman. As she did, the woman looked up with eyes so full of misery she startled Mary. But there was more. Was it anguish, or fear, or humiliation? More like an unfocused dread, maybe. But there was something more. The pleasanter Mary tried to be, the more a sharp edge of some other emotion — antagonism or spite itself flashed out.

Mary found herself remembering the cat they had found caught in a trap that had tried to bite her when she attempted to comfort it while John Henry was loosening the spring. A subterranean river of fury flowed within this woman, Mary realized when, in trying to make pleasant conversation, she innocently asked, "Do you have any children?"

She was aghast to see the woman stifle a look of injury and hate as she opened her mouth to reply and fought for self control. But before she could control her features and formulate a word, whatever emotion had animated her so strangely subsided and she didn't even try to speak. Dully she shook her head.

The man moved in quickly. "She's a-grievin'," he explained blandly, "cause we thought it more Christian to leave our younguns with her ma — just until we git settled, of course."

They all could hear the woman catch her breath, but before she could utter a sound, her husband interrupted with firmness, his eyes hard on her, "As soon as we can git fixed on a homestead, I'm agoin' back and git 'em m'self."

Charles looked off down the river and thoughtfully jingled the keys and coins in his pocket. "A man has to do what he thinks is right," he said solemnly, by way of suspended judgment.

It was, Mary saw, a good answer for them all. You just have to admit Charles is as just as he knows how.

She had not noticed how soon darkness would be upon them and she had lost track of her own children. She excused herself, explaining as she got up as quickly as she could to look for them if they did not respond to her first call. To her surprise, the girls had quietly put themselves to bed and John Henry was just as quietly chewing a stalk of grass as he sat with the Carter boys on the tongue of their wagon and looked off across the Missouri to the myriad of campfires like stars in a low sky over there. They were just waiting to be told to go to bed.

And so was everyone else. In very short order the whole camp settled down to rest against the stern demands of the morrow. The Adamses were no exception.

In the morning they packed up in the best time they had yet made and were soon down at the ferry. The children were rather subdued as the vastness of the muddy swirling water became apparent to them. They jumped to every command and Orthodoxology acted as if they had been trained for this moment as they slowly pulled up onto the ferry. John Henry stood with his arm around Dox's neck most of the way.

THE PLATTE AND THE PLAINS

Before they were safely across on the coast of Nebraska, they were all thoroughly soaked. What the rain did not dampen, the river spray did. But by the sunset the skies were clear and they were drying themselves by a warm fire not even a mile beyond the crossing. Morning would be soon enough to make the new beginning.

Rain and hail, ferrying and fording for the rest of that first week made Mary begin to wonder whether they should not indeed have made a real Ark. The beautiful rolling landscape must surely be completely inundated if the weather persisted. By Saturday, however, they were already beside the Platte and a cool breeze had dispelled the rain clouds to let the sun shine a benediction upon their first Sabbath along the great, gray sluggish water that they would follow for about five hundred miles across the plains.

Here there were flowers for the children to pick, grass enough for the cattle, and fuel enough for judicious burning. Mary's spirits lightened. The Mormons seemed to be sober, quiet folk bent on tending to their own affairs. They had seen no hostile Indians. All kinds of people seemed to be getting along together on the Trail, and most of them seemed inclined, when needed, to lend a hand. There had been some trouble with stampede threats in some of the other parties, but Charles seemed to be very competent. He might not be one to heed his wife, but he listened carefully to advice from the more trail-seasoned menfolk. When John Henry brought in some wild onion for flavoring the stew — ah, life had not lost its savor!

Their Sabbath rest so invigorated them that they went on and on in the moonlight Monday night to reach a campsite one of the scouts recommended.

Tuesday was a beautiful day, too, but Doxology showed some signs of lameness.

"What will we do about it, Pa?" Millie asked with a worried wrinkling of her forehead.

"What everyone else does. Doctor it, if necessary," he replied matter-of-factly.

His answer evidently allayed her concern. She patted the great neck and looked into its eyes, "We'll take care of you, Doxie."

Doxie sighed and looked not at all convinced.

Watching, Mary thought the question is not whether we will take care of Doxie, but whether Doxie will take care of us!

They had been following up the Loup Fork where the fording, though hazardous, was generally agreed to be better than nearer the Platte.

Charles examined the hoof once more and then spoke directly to the great beast, "Doxie, do you think you can go just a little more today? We will see that you get a good rest while we're getting ready to ford, and if you can get us across this afternoon I'll fix that hoof tomorrow and give you a good rest."

Doxie stretched his neck and inclined his head.

Millie took it for assent and thanked him profusely.

John Henry, nearby, snorted derisively.

But Charles slowly patted his massive head, "Good Boy. I think you can do it, and the pasturage looks better on the other side."

Mary was wondering why he was taking a chance when he looked up and evidently read the wonder in her eyes. "We'll be better off fording all together," he said. "Besides, the water may help that hoof. I'll wrap it as best I can."

One party was in the process of fording when they reached the spot. Others were in various stages of unloading their wagons, lifting the wagon boxes, putting blocks of wood underneath, and then tying their wagon boxes with ropes.

Mary sat transfixed, watching the lurching wagons behind the frightened cattle out in the swift current, men on plunging horses keeping them on course as best they could. From a distance, it all had an unreal quality, and the hoarse sounds of men and beasts came back eerily under the bright sky.

Just as Mary was telling herself that perhaps it was not as dangerous as it looked, a wagon tipped crazily, hung for a moment, and then went over. It was almost a half mile away. Objects in the water, unless they showed arms and faces, were indistinguishable. But even from that distance the heroism of men and boys, rushing to the rescue and risking being crushed by floundering beasts and unmanageable wreckage in the swift waters was unmistakable. Whatever was to be rescued would have to be done quickly, she knew, because of the quicksand.

All the while, the wagons that had already started when the accident occurred had to keep coming on because they dared not stop, and their animals were all the harder to control because of the panic of the others ahead, so that it fell mostly on those who had already made the crossing and those unhappily involved to get the battered wagon and its spilled contents ashore.

Suddenly Mary realized that she must have been holding her breath. Slowly she came back to herself. There was the river gushing by, here she was on the wagon seat watching the dreams of a whole family being battered by the merciless waters through which she and her family must go as soon as they could get ready. Over all, ironically, was the sky, blue and benign.

She had lost track of Charles, who had left John Henry to hold the team, but pretty soon he came back.

"Well," he said, "let's get ready."

Through all their preparations from then on not one word did any of them say about the accident. Not, that is, until they were almost at the moment of crossing.

Then Charles spoke directly and sternly to each of them. "If the wagon should tip — but I don't think it will because it is so broad — get free, but hang on to the outside. Someone will get you across safely if you do as I say. Remember, stay with the Ark. It is strong and safely caulked. It will take you over in fine shape. I promise you that I will be right alongside to see that it does."

"Yes, Pa," they chimed confidently.

"Now, Mary," he said to her, "Just hang on. That is all you have to do."

"Yes, Charles," she said.

And in they went, the oxen protesting, the water splashing, sucking, wheels grating, bumping, horses snorting and whinnying, whips cracking, flicking overhead, men shouting, ejaculating. The wagon shuddered and jerked as if it were going over giant cobblestones. The sky was somewhere overhead, but the great reality was this immediate stretch of rushing water, pulling at them, engulfing the team, and splashing into millions of lights that blinded the straining eyes.

Two or three times Mary looked up to gauge the distance yet to be traversed, but before she could focus and find it, the immediate struggle of the floundering team drew her eyes back to will them on. So, when they finally lumbered slowly up the bank, she was at first more surprised than relieved.

"We told you we'd make it," John Henry exulted.

"Oh, Pa, you're all wet." scolded Margaret, impishly.

Mary laughed until Charles looked at her rather harshly, and she realized that she could be close to hysterics. Charles's look took care of that!

Friendly fires were ready to dry out the waterlogged pilgrims and helping hands soon restored the wagon to its normal height. The cold water had been good for Doxie. Mary gratefully set about making camp and getting supper. They would be ready for bed very early that night.

Now that it was June and they had had three days of sunshine, they expected clear weather, but they were sadly unprepared for the fierce heat that assailed them the next day. Fortunately, they had set out at daybreak and put twenty miles behind them before they began looking for a camp — and none too soon for Doxie, who was beginning to show lameness again, even though they were in and out of the water time and again as they forded one creek after another.

As they dipped in and out of the tree-fringed creeks, Mary two or three times thought she heard the sounds of Indians, though none appeared. If Charles heard them, he kept it to himself, and there was never a moment when she felt free to ask him. She was keeping the children very close under the pretext that they could lose their way among the cottonwoods. As an excuse it was rather flimsy, but it served.

By the time all the wagons that were going to stay there had driven in, they added up to quite a village and, as if by common consent, formed a defensive circle. Through the evening the men drifted about in groups, planning definite shifts of guard duty. They were elaborately casual about it all in a terse sort of way. Except for the tension, however, it was an uneventful night.

Doxie was almost as good as new the next morning, thanks, Charles said, to the cool waters and rest.

Off they went at crack of dawn, glad to be on their way with weather just right for the most comfortable traveling. Now, thought Mary, as she tried to keep from jolting too hard with the occasional lurches, if I can only hold out a few more days.

Mary knew that Charles could help if the time came and he couldn't get a doctor, but if he had to, he'd be "put out" with her. There's not much I can do about it now, she told herself. But every time she thought about Charles having to help when the baby came her heart sank.

It wasn't as if he didn't pride himself on being ready to take on just about any emergency, and there wasn't a man kinder to his animals, especially when they were having their young.

She leaned her head against the taut slant of canvas and deliberately tried to summon instances from the past which might have some common factor of making him "put out" with her, especially when she had least expected it.

Instead she found herself remembering that first time Mollie foaled a colt. They'd been married just a few months. Charles had stayed by Mollie most of the night, making many a trip between the barn and the kitchen, where Mary was keeping a fire going for hot water when he'd need it.

She had dozed in the rocking chair by the stove, finally, and, before she knew it, he was standing in front of her laughing, "We're fifty dollars richer, at least, for this night's work, my girl." He looked tall and strong in the lamplight, and a delicious sense of warm content enveloped her. If she lived to be a hundred, she would never forget how, suddenly serious, he had bent to look into her half-awake eyes, and, staying the rocker with a grip on each armrest, moved his lips against her ear to whisper, "I hate to think of you suffering."

How young she had been. Any future suffering was nothing to her then. What would Mary, the girl, have thought if she could have foreseen Mary, the woman, heavy, weary, and worried, jostling across the plains with no home but a wagon and hopes?

Oh my goodness, she thought, pulling herself up as straight as she could, as she realized how close she had come to disloyal, bad thoughts. She looked ahead.

John Henry was walking with Orthodoxology. How manly he looks. I can be mighty proud of him and my girls. And if pride isn't a kind of happiness, it's a pretty close relative.

VI
Quicksands and Cholera

NOTHING MUCH UNUSUAL for the pattern of their days happened until Saturday when they were fording the river. The water was not deep or swift, but there were holes and quicksand. Once the line of crossing was scouted, the main concern was to follow across as quickly as possible.

The fording was not without danger, but they all felt equal to it, even though they would need to take a rather extended, slanting line and be in the water for almost a mile. The three parties had agreed that when they had forded the river they would take the first likely camping place for over the Sabbath. By stopping early there would be time for washing and baking before sundown.

Before the last one had crossed, another wagon, all alone, lurched into sight and came on as if eager to catch up with them. Before long Mary knew who it was. She grimaced to Charles. He nodded back grimly. It surely was the wheedling man and his miserable wife of the week before.

As soon as he got near enough, he whooped and waved as he urged on a team of mules. Evidently he was so busy making his presence known that he did not notice the fording line. Anyway, he did not follow it. Even so, he would not have been in any great danger if he had kept going at an even pace, but his shouts confused the mules. At any rate, they paused and he immediately seemed to realize the pull of quicksand. He began flaying the animals. They reared and plunged just as he either stood up or was bounced up. Before he could free himself from the reins he was thrown forward, his head striking the wagon tongue. The first jerk had thrown his frightened wife backward into the wagon which began to sink irretrievably. There was time, however, to slash the animals free and pull the cowering woman from the wagon.

Mary Vowell Adams: Reluctant Pioneer

The Lights took her in as if she had been their own daughter. Nobody knew for sure what happened to the husband's body. All agreed no life should be risked searching for it in the treacherous quicksands. The horror hung over the entire group, but none of them felt any personal grief. Even the bereaved woman was saying within two hours after the incident. "Maybe I can find some way to git back to my chidrun."

"In the meantime," Father Light said firmly, "you ride with us."

Now that the weather was clearing, the prairie again invited the children to more exploration. When they were allowed to, Millie and Margaret ranged widely.

"Mother," Margaret would draw it out beseechingly, "Millie and I want to look around over there," and sighting down her crooked little forefinger as if drawing a bead on a very special spot which demanded her very special examination, she would hastily interpose, "Keep Pauline and Mary back here, won't you — puleeze?" Millie hadn't really cared about going, but Margaret knew Millie would go with her, once consent had been got — "Oh Margaret, you're the wily one," Mary observed.

"No matter how many times she asks practically the same thing, Margaret manages to make it seem a 'very special' occasion. Already she has a kind of flair," thought Mary.

As her explorers grew smaller in the distance, Mary looked down at Pauline and little Mamie trudging obediently alongside, hand-in-hand, Mamie's fat little legs synchronized with Pauline's thin ones. They both had pushed their sunbonnets back. Mamie's cherubic face was encircled in blond ringlets that pulled out of her short braids. Pauline's thin small face that could have profited from curls, had only wisps of darker blonde hair which the breeze had fingered out of her braids and dangled into her eyes. "I'll get Pauline to brush her hair more and maybe she'll at least get more of it to do something with," she promised herself.

John Henry, meanwhile, had little time for exploration. He was helping with cattle or walking beside the team most of the time. Charles expected a great deal of him and always got what he expected, she thought.

"I guess it's a good thing. John Henry seems to be thriving on

70

it." When she had served his plate last night, she had said,"A man's portion for my young man who does a grown man's work," and he had looked up with a pleased expression on his face.

Before she knew it, her explorers were almost back, flushed and panting from the run. Before she could understand a word they were saying, they began pointing back toward where they had been. Charles, on the other side of the team, paid scant attention to them, though they were obviously trying to attract his attention too.

"A grave — we found a grave over there."

They evidently thought that the whole wagon train would stop and the folks would go over to pay their respects to the dead. Mary guessed that they pictured themselves leading a long procession across the prairies to that sad spot.

Margaret hopped alone beside her father. "But, Pa, aren't you going over to see the grave?" Somehow the child had confused piety with respect for the dead and thought that her father would want to go over and pay his respects, Mary thought.

Charles slipped the goad under his left arm and allowed his right hand to drop gently on the bobbing head. "My child," he said soberly, "if we were to stop at every grave, we'd never get to Oregon."

Margaret walked quietly beside him for a few minutes and then slowly dropped behind, reluctantly accepting the futility of her little moment of excitement.

When the girls were once more out of earshot, Mary recognized the signs that he was about to say something which he wasn't quite sure how to express. Half worried and half amused, she watched him, wondering what could be so delicate a matter between them.

Finally he came out with it. "If we weren't skirting the edge of the Trail, we'd be seeing a good many graves." he said.

So that was it, she thought. She guessed she had known it without really being aware that she had known it. Anyway, she did not feel one bit surprised, but she did sense a sharper definition of her fears.

Yes, Charles explained, cholera was preying on the wagon

trains again this year.

Within three days fresh graves, with their pathetic little markers — names and dates scratched on stone or burned into precious scraps of wood — were becoming more and more frequent discoveries.

They generally let the children inspect those graves, pretending an idle curiosity to cover their increasing apprehension. The children, under strict orders not to approach too close or to touch anything near the graves, got some practice in reading and memorizing. Besides, it made them feel important to bring back interesting information.

Then came the day they had known must come. All their care could not assure them of complete immunity.

As they swung around into position for the night, they passed by nine fresh graves, side by side.

Wordlessly, the message passed from wagon to wagon by casual nods or extended arms. The elders were maintaining a conspiracy of silence, but the children, not inhibited by fear and strongly motivated by curiosity, as soon as they were free to, after helping with the chores, ran over to read the inscriptions and came back asking, "Are they anyone we know?"

"One has our last name. Do you suppose she was a mother?" asked Margaret.

"All we could make out was the name," Millie warned. "It was Nancy James Adams."

Charles and Mary looked at each other in astonishment.

"Must have married one of my cousins," Charles ejaculated.

Mary could see that he was just as surprised as she was.

The children went on with the other names. "No, no others that we know." One was enough. Mary wished she had kept in touch with Nancy.

For Mary the cheerful campfires and all the bustle of women preparing supper, the men and children going off to care for their stock, and all the hustle of the camp seemed more unreal than the cold fact of Nancy's death out here.

After supper, they all went over together to the grave. The children found some rocks with which Mary and Charles created a more distinctive and permanent definition of the grave. It was

72

all they could think of to do until the last. Joining hands, they softly said the old benediction together. "The Lord watch over you ...."

Before the children went off to bed there was another, more pleasant ritual. Sitting quite comfortably in the little folding stool Charles had made for her, Mary, by putting her toes together and, wedging her heels firmly in the ground, formed a little footstool of her toes which the girls thought jolly to sit on while she combed and braided their hair for the night.

As she was engaged so, she noticed Doc Carter and Charles in quiet talk on the far side of the wagon. She couldn't hear a word they said, but she saw Charles put his hand on Doc's shoulder and grip it for a minute. Just the way he would start John Henry on a job John Henry wasn't sure he could do, Mary thought.

Doc had been gone hardly a minute before Charles walked by and spoke in an elaborately casual manner that was intended to fool only the children, "I think I'll go over to the Lights' wagon for a spell and see how everything is going."

"Is anything wrong, Ma?" Millie asked it with a quick show of concern. Mary knew then that the older ones were not the only dissemblers.

"Oh, Mrs. Light told me last night he'd had a touch of dysentery," she answered as easily as she could. "Amos has been driving for him most of the day, you know."

"Yes, he told us," Millie said, in a way that implied he had told them considerable.

Before Charles got back, the children had been in bed long since, and a number of the folks had slipped quietly into the circle of light from the dying fire to ask her about or to tell her about the condition of Father Light, whose malady it was assumed was the dread cholera. He was "being taken" so fast he was not likely to last the night.

Mary sat shivering by the fire, remembering — remembering him alive and happy just two months ago. If only they could all go back to two months ago.

Just two months ago he had come over to tell them the news, so excited that a spot of color flamed along each cheekbone, the pupils of his eyes pinpoints of light in the glow from the open grate of the kitchen stove.

Margaret and Mary were just finishing the dishes when Charles brought him back through the house. Mary remembered how relieved she was when she saw who it was Charles was bringing into the kitchen. She hadn't minded admitting to Father Light that he had been brought into the kitchen because they hadn't bothered with a fire in the front room.

It was one of those speak-of-the-devil occasions, and the children were a bit self-conscious because of their remarks at the supper table.

"Papa, did you ever notice how funny Mr. Light looks when he prays?" Margaret had asked.

Millie had mimicked his invariable conclusion by stretching her neck and quavering, "Bring us at last to the pearly gates and we'll give Thee all the praise."

Even John Henry had snorted appreciatively.

Mary had expected to see a wide swath where the children had been, but Charles, ignoring the other two, slowly brought a long and solemn gaze to bear full on Margaret, "My child," he said with heavy emphasis, "I am not looking around when others are praying, and if God and Father Light want pearly gates — why, that will be heaven to me."

The children knew they had got off easily, she could see. She thought she could see something else, too. Wasn't there a hint of amusement or maybe mild triumph in Charles's face? She couldn't be sure.

"Every one of us is a little bit uncomfortable," Mary had thought as she scanned the faces of her family when Father Light came in the room. But Father Light was not aware of anything but his own excitement.

Father Light had insisted on arranging his jacket around the back of the chair Charles pulled up to the fire for him, refusing to let anyone go to the bother of hanging it up for him. (She remembered how Charles had leaned across the table then and turned down the lamp, since the brighter flame would not be needed for reading, and the softer light was easier on the eyes. For their work, Margaret and Mary had another lamp up on the shelf over the dry sink.) Mary, nearby at the kitchen worktable, was cutting lard into flour mixture for breakfast biscuits, more by feel than by sight, anyway. Millie had finished the skirt hem she had been "catching." John Henry returned to feathering down the kindling sticks with his pocket knife — preparation for a quick breakfast fire in the morning.

Mr. Light could hardly wait. He had crossed, uncrossed, and recrossed his legs, then finally hitched an ankle onto his knee and restlessly fingered the laces of his shoe. Occasionally he'd hitch his ankle a bit closer or straighten momentarily in his chair. Finally everyone was listening and his moment had come.

"Well," he slapped his shoeleather, "I did it: we're going with you."

"Going with us?"

"To Oregon! Hee, hee. I'm going to prove you can teach an old dog new tricks. She won't admit it, but I know she really likes, the idea — just won't give me the satisfaction of hearing her say so!" He laughed and laughed as they made the comments of surprise and pleasure that he had come to hear.

Mary remembered it all. Looking over her shoulder she had seen his goatee jutting out grotesquely and quivering when he laughed. For all, she thought, he could be a leprechaun or a jolly gnome.

As she remembered smiling to herself, she caught herself smiling. How could she smile at a time like this? She was horrified at herself. A sense of guilt overwhelmed her and she covered her face with her hands. She was still sitting that way by the dying fire when Charles returned and helped her into the wagon.

In the morning the bugle called them out of warm beds to as bleak a day as the season could provide. Mr. Light had died early in the night and the train would delay long enough for a burial service.

By tacit consent Mary would not be included in any of the preparations that had to be made in the Light wagon. They did not want to take any chance of her marking the baby. Such things were known to have happened.

The children, sobered and awed, did not resist efforts to make them as presentable as possible for the service. As a labor of love and a penance Mary told over and over to herself all the kindly, lovable things she could remember about the little man. And not one tear did she shed — not until, rounding the wagon, she caught sight of the stiff little figure being lowered from their wagon in a blanket. Then she began to cry, and she couldn't stop.

John Henry helped her up to the seat. There she sat, all alone, looking straight ahead, with the tears in rivulets down her cheeks, for which the soggy wad of handkerchief linen in her hand was of little use.

Presently John Henry was beside her again, this time pressing a man's handkerchief into her hands. Forcing herself to express her thanks, she acknowledged the humor of the gift with a half-chuckle, half-sob. Soon she could say to herself, albeit wearily, "Thank goodness, I'm over that spell."

The men dug the grave beside those others, and now there were ten graves together. It seemed better that way. Charles concluded the eulogy with an adaptation of St. Paul's "I have fought the fight ...."

The idea, she thought, was good, of course, but the words and the figures of speech didn't fit, but what did it matter anyway. That stiff, emaciated little figure in the grave wasn't Father Light.

Sister Light stood alone, but between Charles and Sister Carter. She looked so dazed Mary knew she hadn't yet realized what had happened. Mary remembered her mother saying something about first grief being a merciful lack of realization. For whatever reason, Mrs. Light carried herself with dignity and restraint, and Mary felt pride for the little woman who had, heretofore seemed amusingly birdlike to her.

Since there was nothing else they could do, they left him there, and when they drove off they knew that before they stopped again, the grave would be far behind them and none of them was likely ever to see it again.

For awhile, at least, Mrs. Light would be driving with the Carters. One of the Carter boys would be driving her team for her. The other boy would spell his father.

When Mary told Charles that Sister Carter had told her that her husband was fagged out from tending Mr. Light the night before, Charles was rather short with her.

"Maybe Doc has a touch of dysentery," he said.

By evening they had almost made up the lost time. The Carters were three or four wagons back, and Mary had not heard or seen anything of them all afternoon. As soon as the horses and cattle were safely out of the way, she sent Margaret over to ask how Doc was.

When she returned from the errand, Margaret obviously repeated Sister Carter's exact words, "As well as could be expected."

Mary couldn't find much comfort there, but she tried to tell herself that at least it was not bad news.

During family prayers she knew she had been too easily assured. "Charles is trying too hard to convince the Lord that he isn't trying to convince Him," she thought, as, phrase by phrase, she followed his petition: "our whole dependence on Thee ... divine mercy ... healing benediction on our enterprise ... pilgrims in a weary land ... Help cometh ... Strength cometh from Thee ... in Thy service" Mary listened with increasing alarm to the urgency in his voice.

Just before he finished, there was a long pause. Then, deliberately "And bring us at last to the pearly gates, and we'll give Thee all the praise."

The children got up from the grass, brushing their knees or doing anything to avoid meeting each other's eyes. They didn't want to laugh and they didn't want to cry, either of which they were likely to do if they met each other's eyes.

In her thoughts Mary said, "Amen, If Father Light wants pearly gates that's what we want him to have." Aloud, all she said as she caught Charles's eye was, "Amen."

Charles harrumphed into a big handkerchief he had pulled out of his pocket and disappeared around the corner of their wagon.

Most of the other groups that had camped nearby last night were already out of camp and hours on their way. Of those who were still in camp, clusters of people, most of them children, who had not actually taken part in the burial service, were standing off at a distance, watching. Maybe curious, maybe sympathetic. Suddenly Mary became acutely aware of them.

"They certainly don't give a person any comfort," she thought, and deliberately turned her head away from them.

That movement of her head brought one of the group into action. Coming toward the wagon was a disheveled girl of about twelve. Although she approached Millie directly, Mary could see that she was speaking to them all when she said, "My grandma's awful sick." The poor little thing had been crying. Her nose and eyes were red.

"Grandma drank some of that spring water night before last."

Margaret clapped her hands to her face and peered through her fingers at the girl. "You mean where we thought we heard Indians but couldn't see any ?"

The girl nodded emphatic assent. "Some folks say the Indians poisoned the water."

Amos Carter slapped his forehead. "Pa brought a bucket of the water from that spring. I remember he drank some of it before Ma took it for washing diapers."

From that moment, hours of apprehension became hours of horror. Whether it was poisoned water or a more virulent form of the cholera, one thing was certain. The camp was ridden with dire sickness.

The girl's grandmother did not last long, and it was soon apparent that the horror had a hold on Doc Carter.

Mercifully, it was swift. Before the day that they had buried Father Light was over, Doc Carter was surely dying.

He died in the night. They buried him the next morning. Before noon they tore Eleanor from her husband's shallow grave. Before sunset they had put almost five miles between them and that golgotha.

There was much illness. Many others were buried in shallow graves beside the Platte, where graves became so common they scarce asked "who?" Each day new graves were dug and dreary burial services drained the weary living. It was worse on the south side of the river, they heard.

People passed the word along that, when no regular preacher was available, Charles would read a scripture and offer a prayer just like a regular "man of the cloth." Before long they began to dread the approach of a stranger, so often did it mean someone wanted Charles to "say a few words" at the side of one of those pitiful, shallow graves.

They were losing time, too. Many persons who had become familiar to them in the days before they reached the Platte no longer appeared at camps because they were days ahead.

But those who were ahead had little significance for Mary. She was numb with dread. She could see that both Charles and John Henry were being stretched to the limit of their endurance. The horror, the stench of death, her own physical awkwardness — all oppressed her beyond caring who was ahead or when her own time would come for birthing. Only the habit of their established routine carried them along.

VII

Buffalo Bonuses and Sabbath's Baby

AS THEIR WAGON WAITED to move out Saturday morning, Charles stepped back, reached up, and patted her hand. It was such an unusual display that she began wondering dully what bad news he was attempting to soften this time. Not until later did she realize what he had said. It was that the group which had camped near them that night would be traveling with them for quite a while. Eventually it dawned on her what the significance of that was. The other party had a doctor with them. He was assuring her that there would be a doctor available to deliver her baby. He had supposed she was worrying about herself.

I wonder how selfish he thinks I am, she thought. I ought to be ashamed to let my moods stick out all over me.

As she sat there scolding herself, she thought it might be a sign that she was feeling better physically and the baby was about due.

How long ago it was that she had watched the throng of Oregon-bound emigrants straggling across Van Buren county and had looked down on their campfires flickering through the trees and mists along the creek. Now in this vast, homeless plain, she was one of the alternately moving and camping throng that often stretched as far as the eye could see along both sides of the incredible Platte, so wide, shallow, and almost too full of silt to pass for water. Indeed, it seemed as if the Platte were more than matched by the two mighty streams of humanity flowing out from the States across the country westward.

Their own small nucleus gathered other wagons for a few days or was itself drawn to others, according to the needs presented by the Trail. They became accustomed to traveling with some people for days and sharing camp with them and then not seeing them when they forged ahead or dropped back only to find themselves together again later on. Some, naturally, were more congenial than others, but, by and large, as Charles said, "Birds of a feather ...."

The first Mary learned of The McMillens was through the children. Margaret came up to the fire while Mary was dropping dumplings into the pheasant stew. "Mother, you know the twins?"

"Of course I know the twins."

"Twins are babies, aren't they?"

"The Carter twins are babies."

"Can ladies be twins?"

"Mant and Rand will be ladies when they grow up, I hope. Why do you ask?"

Margaret was bent on pursuing in her own way. "But twins have to have the same last name, don't they?"

"They would be born with the same last name."

Just then Millie moved closer to chime in with "Oh, Mother, she heard those people in that wagon over there when they talked to Mrs. Carter. A pretty woman says she was a twin, too. She said her name was Cecelia Adams and her twin sister's name was Perthena McMillen. One of them is married and the other isn't."

The McMillen-Carter-Adams group became one happily met family before long. Some confusion necessarily arose from the fact that one of them was also another Adams, amusingly. The young ladies were light-hearted and kind to the children. Mary welcomed their influence upon her girls, especially, even though she was dismayed one day to overhear her own children comparing their daily count of graves passed with Cecelia and Perthena as if they had been accustomed to doing so. Perhaps the exact number was no more gruesome than the general sense of being stalked by Death, with every fresh grave another cruel reminder.[1]

1   The diary of Mrs. Cecelia Emily McMillen Adams records for Friday, June 18, "We have passed twenty-one new-made graves today. It makes it seem very gloomy to us to see so many of the emigrants buried on the plains."

Now they were coming into buffalo country. Trees were scarcer every mile. Soon they would have to begin using buffalo chips for fuel, but Mary was determined that she would not resort to burning chips until it was absolutely necessary. Despite everyone's assurance that they really were not at all offensive, she knew it would make her sick. For one thing, her acute sense of smell would probably make what others found mildly distasteful really sickening to her.

Perhaps, she thought, as she jolted along in the wagon, I have become accustomed to so many vile smells that I won't be affected as much now as I would have been. At that moment she had a queer feeling in the pit of her stomach and thought it might be hunger, reminding her it was nearly time to stop for nooning.

But it was not that. Soon she realized she certainly had not become inured to bad odors. A new and horrible stench hit her full force. She watched Charles and the children to see whether it was bothering them. Surely, she wondered, I can't be smelling the chips that everyone else swears are odorless.

Before they stopped for nooning, Pauline was wrinkling her nose and occasionally pulling the corner of her sunbonnet over it.

When they finally did stop. Charles headed off their questions with a sober warning. "There are buffalo wallows ahead, and we must keep the stock away from them."

"What's a wallow?" Mamie wanted to know.

Charles let John Henry explain. "Remember how the chickens like to scrootch around in the dust and sun themselves back home?"

Mamie nodded vigorously, and the sunbonnet slipped back from her flushed forehead where the blond ringlets stuck in moist clusters.

"Remember how, when they got up, they left little hollowed-out places?"

She assented eagerly.

Enjoying his pedagogical role, John Henry assumed a judicial air as he pondered his next analogy. "Well, you know how big a chicken is?"

At this absurd question, they all broke into laughter, which John Henry loftily ignored, his mind on a higher, distant goal of understanding. "All right." he said, "you know how much bigger an ox is than a chicken. A buffalo is as big as an ox, so a buffalo hollow is that much bigger than a chicken hollow. Water stands in these hollows and gets putrid — that's poison — so when the other animals get that water it kills them."

"Pa," Mamie wanted to know, "will we know when we are coming to them? Will we fall into them?"

"You won't want to get any nearer than you have to. They are what you smell now. They have a lot of alkali in them, too."

"And alkali is what kills the cattle," John Henry put in quickly to keep abreast of his father.

Even Millie looked impressed.

John Henry was encouraged to recapitulate. "You see, the water evaporates and leaves all that guck thick with alkali."

Mary couldn't see how her two men could control all the stock, now that Doc Carter and Father Light were both gone. She would have asked, but she felt so miserable she didn't want to talk any more than was necessary. It would have been much easier if she had heard the men arranging a comparatively easy plan of control that would allow the loose stock to graze as they went.

When the afternoon march began, the wagons formed a double line and contained the cattle by driving them in between.

Doubling the line doubled the dust and slowed their progress, however. Everyone who could got out and walked at a distance from the dust-churning wheels. Even Mary tried it for awhile and managed better than she had expected. The ground looked as if a giant rolling pin had gone over it.

However, she so feared stumbling that she kept her eyes on the ground at her feet when she was walking and looked up only when she paused. That is how she almost stepped on the skull before she noticed it. Just seeing it there at her feet was startling enough, but when something within the eye-sockets moved, she froze in her tracks. Then, for a moment, she thought she must be losing her mind. There, on the sand at her feet the buffalo skull started to shake a "No" at her. She stood hypnotized, transfixed to the spot. Then the spell was broken. A lizard scuttled out and away from behind the jaw.

For a few moments the experience left Mary too limp to move. She forced herself to look at the sun-bleached bone structure. Why, it was almost beautiful! How clean the sun's hot rays had kilned the elemental structure of the bone.

The Flesh and the Devil are now cleaned away. She pondered upon the chance association of ideas, warily picking her way among strange thoughts. What once would have been repulsive — back in that long-ago world of shelter and housekeeping — out here in a universe of sky, earth and weather seemed to speak some ultimate truth to her.

She stood there trying, as she told herself "to get a purchase on an idea." She looked up and saw that she was being observed by one of the passing train. She could see Mrs.McMillen watching her and looking worried.

I suppose they'd think I was touched for sure, if they could read the way my thoughts were going, she told herself. She waved reassurance to Mrs. McMillen, glanced back at what was, after all, just an old buffalo skull in the sand, and resumed her slow progress.

The men had been well advised about keeping the stock between the double line of wagons. Because of their measure of prevention, no real trouble developed, but the odor from some of the holes was nauseating even to those with less sensitive noses. They did pass one hole so uncomfortably close that the black, putrid water with the crust around the edge looked like a brooding evil eye. She recoiled as if the Devil himself had winked at her, while she staggered at the noxious breath of it.

As she went on, she thought about the two weird experiences and how differently she had reacted to them. The first one, after the initial moment of horror, she had felt herself approaching a new level of awareness, of seeing new beauty in the structure of life itself.

A stench is a stench, and that is a truth that will make me sick if I let myself think about it. She put as much distance as she could between herself and the evil hole. As soon as she caught up with her wagon, she brushed herself off and rode the rest of the hot, weary day.

That night the word was passed, "Tomorrow you best carry

something with you to gather buffalo chips into. We'll be needing them from now on."

"But tomorrow is Sunday," Millie remonstrated.

"Don't worry, child," Charles assured her, "we have enough fuel for our needs tomorrow."

Mary's practical mind was racing ahead. "Most of these people will not stay over the whole day. Won't they be ahead of us and get everything picked up before we get there?"

Charles answered with a slow emphasis that was evidently intended to give weight to a topic that might develop unseemly levity, "That is one supply which we will not need to worry about."

What grim irony, she thought, that I who have detested the very thought of using dung for fuel should now be worrying about not getting my share of it.

She felt no ill effects from her walking that afternoon. Indeed, she felt surprisingly able. Probably the baby had changed position. The time should be fairly close. Charles had told her that there were two doctors within hailing distance and he would appreciate her having the baby during their Sabbath lay-over so as not to hold up the progress of the train.

Mary rather tartly told him he was no more eager to have the baby born than she.

To herself she admitted one reluctance. She hated to see the look on his face when he learned the baby was a girl, that John Henry was doomed still to be their only begotten son. Mary, the third girl after John Henry, had not been the male Charles had counted on, and neither was Pauline, the fourth. There wasn't much use hoping this time that Charles would have to accept anything but another girl. He blamed her, she knew — as if it were by her will that his was thwarted. Maybe it was, for all she knew. His will was so everlastingly the determined she suspected herself of unconscious subversive tendencies.

Tomorrow would be a good day to have a baby, if it was to be their good fortune to have the miracle of a healthy one in this dry, thirsty land.

A curious sense of well being increased Mary's assurance that this was the day, as soon as she awakened the next morning.

"This is June 20, I mustn't forget," she told herself, and then, "I hope I have time to get a few things rinsed out and dried — it's going to be such a sunshiny day."

She gave herself a "spit bath" in the wagon by dropping three drops of rose water on a dampened washcloth and going over herself as best she could behind the quilt that served as a curtain, and thought, "Now I'm as ready as I can manage." Then she got breakfast while the girls took their turns in the wagon.

The men had rigged up a kind of clean-up area of their own closer to the river. They all used the water sparingly as they could because the alkali in it was making their skins sensitive. As hard on their insides as their outsides, she thought; wrinkling her nose.

After chores and breakfast were over and Mary was putting things away, Charles came along to see how much longer she would be needing the ox yoke for her kitchen table. "You can have it right away," she offered, wondering what in the world he wanted it for now.

She didn't have to wait long to find out. She heard him call to one of the men, "The yoke will make fine pews, since we have no better."

And so they did!

There were some good voices in the crowd. Even those that were not much on quality were enthusiastic, whether they followed the melody or attempted parts. Everyone joined in and they had a soul-satisfying song fest. Mary wondered whether any of them so much as thought about the church controversy last winter about not permitting men to sing with women unless they sing the bass as written in the tune-book. The question would be brought up at General Conference.

Why, General Conference has already met — almost a month ago — and when, if ever, will we ever know anything about it, she wondered. And what had happened about letting men and women sit together or apart in church? But those were questions that belonged in another world.

Out here on the prairie, with ox-yokes for pews, under the great sky, they sang their petitions, their faith, and their praise, each swelling the sound as best he could. *A Day of Rest and Gladness, Sweet Hour of Prayer, Guide Me O Thou Great*

Jehovah. Anyone can see that this is good for us, Mary thought, and maybe it does good for some others — those anxious ones who feel they must press on, even on the Sabbath, though they would like to stop or those heedless ones who don't care. Now that she thought of it, Mary noticed that others of their group, too, evidently had the same idea. They were making a special effort to be heard.

Mary was sitting off at one edge of the congregation, a modest acknowledgement of her condition, and was in a good place for observing the effect of their little service upon others. Occasionally a wagon driver would draw up close enough to hear for a while and then reluctantly move on. Mary observed a variety of responses and became so engrossed with her post as an observer that she almost forgot to bow for prayer. Guiltily she could hear Charles's saying, "My child, I am not looking around when others are praying."

"Oh, Charles, Charles, why do you always have to be so everlastingly right! Despite everything that has happened, this does seem right. At least here in this bright day it does."

Although the baby was active enough to startle her a few times during the day, Mary had only a few false-labor pains which set her to counting more than once or twice. Everything considered, she had managed quite well during their lay-over. She had bread baked for the days ahead, clothing and bedding washed or aired in the sunshine, and the whole family had "at least the worst of the dirt scraped off," as she expressed it.

Almost before sunset, the camp began to grow quiet. The buffalo chips, which most of the camp were already using, burned with so little flame that there was not the cheerful incentive to linger about and enjoy the fire.

By the end of the day their camp had doubled in size, but those who had "kept the Sabbath" and those who had not seemed more set apart than they usually were. They all seemed bent upon "early to bed and early to rise." No one lingered about the fires or found an excuse to carry glowing chips for light about the camp. Just about everyone was in bed by dark.

Mary lay listening to the pleasant sound of voices. Gradually the sound diminished to a sleepy murmur. Charles had taken one deep breath after he hit the pillow and was immediately asleep. That was the last thing she remembered — thinking that she wished she could sleep like Charles.

The next thing she knew, it was time to get up in the gray light before dawn if they were to get a really early start.

As always, Mary kept the girls, especially the two smaller ones, close, while teams were being yoked amid the confusion of horses and cattle plunging about. John Henry, working with his father, was as safe as a boy could be under those circumstances. Charles was not one to let him take unnecessary chances.

Before the sun came up, looking like the sunset in reverse, they had already moved out. As soon as the routine of the march was established, Mary assigned each of the girls a sack for picking up a good supply of buffalo chips. Despite having watched the chips burning the evening before, she still felt reluctant to ask the girls to pick them up. She might have spared herself the hesitation, however, everyone else was, and they were just waiting to be allowed to, all except Millie, who made a bit of a grimace as she accepted her sack.

Mary smoothed the already smooth hair back from Millie's forehead and then kissed the place where her fingers had stroked, whispering, "I guess you and I will have to get over our persnickitiness."

Margaret, seeing only the kiss and not understanding the whispered word, edged her way between them and lifted her forehead, crying, "Pay me, too. Pay me, too."

Mamie and Pauline, not to be left out of the kissing game, chimed in, jumping up and down, "Pay us, too. Kiss us for picking up chips."

As soon as each little girl got her hug and kiss, she climbed over the back of the wagon and out. Mary was inclined to try walking with them again, but she had to wait for a long time when she could be helped.

She did not have to wait long. When she did get out, it was still early enough to be very pleasant. She carried an empty sack with her just in case the girls might be ambitious to fill another. She supposed that the chips would not be too heavy for her to carry even if she could not do the stooping necessary for picking them up. She had even seen some of the women carrying chips back to their wagons in their aprons, but she was not about to do that either. Not for awhile, anyway. She noted with approval that some of the women were fastidious enough to wear gloves as they did their chip-picking.

The children of Israel out picking up their manna in the desert may have looked like us, she realized and thought better of buffalo chips.

As soon as she had put enough distance between herself and the wagons, the quiet of the prairie was lovely, the children's voices blending into the whole as naturally as the chirping of birds. The chips lay like bits of frost upon the grass, but unlike frost, they were dry as well as light. The girls swooped down upon them, cupped their fingers gently around the edges, and lifted. As they lifted each one from the grass where it had dried, it made a little tearing sound, like ladies' skirts brushing across grass, Mary thought. A lady-like sound!

From a distance drifted the sounds of the great beasts, plodding as they kept the wheels, the wheels of progress turning, turning to Oregon. But here in the morning sunshine, she walked slowly, listening to the children's voices and "ladies' skirts upon the grass."

By afternoon the cheerful morning breeze became a rough wind that threatened every bit of loose canvas and made travel miserable. Mary pulled everything as tight as she could and tried to keep the girls entertained and busy in the wagon.

If the wagon had not stopped and they had not heard the voices, she might have missed seeing the packers from Oregon. She looked into their weather-beaten faces and made one of her silly remarks before she had time to think and stop herself from the foolishness that Charles so strongly disapproved of. "So there really is such a place," she said.

They laughed politely, but Charles looked embarrassed. There was an awkward silence, until one of the packers broke it with a wave of his hand and a remark about their having company across the way.

Sure enough, there across the sluggish expanse of the muddy Platte, like a reflection of themselves on its surface, was another wagon train. That meant they were not very many days from Fort Laramie. Maybe the baby would be able to say, "I was born at Fort Laramie."

She rather liked the sound of that and hoped it might be so. But mostly she hoped only the baby would wait until the storm that seemed to be coming on was over. She dreaded "farming out the children" among the already crowded wagons if the baby were born during a storm. Too, there was the awesome thought of asking Charles to go off in a storm to fetch a doctor. Every twinge filled her with apprehension. All through Monday and Tuesday the rain set in and soaked everything it could blow on or soak into. In the wagon, they had to be extra careful not to bump the canvas top. Wherever they touched it, the rain came through.

By Wednesday, it seemed as if everything was soggy, including their spirits and the sand through which the team strained to drag them. When one of the cows started bawling at the early darkening of the sky, Millie scowled and muttered. "I know just how you feel." Her look was so dour it was ludicrous and set the older children to laughing. Mamie and Pauline couldn't see what the others were laughing about, which made it all the funnier.

By Friday, they were almost accustomed to being wet and cold. Mary put out containers to catch whatever rainwater she could, and they put some things out in the rain "to wash themselves." Water from the Platte was so full of sediment they did not like to use it without letting it stand over night for the sediment to settle, often with something in it to encourage the settling. Some recommended sprinkling cornmeal on the top; others, alum. They tried both, the results being about equally disgusting, they all agreed.

To depress them even further the country was getting rougher, the sand deeper; graves continued frequent, and surely the baby would be coming any day. Curiously, though, the more desperate Mary became, the calmer. She considered this development and began to wonder whether she could be in danger of becoming a saint after all.

When they could, the children darted out to pick some of the beautiful prairie flowers which bloomed along their rainswept way. When they brought these flowers back to her, Mary felt their anxious eyes upon her. She had heard Millie whispering to Mamie that "the flowers would make Mamma feel better." The flowers did lift her spirits, and she exaggerated their effects as much as she dared, without overdoing it.

Every day that week, Charles pushed on as long as he could in the face of wind, rain, thunder, sleet and protesting cattle.

As if to reward them, Sunday, June 27, dawned clear and beautiful. This surely should be the day! Almost as soon as she was up — and that was very early — Mary felt a quick, sharp tearing. Although it came before she could serve breakfast, she knew she had better not wait to warn Charles that he would be needing to locate the doctor in a hurry — she didn't care which one, and it would not have made any difference if she had. The head of the family makes the decisions.

The children responded with excitement as soon as they were told. They already knew what each was to do. Millie served breakfast while Charles helped Mary back into the wagon. Millie and Margaret would stay with the Carter twins so that Sister Carter could stay with Mary and help the doctor if he wanted any help. Little Mamie and Pauline would stay with the folks in the wagon just two behind. The little girls had been allowed to ride with them off and on and would not feel strange there.

All seemed to be progressing too well. Mary felt apprehensive. Then she remembered she was upsetting Charles's participation in the Sabbath worship services. At that thought she began to feel that she was operating more normally than she had thought!

"Don't do anything until I get back," he said, oblivious to the humor of the remark. "I'll call Sister Carter as I go by."

He probably did not hear her say "Just hurry" because her voice was rather muffled as she reached down to help herself get onto the low bed. The effort of getting into the wagon had been so intensified by her fear of precipitating the birth that she just sat there stupidly waiting for her head to clear — until an extra hard, wrenching pain alerted her.

She looked about the wagon to be sure she knew where everything was. No point counting between pains. It would not change what would be when it would be.

The little, white, covered chamber pot was at the foot of the bed near the side wall of the wagon. Thank heavens she had thought to take it out and empty it when she first got out of the wagon that morning.

The box with the rubber sheet and the cloths and all was down at the foot of the children's bed. Inside it was a marked box which contained the things for the baby. They couldn't miss it.

Just as she was wondering whether she dared get things out of the box herself, another wrench of exploding pain sent her cowering down on the bed as if thrown there by an external force.

Then she heard Sister Carter's kind, matter-of-fact voice saying, "Well, I'm glad you had sense enough to lie down and wait for me."

She could hardly have known that the smile on Mary's face was as much for the irony of her remark as for her.

"Now, where are the things — or should I undress you first?"

Mary just had time to point out the box and tell her what was in it before another wave of pain had her gripping the sides of the bed as if she expected to be washed overboard.

Sister Carter quickly pulled out the fresh, white flannel gown and slipped it expertly over Mary's head. Almost simultaneously she was undoing the clothing underneath and pulling it off. So quickly and smoothly did she work that by the time the next crashing pain came, Mary's hot, sticky body was gratefully feeling the loose, absorbent folds of the fresh gown.

With almost no disturbing of her patient, Sister Carter pulled off the regular bed covers and substituted, first, the canvas, then a rubber sheet over it. Directly under Mary, she folded a number of worn sheets which could be pulled off and disposed of as they became soiled. The newspapers under the chamber would serve for wrapping soiled cloths when the time came.

Outside, the sun was already serious about making the day a warm one, so Mary had a single sheet over her for the sake of modesty.

"Well," said Sister Carter, sitting down on the other bed and fanning herself with one of the fresh papers she had put there, "I think we're all ready for twins."

Mary didn't have time to find out whether she was just teasing or not before another pain took over, and she hung onto the side of the bed again.

"Now," she said, "I think we had better start counting between pains."

While the two women silently counted, only their lips moving to keep a common tempo, the sounds of the camp became audible to them. Mary gasped, "I do hope Charles has time to get the wagon away from the camp."

Sister Carter snorted, "I just hope he gets the doctor here in time."

Mary laughed in spite of herself. Such asperity was unusual in Sister Carter. A little activity might relieve her tension.

"Sister Carter, may I have a drink of water?"

"How careless of me. I clean forgot you should be drinking water." She hurried out.

But Mary couldn't drink it right away, because she was having another labor pain. They were both so intent on Mary's getting a good drink of water, they forgot to count the time between pains.

Each time Mary went into a pain spasm again, they would start to watch the time interval, but too often something would interrupt them — outside sounds that made them think the doctor was coming, or some detail about plans for the day would occur to one or the other of them. They were just assuring each other that this time they would watch it, when they heard the horses up close and they could hear Charles saying "Let me know if there is time to hitch up the team and drive the wagon off a little way."

Then the Doctor's bag came through the back opening, followed by the Doctor, a dark little man, peering through thick-lensed spectacles. He was having some difficulty adjusting to the interior of the wagon after his ride in the bright sunshine. He hunched his shoulders and rubbed his hands nervously before he picked up his bag. "Mrs. Adams?" he asked, peering rather blindly. Then, with more confidence, he moved a step or two forward and bowed. "Doctor Schmidtttt," he announced.

Sister Carter pushed herself up from the bed. "I'm Mrs. Carter," she said, and hurried to get to the end of the bed and out of his way before he could advance and create an embarrassing collision in the narrow space between the two beds. "I'll be right outside if there is anything I can do," she assured him in passing.

"And here I am, Doctor," Mary answered wondering whether he could see her.

"Fine, fine," he responded quickly, and lifting his bag gingerly before him, he came down the narrow aisle and settled himself on the very spot Sister Carter had vacated.

The amenities over, his manner became brisk and confident, "How long have you been in labor, Mrs. Adams?"

Before she could answer, Mary was awash with another crashing wave of pain. As she came up gasping, she saw that he had his watch out and was peering with great concentration. Heavens, he is either half blind or he had never delivered a baby before and is embarrassed, she thought. But the next minute his hand was on her stomach easily and confidently, and she was too busy trying to read his reaction from this to worry about his qualifications.

He had moved over and was sitting on the bed beside her. He repeated his question with business-like emphasis, "Now, Mrs. Adams how long have you been in labor?"

Mary had lost all concept of time. "Um, how long has it been since my husband reached you?"

"Roughly, a half hour."

"Then, about an hour, I guess — eeyehe." She was in another whirlpool of pain.

"Umhum," he nodded to the watch in his hand, as if it had told him a message of good news.

Mary could have allowed herself to be very much irritated by his satisfaction coincident with her distress.

"You are having very good labor pains," he beamed.

Mary bit her lip.

"Any show of blood?"

"We just padded me and didn't look," she admitted.

"Well," he said, without any further sign of hesitancy, "I think we'll listen first." He reached into his bag and the stethoscope writhed out of it. In the silence, he adjusted it into his ears.

She watched the end dangle over her. It was cool. Her skin

jumped at its first contact. She almost laughed. A little extra authoritative pressure brought her under control as he began placing, listening, placing, listening — very deliberately placing, listening — and then the next wave smashed into her.

Shoving the stethoscope into his coat pocket, he stood up and went to the back of the wagon and spoke decisively, "I think we will not bother with moving this wagon."

"Now, if I can only keep quiet. I'll *have* to keep quiet," Mary thought.

"Now, he said, as if echoing her thought, "I think you and I can take care of this in great shape."

"Great shape!" she thought.

He took one of the clean cloths Sister Carter had left out for him; spread it out for a white surface on the other bed and brought out a pair of scissors and cord from the bag and placed them on the cloth. The stethoscope he put back into the bag, which he then also put on the bed within easy reach.

Then he removed his coat and carefully laid it across the front seat of the wagon. Since there were plenty of places he could have hung it inside the wagon, she suspected that he was using the coat as a signal.

When he returned to sit along the edge of the bed at her feet, she noticed how his black, curly beard contrasted with the whiteness of the stiff collar that he had loosened and was letting wing out, threatening to fly loose. He hesitated a moment and then reached up and took off the whole collar and tossed it over on the foot of the other bed.

"Now, Little Lady," he said, returning his attention to Mary, "Let's go to work."

Drifting off in one corner of her mind floated the thought, "He can't think of my name." Not that it mattered at all, at all.

Mary shut her eyes and listened to the little song he started to chant, something about "an upptiddi-ump Now and an umptiddiyump Now," over and over and over. Forever and ever umptiddiump Now. Then, NOW. NOW. NOW .... And the battle was over.

She was too tired to open her eyes, but she was listening. She heard the baby cry, and she heard the Doctor say, "You have a fine boy."

A boy? She wasn't sure whether she had drifted off to sleep and was dreaming or not. She was too tired to care, as long as she had done her part and all was well.

Far, far away, she heard voices, felt ministering hands, knew that people (who couldn't be as tired as she was) were taking care of everything. Let them take care of things and let her sleep ... sleep ... sleep.

When she finally awakened, the Doctor was gone and Sister Carter was dozing on the other bed. They shared a mutual guilt at having slept, but the wagon was hot, dusky and sleep-inducing, they both agreed.

The rest of the camp had gone right on with Sunday service. Mary had not disturbed them, and they had not disturbed her. Afterwards, all the women in the camp went to work to put on a real celebration dinner.

Mary awakened from her deep sleep refreshed and ravenous, just in time to enjoy the bounty while it was still hot and delicious.

Sister Carter, seeing how hungry she was, said "If I'd known you didn't have breakfast, I wouldn't have hesitated about waking you sooner."

"Oh," laughed Mary, in high spirits, "I had Platte ambrosia, remember."

She was so hungry she almost forgot to look at the baby, and right then she knew she did not deserve to have such a beautiful one. There wasn't a scratch or a bruise on him.

Charles came in, pleased and self-conscious, evidently quite set-up about the attention and the fact that he had a son, after all. "Well, what shall we name him?" he asked.

Mary knew perfectly well what he wanted for a name. "Why, I won't stand for naming him anything but Charles," she said.

That night, as Mary lay awake listening to the sounds of the camp gradually subside, she thought having the baby come that Sunday was as nearly like having a baby at a picnic as it could be, even if having a baby is no picnic. She had slept too long in the afternoon to go right to sleep even though — or because — Sister Carter had warned her that she must get as much rest as she could because there was a hard day ahead for Monday. In the darkness, her weary, wrenched body was creaking and sagging - pulling itself together — like the wagon after a long pull. Only wagons don't give milk. At that silly thought she almost giggled aloud.

The baby was stirring. She caught a little muffled sound. She reached out her hand and skirted with her fingers where his head should be to assure herself that he had breathing space. Without touching him, her fingers probed the contour of his head by feeling the warmth on the back of her hand. Now she could hear the sound more clearly and she smiled to herself that it was a strong, healthy sound. He was smacking his lips!

She felt her breasts and wondered whether the milk was beginning to come. She certainly hoped he wouldn't start crying before she had something for him. She would not use sugar water unless she had to.

If the baby fussed in the night, she did not know it. Guiltily, she awakened when Charles got out of bed at daybreak and the baby was just "tuning up."

While she had slept, her body had labored on, and now there definitely was milk in her breasts. She had heard Sister Carter say to Charles last night, "You all come over for breakfast." Now Mary leaned over and whispered, "You-all come over for breakfast."

He was very, very wet, but she didn't have any argument with herself about whether to change him before she fed him. Better wet and warm than cold and dry at this hour. Anyway, he'd have to be changed again soon after his breakfast.

She pulled a dry blanket around the wee fellow and pulled the whole cocoon into bed beside her. She unbuttoned her gown as far as it would open, laid her right arm above the little tuft of hair as she turned toward him on that elbow, and laid the first two fingers of her left hand across the lower breast in order to guide the nipple to the cunning little mouth that was already making aimless motions. The miserable contrast between the weather-beaten fingers and the creamy whiteness of the rose-tipped breast shocked her. Those fingers were no more like the ones that had held the same breast for her first-born son than if they belonged to some old crone. She kept the fingers away from the tender skin of the little face as much as she could, as though those alien hands had no business near her little son, who needed surprisingly little guidance.

You act older than your age already, she thought. Maybe you'll make it all right.

On their bed, Little Mary was helping Pauline to dress. Outside, in their lean-to tent, Millie and Margaret were chattering to each other. John Henry had silently joined his father for the chores, she was sure.

The little girls eyed the busy baby as they dressed, but not for long. Millie soon washed their faces and marshaled them off to breakfast.

Before they were back Mary had given the other breast to the baby and dozed off again, hypnotized by watching him slowly drop off to sleep as his stomach grew full.

Millie was back with warm mush, rich milk, and hot coffee before Mary had even sponged off her face.

The baby had not awakened when she lifted him back, so she went ahead and had her own breakfast while it was warm and palatable.

Almost immediately the camp was full of the usual noise and excitement as the teams were driven in and hitched up. Perhaps the baby had heard enough of these sounds before that they did not seem to frighten him unduly. Whatever the reason, as long as he was healthy, Mary was grateful, because there seemed to be more noise and general commotion than usual. Of course it could be, she thought, that she was just more sensitive to it this morning.

But then she heard someone say something about "Ash Hollow." She had heard women whose husbands let them see the guide book tell about the steep hill down to it. Can my luck hold out another day, she wondered.

In a minute or two Charles climbed into the wagon and looked around. "Sister Carter will be here in a minute," he said. "She has offered to keep Little Mary and Pauline with her today. Millie and Margaret are to ride with you and look out for things. You best take it easy as you can. There's some rough going before the day is over."

She wanted to beg him to lay over just one more day, but she could see that he had thought it out and determined to go on with the rest. She might as well save her breath and her strength for what she could not delay.

That afternoon she was able to sit up on the front seat for a little while, just in time to watch the sky hatch a storm that grew to be a monster before her eyes, its great, purple streamers fingering the plains tentatively before the whole world darkened with dramatic suddenness. Then came the crashing volleys of thunder, rolling along the ground. It sounded to Mary like some great beast growling in its throat as if unwilling to give up the threatening sound, which seemed to intensify and not die down.

The baby commenced to cry. Mary got back down on the bed as quickly as she could and drew him to whatever comfort the warmth of her body might offer.

The girls scrambled into the wagon just in time.

The wagons were drawn into a circle and chained down against the storm as fast as the men could manage it. Neither Charles nor John Henry took time to get protection and Mary lay there dreading to think how they would ever get dried out. Then the hail began to pelt the canvas like bullets; and the rattle of the hail, the clanking of the chains that the men were staking the wagons with, and the sounds of frightened animals blended into a hideous cacophony of fear.

Finally, first John Henry and then Charles climbed into the wagon and sat along the edges of the beds. Charles said they might as well wait out the storm inside as out, but Mary suspected that they were giving whatever additional ballast they could, for the storm was buffeting their ark, coming at it again and again with rushes that seemed bent on tipping it over one way or another.

After an hour the worst of it was over, but there was no use to try to make a fire. They munched on some dried fruit and some biscuits and called it supper.

"Get your rest," Charles said, with an unusual show of tenderness as he jabbed at the covers to tuck them around her. "We will have to do considerable repacking anyway when we get to Windlass Hill."

"And the baby and me? How will you repack us?"

"You? Why, you'll be no problem at all. We'll just strap you in snug as bugs in a rug."

Bugs in a rug, yes. Snug, no, she thought.

Then Charles pulled himself wearily up off the bed. "If the cows are where I staked them," he said, "I think I can milk them in the dark."

"I can do it, Pa," John Henry offered.

"That's all right, Son. I think I ought to go over and see how the Carters' wagon weathered the storm, anyway, and no need for both of us to go out again."

John Henry was so tired he folded up a blanket and crawled between the folds without undressing and was asleep before his father returned and almost stepped on him getting into the wagon. Even if he had been stepped on, it was not likely he would have awakened.

"Mother, it's so cold. Do we have to undress?" whispered Millie.

"Can't we all sleep crosswise on top of the bed with something extra over us?" chimed in Margaret.

"Well, this once," Mary agreed reluctantly. She didn't see what else she could do. Just this once, she promised herself.

The little candle they had lit when the worst of the storm seemed to have passed was burned far down when Charles did eventually get back. He stepped gingerly between the two beds, over the crib, and didn't even take down the holder to blow it out. Even that sounded more like sighing than blowing. Then he turned and simply dropped on the bed without even taking off his boots.

Mary pulled herself down far enough to loosen them and get them off so that she could get a blanket over him. Tomorrow they would worry about getting things dry and clean again.

As Mary lay listening to the heavy breathing and smelling the wet, dirty clothes, she thought of the circle of wagons, each with its cargo of wet, dirty, weary people, curled around the motley herd of weary, frightened cattle, with the whole black sky bent on beating them all into these sandy mounds along the Platte, and it all seemed so pathetically ridiculous that she wondered how they ever talked themselves into thinking they were undertaking a good and patriotic task for which they would reap rich rewards. Monstrous human vanity!

VIII

Blackeyed Siouxians

MARY DIDN'T NEED to be told when they came to Windlass Hill. Exclamations and preparations were sufficient, but Charles came into the wagon and sat down on the edge of the bed with his hat shoved to the back of his head. He looked rather shamefaced, as if he had tried his marksmanship on a robin and had brought it down, she thought, as he nervously snapped his suspenders and then rubbed his hands.

Finally he came out with it. "Our team is the best and our wagon is probably the heaviest. The other men think our wagon should go down first while the ropes are good."

"What ropes?"

"The ropes that hold the wagon back."

"Back?" She sounded like a parrot.

"We'll have the wagon roped to the top of the hill and the men will play out the rope just enough to let the wagon down safely. We'll use Ortho-Doxology to hold up the wagon tongue, mostly, and I'll be beside them every step and talk to them to keep them from becoming frightened."

"Frightened of what?"

"Well, it is pretty steep and they'll feel the weight of the wagon pressing them once in a while." Then his chin lifted: "Once I get you and the children down safe and sound, I'll feel freer to lend a hand to the rest of the folks."

Then he added the clincher, "Everyone was so nice to us Sunday I'd like to pay them back a little for all their kindness."

Of course, of course. What can I say to that, she thought. Aloud she agreed, "Might as well get it done with."

And before she knew it, almost, Sister Carter was in the wagon helping Charles pack their things forward, shoving and stuffing every piece in tight so that it would take a lever to get any of it loose.

The bed was already against the front of the wagon, but it was headed the wrong way. They just opened up the foot, put the pillows down there, and pivoted Mary 'round. Then, at Mary's suggestion, they tied her down first with the baby in her arms, so that little Mary and Pauline could watch the process, before they, too, were tied down.

Finally, after much todo outside, she heard Charles say, "Are you ready?"

"As ready as we ever will be," came a nearby answer and a short laugh.

Then she could hear Charles talking to the team. She couldn't hear exactly what he was saying all the time, but he sounded as if he were talking to John Henry instead of oxen as the wagon began its slipping, lurching descent down the rough hillside. She did not have to see out to know full well what was going on. The men whom she had heard answer Charles were doling out the rope that held the descending wagon from crashing down against the team — even held the team if they should slip or plunge. The rope could not hold the wagon upright, however. At this angle of descent on rough ground a comparative slight jolt could tip the wagon over. Each jolt made her wonder whether this was the one that would do it, but even while she was wondering she was telling the girls how carefully Ortho-Doxology were placing their feet and how well they were doing. "Listen to the way your Father is talking to good old Ortho and good old Dox. Aren't we lucky to get down first! Poor Brother, having to wait back up there with the stock. I do believe we must be halfway down already. Scared? Us scared? Why, your Father himself said we'd be snug as bugs in a rug! Creak, creak, poor old wheels, working so hard to get us down safe and sound."

Finally, there was a shout, "That's it." and answering "Hurray!"

When Charles untied the rope he looked in. "Everyone all right?"

"Of course, Pa, we're snug as bugs in a rug," the girls laughed.

"If you can untie yourselves, I'll go on back," he said, and

103

did not wait for an answer.

The girls quickly freed themselves and Mary so fast that they were almost over the back gate before Mary reminded them to roll up the rope and put it back in the box where their father would want it to be. While they were engaged in the rolling up process, she had time to caution them about getting in the way of danger.

"Oh, Mother," Millie remonstrated impatiently, "don't you think we know anything?"

"Well, Millie dear, this is the first time we have gone down such a hillside, and oxen will be frightened. Besides, if the rope that holds them back should break, who knows which way they might roll."

Millie's eyes grew big for a moment. Then she darted to the back of the wagon just in time to see the next wagon descending. Only then did the reality of the danger come through to her, and she watched the laborious descent in fascinated silence.

This won't do, thought Mary. The child does not need to worry like that. "Millie," she suggested. "I'm sure your father secured Orthodoxy, but do you suppose you could stand near to them and talk to them a little while to keep them from worrying?"

"I'll help, too," chirped Margaret, as the two girls scrambled out eager to have a part.

Only then, alone with the baby, did Mary realize how completely drained she was from the ordeal. She was glad to lie still and listen to the girls carrying on loving, earnest conversation with the team, telling them how good and strong they were, how God was looking after them all, and that soon they would be unhitched to enjoy the grass and water and have a good night's rest.

Mary had thought she heard the sound of water and the rustle of leaves. She loosened the canvas to glimpse the place.

They were indeed in a hollow backed by cliffs where swallows swooped and darted with joyous abandon. She could not see water, but she could hear it, and she could smell wild roses. Quickly wearied by having stretched and propped herself on her elbow, she dropped back and lay sniffing the faint fragrance of roses which had so long since passed their prime that now the scent was more of a faded remembrance of the earlier blooming but by concentrating on it, her imagination pumped out the dry essence. She dropped off to sleep, smiling.

That is the way, Sister Carter and the children found her — even though the baby was beginning to fuss — when they came in to assure her that they, too, were down safe and sound.

Shamefaced, Mary struggled to sit up, avowing that she was going to get up and start taking care of her own children, but Sister Carter intervened.

"Now never you mind about a thing," she said smoothly. "The boys have brought in pheasant and rabbit, already dressed, and Millie has a fire started. It won't take me very long. You just rest and get your strength back. There are plenty of hands to make light work of supper tonight."

"But how can I ever repay you for all your kindness?" Mary worried.

"There will be plenty of time for that," she replied.

As she started to leave, she turned back. "As soon as the milking is done, I'll send some fresh milk. Drink as much as you can and don't you stint yourself. You don't want the well to run dry."

Mary laughed at the homely imagery of the woman-type joke. "You're spoiling me," she warned. They both had heard women boast of getting their family's supper the very day of giving birth, but she was glad to accept the role of indolence, not only to indulge her own lethargy but to give her body a chance to manufacture the milk supply which being on her feet would reduce. How nice, she thought, to indulge my own laziness — unselfishly.

She wondered what Charles would think about her lolling in bed and letting Sister Carter wait on her.

Later, when he finally came to help her out of the wagon so that she could eat with the rest of them, and they could see the new member of the wagon train, he seemed to be enjoying his role, what ever it was. Whether that role was tinged with gallantry or martyrdom she could not be sure. That he was rather self-conscious she was certain. No, she decided, he is just proud of the baby and pleased with a namesake. Everyone made a fuss

105

over "Baby Charles" as they called him.

The fresh game gave abundance and further festivity to their supper. Their relish was the sauce. The fact that there was ample to satisfy the huge appetites they had worked up that afternoon was the subject of Charles's lengthy blessing, to which masculine voices added an especially devout "Amen."

Mary's appetite was not as lady-like as she would have wished. She apologized for accepting a second helping.

"Just a case of somebody else's cooking," Sister Carter assured her.

"No," said Charles, waving a spoonful, "this really is delicious."

"Why, thank you, Brother Adams," she responded, really pleased.

Mary wondered whether Charles's remark was a kind of back- handed compliment and if so whether it was intentional, or not. She could not tell.

However, she was too much at peace with the world at the moment to give it more than a passing thought, and Charles's next remark would have surprised it out of her mind if she had been inclined to dwell on it.

"Yes," he said, "very tasty. Your fright didn't scare you out of your cooking wits." He was pleased with his phrasing.

"What fright?" Mary had to know. Sister Carter had not mentioned having any fright and had no intention of telling her about it, evidently, but now trapped, she explained with careful lightness, "Oh, our wagon almost went over on the way down this afternoon — but a miss is as good as a mile, I always tell myself."

Not wanting to probe if Sister Carter did not want to talk about it, Mary let the whole matter drop, but she could not help wondering what lay behind the placid surface. She knew she would not have been able to keep from chattering about it. Sister Carter evidently ran deeper than she had supposed.

It was that evening that Little Mary made an amusing mistake which gave them many a laugh at her expense. She brought her mother a bouquet saying "Here, Mother, are some daisies for you."

"Oh, dear, how nice," exclaimed Mary. "I didn't know that Black-eyed Susans grew out here."

Little Mary chortled, "That's a funny name — Black-eyed Susans."

When the adult conversation turned to the days ahead and Little Mary heard discussion of "going through Sioux country," she made a phonetically reasonable mistake. The next day, when she saw a Sioux lodge by the bank of the Platte, and she heard her father say "Sioux," she called out gaily that there was a Black-eyed Sue's house.

Little Mary was so disgruntled at finding herself the cause of general laughter that mother Mary promised her that she could have the first moccasins if the Indians were still in the mood to make them for children, as she had heard. However, she was afraid to have the Indians see the child's blonde curls and at the same time she did not want to frighten the child needlessly. She finally hit upon a story that was not too blatant a lie for her conscience.

"Mamie," she said confidently, "you know that God has given you prettier hair than the rest of us; you know that you should be grateful for it, even if it is sometimes harder to comb than Millie's or Pauline's?"

Little Mary nodded solemnly.

"You know that the Indians don't know very much about God."

So far, so good.

"You know that Indians have black, straight hair. Since they don't understand about the Will of God, they might be jealous of your hair. You don't want to hurt their feelings and make them jealous, do you?"

Mary shook her head.

"Alright, then, promise me that you will keep your sunbonnet on so they won't see your hair."

Mamie did keep her promise, though that did not keep Mary from using every pretext to keep her close as they went through the country of the Sioux. If she wasn't with her mother, one of the other women took her under her wing. A large, raw-boned woman whom Mary knew only as "Mrs. Baker" undertook to keep Mamie with her quite often during those days. Surely the child was safe as could be with her, for she was strong enough in appearance to awe any would-be Indian kidnaper.

The Sioux proved to be friendly, however. Before the train had traversed their country, they had made moccasins for each of the children at a price of about seven pins apiece.

– U.S. NATIONAL PARK SERVICE

Courthouse and Jail Rocks, a pioneer landmark near
the upper Platte River.

IX

Millie's Birthday Present

POOR MILLIE HAD BEEN counting the days until her eleventh birthday, on July 2. But on that day there was another sad burial. Although it was for a man they did not know, the whole family became involved because Charles was asked to say those pathetic "few words." They all stood soberly by as the body, wrapped in bedclothes, was laid in a shallow grave with no more ceremony than a hymn and a prayer. Then the wagons, the voices of their occupants muted, pulled away to get as much travel into the remainder of the day as possible.

Millie whispered to Mary that she "didn't feel like a birthday, anyway." But later in the day, when Mrs. Carter suggested that if the weather were clearer they might soon see Chimney Rock off in the distance, Mary soberly confided that seeing it would be a good enough birthday present for her.

All in all, it was a most depressing day — sultry weather, sparse grazing for the weary cattle, and only the distant landmark, not yet visible, as the symbol of progress for a dreary day.

FORT LARAMIE

By the time the train approached Fort Laramie, Baby Charles was almost two weeks old. Mary laughed to herself about having thought how nice it would be for him to say he was born there. She felt she had been as fortunate as an emigrant mother could hope to be, and when she compared herself with Sister Carter, she wondered how she deserved to have come this far so well. Sister Carter could have turned back, like Mother Light and plenty of others, but she hadn't. Mary could not imagine herself all alone in a strange land, and the children to look out for.

Well, Mary thought, maybe there will be some poor widower who needs a good wife out there. Sister Carter certainly would be that.

As if by some mental telepathy, Millie evidently was thinking about Sister Carter. "Mother," she asked, "have you noticed how much Mrs. Carter has walked by her wagon this week."

"No, I had not noticed," she said, startled.

"Ever since she got that scare on the way down to Ash Hollow; do you suppose she plans to walk all the way to Oregon?"

Mary considered Sister Carter, herself, and the lot of women in general. "Sometimes women just keep going and let things work out," she suggested.

Millie made a grimace as she finished smoothing down her side of the bed they were making. "Well, I don't think I'd walk to Oregon carrying one of those twins."

Mary laughed, "You better be careful what you say you won't do. Very often that is exactly what you'll find yourself doing."

Millie planted her feet squarely, her hands on her hips in mock defiance, "Can you imagine me carrying one of those twins to Oregon?"

"My imagination doesn't seem to be in working order, where Oregon is concerned," she laughed. Then, more seriously, "I can imagine you doing what needed to be done if you possibly could." And she leaned over and gave the surprised Millie a resounding kiss on the end of her nose.

The wind was beginning to come up again as they sat around the fire of cottonwood, the first wood fire they had enjoyed for two hundred miles, and ate their supper. Tomorrow they would pass the fort and perhaps get up into the Black Hills.[1] Mary had made a stew of the game they had been enjoying lately — a bit of rabbit and a bit of prairie chicken thrown in when the side meat was sizzling. When they were all good and hot, she lifted the pieces of meat out and put them in a pan at the edge of the fire to keep warm while she stirred in flour to brown in the grease before she added a few dippersfull of water and milk to make a rich

1   The McMillen diary for Saturday, July 10, records, "Today we came into the Black Hills." The area, of course, is not that known as the Black Hills today.

gravy. She had already crisped the cornmeal mush left from breakfast. As soon as the meat was back and bubbling in the deep pot, she called the family to eat, a call they were all washed up and waiting for. Each brought his own plate to Millie, who put a brown slice of the crisp mush on it and then handed it to Mary, who ladled the stew over the mush. After everyone was settled down wherever he chose to sit, Margaret brought the milk or coffee. Mamie and Pauline had the baby, in his Indian basket, between them.

Mary watched the little girls divide their attention between the food and the baby. They were not very clean and not at all well-dressed, she thought, but as long as they keep healthy and kind to each other, perhaps we'll come through all right. She got to watching the little girls and thinking about the adjustments they would have to learn once they were living in a more civilized manner again, and before she had finished her own plate, Millie was reminding her, "Don't forget the dessert!"

"When everyone's plate is nice and clean, Millie and Margaret have a surprise for you."

"You mean they didn't eat all those berries they were picking this afternoon?" John Henry teased.

"Not everyone is a selfish pig," Millie hissed at him.

"Now, John Henry," Mary gently brought him into line, "the girls not only picked them for us, they cleaned them and sugared them early, so they really should be delicious. If you can find some more tomorrow while your father stops at the Fort, perhaps I can bake some pies of them."

Millie brought the bowl that had been covered with a plate and a drying cloth. She proudly dipped out servings with a big spoon onto their eagerly held-out bowls. Margaret followed with a pitcher of cream and soberly advised each to "Say when" as she began to pour it on the berries.

Mary was relieved to see that Millie did a good job of measuring out the berries. There had been none to spare and she had feared Millie would not come out even.

When he had finished, Charles carefully wiped his mouth, first to the right and then to the left, with his big pocket handkerchief that had not seen an iron since they left "home," and considered aloud, "Now, if there were a nice big mess of berries ready *before* I go to the Fort, the berrypickers could go to the fort with me."

Bedlam broke loose the moment his words were out. There was so much jumping up and down and shouting that Baby Charles began to cry.

"Poor Baby Charles wants to go, too," they laughed, clustered about his basket, elaborately reassuring him that they were sorry they had frightened him and that there really was nothing to be afraid of.

Then they began putting their "dibs" on the containers they would use for their berrypicking, leaving Mary to pick up and quiet the baby before she put away the supper things.

As she held him close for a minute or two, she felt a wave of gratitude toward Charles. He didn't need to take them with him, but the children would love it.

As they neared Fort Laramie, Mary felt a peculiar sense of homecoming as she considered the great white adobe walls. Here was a sanctuary to which citizens might come. The armed sentinels walking the palisade atop the walls represented law and order to her. The brass guns on either side of the main gate were the voice of authority, polished and ready. Perhaps the sight of the Fort would not have stirred her so deeply if it were not for the beauty of the spot in which it was set. The lush grass, the flowers, and the tree-covered hills behind seemed all one weary pilgrim could ask of Paradise.

While the family made their trip into the Fort, she made pies and bread. She even did a little washing that could be rolled up and dried later, if need be. Indians were everywhere, handsome and seemingly friendly.

Being alone with the baby made her rather wary, however, and she kept the baby in his basket at her side every minute.

As watchful as she was, the young squaw was at her elbow before she knew anyone else was near. She jumped and stifled a scream as she looked to see whether the baby was all right. When she regained her composure and looked into the young woman's face, she was amazed to see a look of amused pity. Then she saw the papoose and she understood. The young mother had come

112

over to compare babies.

The only reason that young woman did not get hugged and kissed was her own dignity. She pointed to herself proudly. "Dakota," she said.

"Not Sioux?" Mary asked.

She shook her head and pronounced firmly, "Dakota."

"Won't you sit down?" Mary asked, making exaggerated motions to clarify her words.

Mary was glad her work was done so that she could enjoy her guest. Without knowing each other's language, they compared babies, discussed how big they were when they themselves were pregnant, how long they took in labor, their babies' clothing, how they held them at feeding time, and any number of topics of interest to them both. They even had tea together, (although the tea was coffee). Mary had made some tarts of leftover piedough, and when she served them she thought that she had never had a guest who accepted hospitality with more natural grace than her new friend.

Suddenly, the young woman looked up and said, as clearly as if she had spoken the Queen's English, that she really should be going, that she had stayed much longer than she had intended, and that she had a delightful time. Almost before she knew it, Mary found herself alone.

Alone, but only for a little while. Mary had not noticed, but the young squaw somehow knew her family was coming back and that introductions might be difficult.

When Charles and the children did get back, instead of telling her all about the Fort and what they got, they stood back and let Millie hand a small package to Mary. A young squaw, they said, had stopped them and handed the package to Millie, motioning her papoose and then toward the wagon until they understood that she wanted something taken to the baby.

In the package were exquisite moccasins, baby-sized. Not one of them could understand why Mary took one look at the cute little moccasins and burst into tears!

X

Ox-Mocs and Dust Masks

ALTHOUGH THE REST of the week was mostly pleasant, there was enough wind and rain for the other women to keep on "spoiling" Mary. "You must not chance getting chilled," they reminded her and, in the goodness of their hearts, they took turns inviting the girls to ride in their wagons when the weather made walking disagreeable. The girls enjoyed the attention and eagerly accepted every invitation until Mary realized they were overdoing it. By Friday she imposed a strict rule that they were not to ride in any other wagon more than once a week. "You will wear out your welcome," she explained.

The girls muttered, but they understood how such a thing could be and kept a strict accounting among themselves, under Millie's quick eye. Millie was never far away and almost always right at hand when Mary needed her to set by water for over night, to hang clothes on bushes to dry, to hold the baby for a while — to be "another pair of hands and feet for me," Mary told her. The other women obligingly told Millie what a fine daughter she was. With that accolade upon her, she outdid herself and won a few jealous sniffs from Margaret whose temperament was less docile.

Margaret and Little Mary had just formed a coalition for dust-kicking on Friday when Charles diverted them to look off "there." That is how they became the proud heralds of Chimney Rock, still about two days' march off but the landmark to which everyone had looked forward. They tore along the train making a spectacle of themselves as they announced what many a wagon load had quietly been watching gratefully for miles.

Pauline had been having a nap in the wagon and was miffed to find herself in the class with Baby Charles, having everyone else see the landmark while they napped.

Maybe it is wholesome, Mary thought, that the children

think as children and are not so concerned, as we older ones, with the sound of wolves at night, and lame oxen, and cholera.

By the weekend when they stopped for the Sunday layover, Mary was about ready to catch up with some of the chores she had been letting slide. The weather was fitfully improving, and so was her figure and so was her strength.

After the ones who did not choose to lay-over for Sunday had moved on out and there was a little spare time for a few extras before their Sunday service, she noticed a crowd at the edge of the camp on the west side. When she moved to where she could see better she recognized that it must be a train from the West, bound for the States. They seemed to be pausing, not stopping, and seemed to be impatient to be away. They left a serious- looking group of emigrants behind them as they cracked their whips and rattled off toward the East.

The men were talking earnestly, and she heard Charles remonstrating, "You have seen how those who would not rest for the Sabbath have wearied by the end of the week. Almost every Saturday night we have overtaken the ones who would not wait over, haven't we?"

The others admitted he was right, but —.

By this time Mary was not the only woman who stood at the edge of the group listening.

"But the Californians say we are going to be getting there late in the season for crossing the mountains if we don't pick up some time." They evidently repeated the warning they had just received.

"Well, at least I didn't hold them back." Mary thought. She knew they would be coming to mountains soon after Chimney Rock, but they were talking about other mountains beyond, which she had quite forgotten about in her more immediate con-cerns of the past few weeks. She simply could not imagine that far ahead. Somehow it seemed as if the edge of the world loomed out there. Being a practical woman, she shook herself free of the thought and inspected ears, especially middle-sized ears which seemed to be sandtraps.

Going into the Black Hills would be a new chapter of their saga. That would have been apparent from the moment they left

Fort Laramie if no one had ever heard of a guide book. The plains were abruptly climbing into ridges. It would be up and down the gray granite canyons that bristled with stunted growths of pitch pine and cedar. The grass along the Trail was thoroughly grazed over and the oxen would have a rough time of it, unless some trails could be found where the grass had had time to grow. The girls could pick bouquets of blue, white and yellow to their hearts' content. Pa could use some of that pitch, and if John Henry could get a wild hen or two, Mary could have something to season with the sage.

They had all had a delightful morning, which had extended well into the afternoon, so that they decided to take the shortest way through the Black Hills, getting to Warm Springs canyon that evening and to Bitter Cottonwood Creek for over Sunday.

The children had begun to feel the cold as soon as they were in the Black Hills, and by Sunday morning they were really shivering, especially John Henry. When he came in after looking out for the stock Sunday morning, his nose was red and his cheeks were tinged with blue. He seemed to relish the warm mush, however, and Mary took a good appetite as a good sign.

The McMillens wanted to be on their way, but they waited to have Sunday services beforehand. The children waved them out of sight, as they moved out of the valley, buzzards slanting in the blue above.

Millie turned to her mother soberly, "Do you suppose we'll ever see them again?"

Mary was glad to be able to dredge up one of Charles's remarks for a reply, because she had been thinking the same forlorn thought as Millie. "Your father thinks we make better time by stopping for Sunday so we'll probably catch up with them when they do have to stop and rest."

"I do hope we shall," Millie answered, wrinkling her forehead for all the world like a little, old woman.

Sister Carter came over with one of the twins riding on her hip. "She'll warp herself for sure," thought Mary, and wondered whether she would be carrying Baby Charles along the Columbia four months from then as Sister Carter had carried one of the twins along the Platte. She hoped not. Aloud she suggested, "It's

116

getting so cold we'll all have to go hunting to get enough buffalo robes to keep us warm."

The north wind was still blowing when they broke camp the next morning, but the children decided they could keep warm enough walking. Mary was glad they did because it was easier to feed the baby and let herself rest beside him when the wagon was quiet. She wasn't quite sure whether she put the baby to sleep or he put her to sleep. The upshot was that they both slept for at least a little while then, and the older children seemed to think it was part of the ritual of feeding a baby.

When Mary awakened and looked out of the wagon to see that all was well, Millie called, "Did you find the flowers?"

"Flowers?" Mary looked behind her. Sure enough, there they were, a pretty bunch of yellow daisies lying across the foot of the bed. How like Millie, she thought, wanting me to have the pretty things but considerate enough not to waken me.

"Thank you, Millie," she called as softly as she could and yet make herself heard. "Where's our vase?"

"Come to the back and I'll hand it to you. I let it hang on there until you were awake."

"Shall I hang it toward the front or toward the back?"

Margaret had an answer for that. "T'ard the back," she commanded, moving her arm in a generous arc to include John Henry, trudging along behind them. Mary could see him not too far back. She held the flowers up so he could see them.

He responded with a nod and a grin as he waved back, good-naturedly humoring their womanfolk follies.

As she looked back at him it struck her how different he was from the playful boy of a few short weeks ago! He looked taller. She knew he was thinner. What was there ahead for him in the new country? Would there be any getting him back into school after having done a man's work with men along the Trail?

Suddenly her thoughts were interrupted by screams from the girls who had evidently forged a little way ahead when the pace of the oxen, now beginning to pull harder against an uphill grade, had slowed. Mary could not understand what they were screaming, but one word, or name, recurred. Something had happened to someone. As she hurried to the front of the wagon, catching the

117

straps as she went to maintain her balance, she assured herself that it was not a name that sounded like any of her own. It sounded like "Sookey," but that didn't mean anything to her — until she saw what they were all pointing to.

There was the McMillens' ox, Sukie!

She looked at Charles.

"Lame," he said, laconically.

Millie, returning, heard his answer. "We can't leave Sukie behind. Can't we take him with us?" The other three were near enough to understand Millie's plea and joined in a chorus of pleading.

Mary could see Charles bracing himself as he answered a sharp "No."

Only Margaret was foolhardy enough to ask "Why," but for once, at least, Charles was ready, and willing to supply the answer to that usually irritating question. "I looked at that foot Saturday night," he said. "It isn't very bad, and if Sukie can just forage around here for himself a few days, he'll probably be as good as new. Then, someone will come along and let him take the place of another lame ox. If we made Sukie keep going on the rough road ahead, he might get worse. Now, you just tell him to stay here and get well."

Their father's reasonable explanation seemed to calm the girls' anxiety. As the wagon started up again, Mary could hear them admonishing the big fellow to rest his foot and get well.

Sukie rolled his eyes and dropped his head non-commitally. Mary thought he looked as if he were thinking, "Well, if you are going, get on with it."

That was the day they began to see Laramie Peak, "peeking," as Pauline insisted, over to their left.

At nooning, Charles and John Henry discussed the grazing situation with the Carter boys. Such large numbers of emigrants had recently gone through ahead of them that grass was thoroughly grazed off along the trail. "They tell me," said Charles in his man-to-man tone. "That we will have to seek camp off the Road or swim the cattle across the Platte all the rest of the way along the river. If you had your choice, which would it be?"

Amos spoke up first, surprisingly. He usually gave John

Henry precedence. "Mother wants to stay with as many wagons as possible. She's been listening to talk about extra guards at night," he explained. "She says she wants the safety of numbers."

"I was not thinking of separating from the main stream," Charles quickly assured him. "I was just getting the feeling for Mr. Hanna, so I could tell him 'as for me and my house'." None of the boys got the Biblical reference. They merely looked puzzled. Mary would have quipped, "You have been too long on the Mormon Trail, Charles," but she didn't dare. The things she said without thinking were bad enough.

Tuesday the weather was pleasanter, but the road wasn't. The rains were just recent enough to have laid the dust, somewhat, and not recent enough to have the road muddy. Ortho-Doxology were finding it bad enough as it was, and so were the other teams. Twelve miles was more than enough for that day.

Mary was the first one to notice the hunters coming back with buffalo enough for the whole camp. "Maybe I'll get that buffalo robe I've been wanting," she hinted.

"Enjoy the meat, but don't ask for any of the hide," Charles advised. "The oxen need it more than you."

"Why, Pappa," laughed Mary, positively crowing with the absurdity, "They have their own hides."

John Henry quickly intervened to keep his father from chiding her for impudence and to ease her chagrin at being naive. He did it so deftly by channeling their laughter that Mary was amazed.

"Didn't you ever hear of Ox-Mocs?" he asked. "You tell them, Pa," he said, "how they make buffalo boots for the teams. You know how it's done — I don't."

Charles obliged, "The idea is to make a bag of buffalo hide for each hoof. We figure we can do better than two teams per hide if we're careful, and that ought to carry us through the rockiest stretches of the road ahead.

"I'm counting on some boys working late tonight getting those hides cleaned up."

"Without any tanning?" Mary had to know.

"They won't smell too bad, if that's what you mean. If they did, we wouldn't have much choice."

Mary had no answer for that. He can make me feel so cheap, she inwardly rebelled, and when did I have a choice, anyway. Having thought it, without having to take the consequences of saying it, she felt a little smug. But as she lay alone in bed while he stayed up working on the skins and the others went on guard, she suddenly realized how much she had been "talking back to him" in her mind lately. She was aghast to think how much she had set herself up against him. In the comparative silence of the wagon, she thought guiltily of how someone like Sister Carter would feel lucky to be in her shoes. With that thought for flagellation, she resolved some of her inner conflict and fell into such a deep sleep that she didn't even know when Charles finally came to bed.

The next morning the girls were disappointed to see that the oxen were not wearing their new shoes.

"We will save them until we really need them," Charles explained, dropping eight raw bags into one side of the front box and tossing eight more over on the other side.

So there, Mary told herself, they don't offend even your sensitive nose!

But it wasn't long before the "Ox-Mocs," as the children called them, had to be put on. Every mile seemed more and more cruel. Mary would have welcomed anything to make the teams' work less bruising and grueling. Even the wagon creaked and groaned as it had never done before. Going up the steep, rocky hills threatened the strength of the team, and going down steep, rocky hills threatened the durability of the wagons and the courage of the voyagers, old and young. Those in the middling group were too much involved in warding off the threat of the moment to indulge themselves in fear. After hours of slipping, straining, lurching, grinding effort they were only seven miles nearer Oregon.

That night there was so little to make a fire of that they ate mostly dried fruit and cold biscuits. Mary grimly washed the diapers out in cold water and tried to tell herself that she could be grateful that there was water enough for that chore.

Charles came wearily by as she began draping the white squares about to dry. "We are all agreed to lay over and recruit tomorrow. If the womenfolk of three or four wagons plan together and make-do with one fire for the day, it would be wise."

"Maybe the children could fix some rocks to hold the heat," she suggested.

His face brightened so it did her heart good. "If our hunters or fishermen bring in anything, that will help." He sounded almost buoyant.

The sun was dropping fast. As soon as the sun was gone the air would begin to chill. All those who were going to bed, turned in quickly, considered themselves lucky, and felt sorry for those out in the chill night on guard duty for the cattle across the river.

And after all other sounds had ceased in the camp, those who lay awake could hear the poor, tired cattle-sounds across the water.

"Tomorrow is the middle of July." thought Mary. "How can we keep this up for two more months?"

The baby whimpered in his sleep. "I know, I know," she answered. It was the only comfort she could offer, but it seemed to help. He sighed and then slept quietly.

The next day dawned smiling warmth but caressing with a gentle breeze that continued all day and made pleasant even such worrisome chores as mending wagon wheels, canvas tops, and clothes. The smaller children who were not helping in the special assignments happily scoured the stretches of desolate land for anything that would burn. By the time the hunters and fishermen had brought in their contributions there was enough for handsome meals and the wherewithal to cook it.

Meanwhile, washings, hung from wagon to wagon or spread out on scanty vegetation, had bleached and dried in the sun. Many of the wagon canvases were rolled up to let the breeze air out the wagons. Bedding, hung on or from the great ribs, and gently flapping, added carnival color and movement as of banners flying.

Sometimes spoken, mostly not, the mood seemed to be: This is a good day; let not grief for what has been or dread of what may yet be spoil the healing beauty of the blue sky bending over us on this warm wasteland beside the slow Platte. It was not a place to gladden the slothful or the fainthearted, but it was a great day to renew strength and faith. One day is not much time to fill up a reservoir that must be drawn on right away.

The beautiful day had dried the pulverized road ahead! Almost as soon as the wagons started to roll the next morning, the dust began to billow around them. Mary closed up the wagon as tight as she could. If she and the baby were going to smother, they would at least smother as clean as possible. The girls chose to walk off the road and promised that they would stay where Charles could see them. They would hurry back to the wagon the minute any Indians appeared. As long as they thought their father could see them it would be all right, Mary decided. Both he and John Henry were right in the midst of the billowing clouds of choking brown dust. More by instinct than by sight they were keeping the animals on the road.

Whenever Mary peeked out she could see, ahead or behind, little but the dust-bronzed tops rocking through billowing clouds of dust. She felt so gritty she hated to pick up the baby when it was time to feed him. Of course, the only "time" for feeding was the timer in his tummy. When he began to fuss, she gave him a breast, changed him, and put him back to sleep. His soiled diaper she would put in the covered pail with a little water and sal soda in it. When she could, she'd drain it and put fresh water and soda over the soiled diapers, if she couldn't get them rinsed out. All this week, she had been able to rinse them out at nooning and at night and have at least some dry enough to use before the train started up again.

By noon her husband and son were hardly recognizable, their faces masks of dust, "If you weren't my own children, I might not even want to recognize you," she told her grimy little girls, grimly.

"Well, Mother, I don't see how Ortho-Doxology *stand* it," shrilled Margaret, as she bent over and swung her head back and forth so low she almost lost her balance. "How do they *breathe?*"

Dirty and tired though he was, John Henry found her imitation of a plodding ox highly amusing. "Go look at their nostrils," he said. "There's lots of room in there. When the dust gets caked around the skin inside they just snort like this (he snorted gustily) and blast it out."

"They may have good blasting equipment," Charles pronounced, "But we shall not put it to too great a test. Our scouts have already settled on a camp not too far ahead."

Thirteen miles was enough of dust for most of them. When they did stop to make camp, every woman in the train spent about the first half hour shaking out the layers of dust. A stranger, riding by, laughed at the sight, "Jest swapping dust with each other," he called.

Mary and her neighbor paused. "Do you suppose we are just doing that?" Mary asked.

"My guess is that we were shaking so hard the dust particles collided half way and dropped between us," she laughed. "At least, it's dry," she added.

"That reminds me — my baby isn't," Mary laughed back, and called to Millie who was holding him for her.

Millie, with a pleased expression, had been watching her mother bantering lightheartedly. "Mama," she said, "you have a little fun. I think I can change him for you."

"In another month, I'll probably be asking you to take a good deal of care of him." Mary kissed her lightly and collected the little bundle in her arms.

As she did so she was surprised at her buoyancy. She might be a dirty emigrant, but she felt fit and easy on her feet. There's a lot of life in me yet, she thought.

The next day the dust was not so thick but the sand was deeper and the oxen struggled and strained. Everyone who could got out and walked to lighten their load as much as possible. Mary felt a terrible guilt to be riding.

Those two days they had made but twenty-five miles in all, but the teams were pitifully tired. "If I weren't a religious man, this is one Sabbath I'd sure-nough want to lay-over," she heard one man say to another as they passed. She looked up and saw it was the same man who had laughed about the women shaking dust at each other the day before. Though he gave no sign of seeing her, she had a queer feeling that he had spoken for her to hear. But there wasn't any sense to a thought like that unless he was one of those that just has to have an audience, she thought.

And thinking less of him, she thought better of herself.

The girls had discovered berries — currants, to be exact. They came racing back to get something to put them into and raced off again to get enough for a mess before supper.

"Ma'am," she heard that man's voice again. She looked up and there he was speaking to her. "I notice your husband is busy. If you'll give me something to pick into, I'll go along and keep an eye on your little girls for you. We're rather close to the Upper Ferry, you know."

She did know that, but she wasn't sure just what significance he meant to imply, but he seemed to have joined their train.

She looked at him directly and got a little shock to find his eyes eagerly looking into her face.

She didn't want him to think her bold, as he probably would if she looked back into his eyes, she thought. Instead she looked industriously for the right utensil for him to pick into, gave it to him with a sliding glance, and thanked him kindly.

Charles got back almost the same time the girls and the man did. The two men had evidently met before, and Charles assumed, because he was with the girls by Mary's consent, that she had met him.

He lingered, and Charles, with hardly a by-your-leave to Mary, invited him to share their supper and family prayers.

Her first impression of him as one who enjoys being heard seemed to be wrong. Really, he was extraordinarily quiet but very observant. He was right there when Mary needed someone to steady the yoke while she was stirring the batter for fruit dumplings. It was he who lifted the kettle over to the fire for her, and he who lifted it off. And he complimented her outrageously. She knew she wasn't that good a cook.

Charles actually seemed to be encouraging him, too, she puzzled. Well, if Charles enjoyed it she could, too. And she did.

That night, in the darkness, after they had all gone to bed, Charles said, "I'm glad that boy (she hadn't thought about his being that young) could have the evening with us. When he told me how homesick seeing you made him, I vowed we'd have him for a meal."

"Homesick?"

"Didn't he tell you that you looked enough like his mother to be her sister?"

"No, he didn't tell me."

She grinned at herself in the darkness.

Chimney Rock today.

XI

Goodbye, Platte

FOR SOME REASON, the children had supposed that the end of the week and the end of their trek along the Platte would coincide so that the Sunday lay-over would be near the ferry. They were, therefore, disappointed when they realized that the Sabbath had come and they were not to spend the day at the ferry.

"Goodness knows you've seen plenty of ferries, and where you ever got the idea we would spend our last Sunday on the Platte there, I'll never know," Mary exclaimed.

"Be satisfied that we are all better off here for the day," Charles admonished mildly. "I may have mentioned that we would leave the Platte after Sunday lay-over, and that is exactly what we will be doing," he added with an accent of finality. He is always careful about keeping a promise, but he doesn't like the idea of the children even giving a hint of calling him to account, Mary thought. Many men would have flown off the handle for no more than that after a week as hard as this one, she knew. For a man as stern as he, he was not easily provoked to anger. For this she would be forever grateful.

Sunday seemed almost a repeat of Thursday because of the weather and the deep emotional undercurrent this time for leaving the Platte. As they were beginning to congregate for their Sunday service and were arranging ox yokes and pillows, Sister Carter came over and sat with Mary, arranging the twins between them. The three boys were nearby with the yoke they would sit down on when they had to. Mary looked down over the baby at her own four little girls, arranging themselves to use the two women's knees as backrests while they sat on the ground at their feet. They are all good children, she thought, and they get along as well as anyone could expect them to. Then a vague question formed in the back of her mind. Perhaps it came with the sense of

Oregon's being more imminent now that they were leaving the Platte. Once they got to Oregon — if they ever did — would Sister Carter live next door to them?

The thought startled her so that the question must have been written all over her face when she turned. Sister Carter was speaking to her, but not looking at her. Sister Carter was looking off at the muddy waters of the Platte.

"I was saying." Sister Carter remarked, "that saying good-bye to the river is a little bit like saying goodbye to a black sheep relative. You feel it's good riddance, and yet he's your kin."

Mary, thinking of all the grief and hardship that she had expressed so mildly in the homely figure of speech, felt a surge of loyalty to this stoic woman, and she thought I should be glad to share even my home with this good friend.

Aloud, Mary said warmly, "You're so charitable, I'm surprised to hear you'd ever admit anyone was a black sheep!"

For once, she thought to herself, I've said the right thing. It was the right thing, surely, for Sister Carter gave her a warm, happy smile.

Keeping the personal conversation light was a good idea, because the service stirred pretty deep. Just reciting the Twenty-third Psalm brought out some handkerchiefs, and singing didn't help much. "Shall We Gather at the River," that used to be so joyous, now reminded them of many who were forever gathered at this very river. It also reminded them of the rivers yet to be crossed and the dangers that lurked even in shallows.

But whatever possessed Charles to read about poor old Aaron not getting to the Promised Land? She wasn't one to question Divine Justice, but it always did seem awful to think of Aaron, by decree, getting only a glimpse of the Promised Land.

The baby stirred fretfully. Humph, she thought, who am I to worry about Aaron! Me with a baby to think about. She signaled the girls at her knee to let her get by, and then she slipped out as quietly as she could to take the baby over to the wagon for a feeding. Some of the women would not have bothered leave. They often gave their breasts to their babies right in church. Mary hoped they didn't think she was uppity, but she preferred more privacy.

After the emotional tension of the service, the grownups were determined to make the rest of the day as gay as possible, and they had a "regular church dinner" together afterwards. For blessing, they sang "Blessed Be the Tie That Binds," thinking, Mary felt sure, of many ties the songwriter couldn't have understood at all — unless he, too, had been traveling along the Platte on a plague-ridden pilgrimage.

As usual on Monday, the next morning they got off to an early start and got to the ferry by nooning. Such a motley crowd there! All kinds of foreigners, as well as Indians — all swarthy and cunning-looking to Mary. She was glad when they left the place far behind and the last savage had given up following them.

If she had known what a miserable camp they would be setting up that night she might have felt more kindly toward the folk at the ferry. The springs looked good enough, but they had been warned against them. Nothing to burn but sage. The grass cropped down to the roots almost everywhere. And once again they were traveling with a large number for safety. That meant more animals needing grass in the same place. None of them felt easy that night, for the teams on which they were depending were tired, and hungry, and thirsty. Tuesday night they would be camping at Willow Springs, but how can you tell an ox that tomorrow he can count on good grass and water?

When they did get to Willow Springs the next day, the children were bitterly disappointed. No one had thought to tell them that the willows had long since been cut down for firewood, and there was nothing to burn but sage. The water, however, made up for any number of other deficiencies.

"Enjoy it while you can," Charles told them at supper, "and fill up everything we have that will carry water. We are in for a bad stretch when we leave here. Nothing but alkali between here and the Sweetwater."

Mary, not sensing the gravity or not accepting it, chortled, "Will the Sweetwater be as sweet as the Willow was?"

Charles looked at her, but he was warning the rest of them, "That we shall find out if we have care between now and then."

If we have care! What else have we, Mary thought. But it was nice to have good water — as good as the water in the old well

128

back home. Home — now there is a dangerous word. All it means is what I don't have. And what I don't have is wrong with what I've got, which makes me a discontented shrew.

When she was taking some things back to the wagon after supper, she noticed Charles seemingly counting something in the front box. She could see his mouth working as he laid unseen objects from one part of the box to the other. He looked concerned.

"Is there anything I can help you with, Charles?" she asked.

"Not unless you want to make some more ox-mocs," he said, not even noticing that he had used the children's names for them.

"I guess I could if I had to," she answered straight.

"These won't hold out the whole way, I'm afraid."

"Whole way to where?"

"To the Sweetwater."

"How far?"

"The longest day's travel yet."

As it so often did, his soberness roused some flippant demon in her. "Where's your faith, Charles?"

Without so much as looking up, he gave her tit for tat: "I have faith. It's oxmocs I'm running short on."

In the early morning light, they ate their mush without cream and drank strong tea to wash it down, then more tea to quench their thirst after finishing up the side meat from the night before, having been warned repeatedly that they must not drink milk from the cows until they reached the Sweetwater. Breakfast had been a rather grim meal, for which Charles had set the tone when he asked the blessing. He had made it very clear to the Lord and to his family that they were going to need extra-ordinary fortitude for that day which, at best, would be rough and long.

As he finished cleaning his plate, Charles looked around at his brood until he had everyone's attention, and then he cleared his throat as if the words were stuck there.

"The only water we will have until we get to the Sweetwater tonight — or whenever we get there — will be what we carry with us. Anyway, we can't count on any fit to drink, either for us or for the cattle. Any animal that gets any of the alkali water will probably die right away. I am going to tie the cows behind the wagon, and they must not get loose. If they should get loose, yell

129

as loud as you can and try to keep them in the road until I can get there. Now, the oxen must not be left even for a minute, so if I should have to leave them, John Henry or Millie will have to take my place.

"Do you all have your heaviest shoes on? If not, get them on before we set out. I'm told the alkali dust will eat right through thin soles. If the dust billows up from the road, keep handkerchiefs over your nose.

"One more thing: if you girls see a dead cow or an ox by the side of the road, get John Henry or Amos to cut more hide for oxmocs. And, John Henry, I understand they are better if they aren't cleaned off the way ours are. I'm told that if they are put on flesh-side out and not too well scraped, the flesh helps cushion the hoof."

Human carrion, that's what we are becoming. Mary gagged at the thought.

"Oh, one more thing to remember." This time he centered on Mary.

Now what? she thought. I suppose I'm to sit in the wagon poking holes in the edge of the hides, running ribbons through them; she knew she could get hysterical without half trying.

"If all our prevention fails and one of our animals does get into alkali water, I want your mother to be ready, on a minute's notice, to have big chunks of bacon ready for us to push down its throat as quickly as possible, and then to have vinegar ready to pour down after that.

"If we are where we can stop and make a quick fire with some sage, there's another remedy we could use. Then, Mary, I'd like you to mix a cup of lard with a cup of syrup and warm it enough to blend it together, but not hot, of course. That we could pour down its throat instead of having to push the bacon chunks down with a prod.

"Well," he said, finally, to the circle of concern around him, "I think we are as ready as we can be for this day. Let us be on with it."

"On with it, or done with it," Mary thought nervously, as she packed as quickly as she could and mentally practiced diving for the lard and syrup. Then, thinking how long it would take to get a fire started unless someone had a fire going, she mentally rehearsed grabbing the hatchet and chopping the slab of bacon.

Hitching up and moving out was a subdued, sober ritual. Alkali had been bad enough before this to fill them with dread at the thought of a whole day of fighting it. But as they plodded up the hill from Willow Springs they began to get glimpses of the Sweetwater Mountains, bathed in the rosy light of a beautiful dawn. To the worried pilgrims the sight was as inspiring as a vision of the Celestial City, mitigating the miserable effects of the sun-baked, dust-ridden plateau over which they slowly plodded, listening to the repulsive sound of the crickets being crunched under the wagon wheels, or watching the landscape waver in the heat. Even the occasional breeze from the west brought no comfort — only more dust into their faces. Even nooning was a kind of exquisite torment because the rationing of water made them even more thirsty than they were on account of the alkali dust. They all washed their hands in the same small basin of water, which Mary then poured over the soiled diaper's in the pail.

The girls were content to stay in the wagon most of the day, taking turns at sitting on one bed or lying on the other, telling each other stories or playing with clothespin dolls. When the baby was awake, they talked to him, and when he was asleep they were careful to lower their voices.

By keeping the front of the wagon closed and mostly the back open, Mary got the most air and shade with the least dust, at best, little less than stifling. She could hardly imagine how Charles and John Henry could endure walking all those weary miles over the rough, rocky road, now becoming rather sandy and dusty.

It was almost sundown when a shout came down the line, "We see it. We're almost there."

Mary got to the front of the wagon as quickly as she could and pulled the curtain. Sure enough, lying in its own shadow, a little bit like a dog with its nose on its paws, was the big granite mound. Millie came to stand beside her, and between them they swung Mamie and Pauline up onto the front seat. Then Mary stepped back enough for Margaret to stand beside Millie. That is the way they were standing when Charles looked back and saw them there.

"We made it," he called. He was covered with dust and stained with perspiration, a sorry spectacle, like all the rest of the men, and yet, Mary thought, there is something truly heroic about him. He doesn't swagger or brag — he just says he'll do a thing and he does.

The wagons were stopping. Charles stepped in front of the team and held out his arms. They stopped as if that was what they had intended to do anyway, and tried to find a blade of grass long enough to get their teeth on it.

Charles was watching them as John Henry came up, and he turned to the boy with a shrug, "No telling how far we'll have to go with them to find grass." They stood there looking around at the barren ground.

Then one of the men who had been ahead scouting, rode up. "Brother Adams," he said, "Most of the womenfolk want to keep the wagons right by the water here so they can do their washing and all handy. There isn't much grass, but yonder there is more than here, so put your wagon wherever you fancy and we'll drive the cattle where they can get a little forage anyway."

"Um-yummy, doesn't that water look good," Margaret called to John Henry.

"I'm going to find a shallow place and just lie down in it" he answered, "and I'm going to climb the rock and carve 'Maggie Adams'," he teased.

"That will do, Son," Charles said to him and in the same breath to Mary, "This will do right here, won't it?" His tone suggested that of course it would.

Mary looked at the lovely, clear water, hardly more than a foot deep and all of sixty feet wide. "If the children can scare me up some sage for fire, it will be good," she said. Margaret was already sidling down the dropped wagon tongue and Mary didn't want her to get away while she and Charles were talking.

Charles took the cue and reminded her that she was expected to help.

Margaret looked aggrieved, but Millie made a triumphant grimace to her mother.

As Mary climbed out of the wagon, the cool sound of the rushing water, the brooding presence of the great rock and the

canvas-freckled valley with wisps of smoke from a hundred supper fires rising into the upper sunny air while the shadows
fingered a dusky pattern below — all produced a serenity within
her somewhat akin to the way a woman feels when she surveys
her kitchen all clean and ready to be put to service for the evening
meal.

The children, too, were beaming around. Pauline was hopping up and down on first one foot and then the other, making a
great thing of catching the up-ankle behind her with her hand as
she alternated.

Mary watched her for a minute, trying to remember whether
she had even seen her do that before. I am afraid I have allowed
myself to be isolated too much of these weeks since the baby
came, she thought. I don't want to let them get along without me
just yet awhile.

The thought may have prompted a more outgoing manner on
her part to which the children responded that evening, or they all
may have been responding to the pleasant surroundings.
Whatever it was, the brief evening was one of those happy ones of
content before they stumbled into bed.

The next morning no one was in any mood to move out
early, and many of the train wanted to climb the great rock, some
to look for the names carved all over it, some to carve their own,
and some just to climb up, wave their hats, and come down.

Charles's hat was pushed far back on his head, a sign that he
was feeling unusually debonair! "I think the whole train would be
for laying over right here through Sunday if it weren't for the
grass being all grazed off," he said.

Sister Carter came by just in time to hear his remark. "Too
bad we couldn't have been here twenty days ago," she said.

"The Fourth of July?" Charles was not asking whether it was
— just giving her conversational encouragement, Mary noticed,
rather amused at his unusual gallantry.

Sister Carter looked pleased. "You just couldn't believe the
celebration they had here. They even took apart wagon beds to
set up for tables."

"Tables!" Mary exclaimed, as if she had never heard of such
a thing.

"And they made a flag."

"What with?" Mary had to know.

"They started with a sheet, then a red skirt, and finally a blue jacket."

Mary sighed. "Their clothes must not have been as dusty and dirty as ours. Seems to me we're all one color!"

Sister Carter was not through and she was not going to be sidetracked from sharing a good story. "They even set up a forty-foot pole for their flag and shot off guns that morning.

"They must have had a wonderful celebration — speeches, singing, and my land, the food!"

"The men made the speeches and the women cooked?" Mary asked, very sweetly.

The other two silently measured her. Instead of shaming her, however, their staid manner seemed to evoke heady impudence. "What can you expect of a rib?" she laughed. "Anyone want another cup of coffee before I have to throw it out?"

"Why, yes," answered Sister Carter, glad to have the conversation running in smooth channels, "I am all packed up and put away."

"We should be, too," said Charles, a bit shortly, "but there's time for another cup of coffee, I guess."

Mary poured their coffee and was ready to pour a cup for herself, when the baby began to fuss. "Oh, bother," she said, "I thought he'd wait, but I guess he won't and Charles hates to have a baby cry. Excuse me, please." And she carried the baby to the wagon to feed him, leaving the two rather self-consciously by the fire, drinking coffee together.

But not for long. In a few minutes Mary heard Mrs. Baker's hearty voice announcing that she would like to finish her coffee with them as her boys had already put out her fire.

"Bless you, Mrs. Baker," Mary thought.

"It does seem a pity to hitch up and move on for just those three or four miles to Devil's Gate," Mary sighed, when John Henry, returning with the oxen and the cows, came by to see whether she had saved out an extra bite of something for him.

"Where could you find a better place to spend Sunday than at Devil's Gate?" he grinned.

"I wonder why they gave any place a name like that?"

"Some of the men tell me it makes a hell of a lot of noise."

"John Henry, don't let your father hear you say a thing like that!"

"He just laughed when one of the men said it to him a little while ago," he smirked.

Mary raised her eyebrows in mock horror and let it go at that.

Going the short distance to the Devil's Gate proved of more consequence than it had seemed in prospect. They forded the river and Rock Creek. Mary noticed that they had left the main trail and were evidently going to camp off the beaten path. The day was lovely and she was enjoying the front seat again. Just as she was beginning to see enough shadows to tell that they were going south, the train pulled into a lovely little valley, lush with deep grass and a sparkling stream.

"Oooh," Margaret exclaimed, "I want to roll in that beautiful grass."

John Henry, coming abreast with the cows, heard her. "You and the cows," he laughed. "They're going crazy."

Charles looked back. "We'll have to be careful or they'll make themselves sick, Son."

"What a wonderful worry," Millie sang out.

All up and down the line of wagons, people were leaving their wagons to get out and walk in the grass as if it were a wonder they needed to feel to believe.

As soon as the tongue was down, Mary walked down it almost as lightly as Margaret would, and she stopped beside Charles to share the moment with him. "Well, Charles, I thought we were going to Devil's Gate, and I find myself in Paradise."

"Thanks to Amos," he said. "The boy went over to the trading post as we went past and I guess this man Schambau took a liking to him and the fact that he's trying to take the place of his father; anyway, he told Amos about this place. Judging from the looks of the grass, I'd guess he doesn't tell many emigrants about it."

"Let's send Amos in to every trading post from now on," Mary laughed. She felt so elated that she began to wonder whether she was giddy, but she had only to listen to the other voices around her to guess that if she was, she was not the only one.

The spell of the beautiful little valley was upon them all. In the wondrous reality of it, the weary miles of alkali dust, arid wastes, and dunes of sand were as a half-forgotten dream. The children galloped about like frisky little colts and the grown-ups relaxed and softened. By Sunday evening even the cattle looked like new animals.

Mary heard Pauline say as she and Mamie were getting ready for bed, "I hate to go to bed tonight."

"Because you want to stay up and play?"

"Because when I wake up it will be Monday morning and we'll never see this place again."

"Then let's notice everything in the morning so we can remember it."

Mary forgot all but the compassion she felt for them at the time until the next morning when they were leaving. The two little girls were solemnly pointing out what they wanted to remember as they trudged along beside the wagon. Before long, Millie and Margaret caught on to what they were about and joined in, making it more of a game and less of a sorry ritual.

Meanwhile, Mary had begun feeding the baby in the wagon. "The more, the merrier," she smiled down on him.

Just as their train moved back onto the main trail out of Devil's Gate, they met another that had evidently encamped there the night before. The children began to shout, and then some of the older ones began to "Halloo" back and forth. It was the McMillen train.

"Pa was right. Pa was right," John Henry shouted.

Mary knew what he meant, and she knew that Charles knew what he meant. She could tell by the half-smile on his face as he called back, "Right about what, Son?"

"Right about making better time when we observe the Sabbath." The boy was so happy to have obvious proof of his father's superior judgment that it was a pleasure to see.

The McMillens were tired and their cattle were the worse for wear.

136

Mary couldn't help feeling a little embarrassed for the freshness and gaiety of those who had had their Sabbath rest in the little valley. The McMillens traded off their footsore team of oxen for a yoke of cows that day. Mary did not need to feel embarrassed very long, because, in a few miles of the sandy roads they had to travel together, they all began to look about the same again.

They all camped together that night, happy to be in each other's company once more. They oh-ed and ah-ed over the baby, reassuring Mary of what she herself had thought to be true — that he was indeed a very fine specimen of young manhood.

Their campsite had good grass, they were by the Sweetwater, and, after a sultry day of plodding through sand in the face of a west wind, the evening was delightful. However, the McMillens were very tired and went to bed quite early, to Mary's disappointment.

As they toiled into the mountains on Tuesday, the children discovered gooseberries.

Mrs. McMillen came over to the wagon, calling, "Sister Adams, why don't you let me stay with the baby. You get away for a little while and pick some berries. I should think it would do you a world of good."

Mary had been wanting to get out and walk a little, but she had not wanted to carry the baby, or leave him alone, or ask anyone else to mind him for her. She suspected that this kind lady would enjoy the baby as much as she herself would enjoy getting out. She accepted the offer happily.

The response of the children to having her venture out was rather humiliating. It was as if they expected her never again to enjoy an active life. In the past ten months, they had all but forgotten that she had ever been able to jump from one rock to another or climb a steep path. One would think she was a hundred years old!

Perhaps she overdid the climbing and stretched herself a bit. She felt she had by the time they had picked enough gooseberries for three or four pies and got them back to the wagons.

With enough sugar, the gooseberries made excellent pies that night, and Mary was quite set-up at the way the children bragged of her gooseberry picking prowess.

The next day she felt some after-effects, but that was to be expected, she knew. What really made her feel bad was to see that the McMillens were lagging behind. All evening she kept hoping to see them come into camp. Evidently the bad roads of the day had discouraged them from forcing their team too far.

Before the end of the week Mary began to wonder how they ever could have made it had they not had the recruitment of that refreshing lay-over in the valley. The grass was skimpy and the roads often almost as bad as any they had seen.

– OREGON HISTORICAL SOCIETY

Famous Independence Rock, on which pioneers carved their names, as sketched by the Cross Rifle Regiment artist in 1849.

– OREGON HISTORICAL SOCIETY

Devil's Gap or Gate, formed by the Sweetwater River,
as sketched in 1849.

– U.S. NATIONAL PARK SERVICE

South Pass, over which the Overland Trail crossed
the Continental Divide.

XII

The Top of the World

THE MORNING THEY STARTED up the Great Divide, everyone was excited. "Goodbye Sweetwater, Goodbye," sang Margaret.

"Goodbye, Sweetwater," echoed Mamie and Pauline.

"And Hello, South Pass," amended Millie firmly.

Listening, Mary thought, Why, their voices are at least three notes higher than usual. To her, even the sounds of the chains seemed sharper. The oxen sounded the same, though — and smelled the same, poor beasts.

While Mary packed away the breakfast things, Millie held the baby for her. Fortunately the chore was routine, because her mind was not on the task at hand. All the time she was thinking, I have cooked my last meal on this side of the Rockies.

Margaret was hopping about when Charles came to help Mary into the wagon, "Pa, are we going to noon at the Pacific Springs?"

"Not if we don't get started shortly," he answered drily. It was exactly the same thing he said often enough before, but there was something in his tone that Margaret, too, noticed, for she glanced quickly up into his face to read the expression there. He was busy tightening the ropes around the kegs along the side and appeared not to notice.

"He is sure-nough tense," Mary thought, and she visualized steep cliffs and ravines ahead in the day's travel.

As soon as she had checked up on the children and had had a clear understanding about how far from the wagon they would be allowed to stray, they were on the move again, and Mary lay down beside Baby Charles to give him another feeding before he set up a clamor. When Charles was in front, John Henry not too far behind, and Millie nearby, it worked out pretty well, she thought. Once there was a time I would have worried about mussing my dress, she thought ruefully, but now a mussed dress is of no consequence — no conse–quen–ce.

Watching the baby always made her drowsy. Slowly his little hand stopped waving, and as soon as his little stomach was full, he was sound asleep.

Mary was almost off to sleep herself, but she managed to fasten her dress and lift him into his basket without disturbing his sleep. Then she let herself drift back into a delicious snooze.

When she awakened, she was thoroughly chilled. She pulled a shawl about her shoulders and looked out the front of the wagon and could hardly believe her eyes. How long had she slept? They were in a high broad valley, maybe thirty miles wide — she could not be sure. It looked almost as if the mountain had stretched out on either side to touch the extremities of the sky and had thus left the straggling line of men, wagons, and beasts peculiarly exposed to the heavens in this great barren incline. Some snowy peaks off in the distance gave the only evidence of the rest of the earth.

John Henry had changed places with Charles and was ahead with the oxen. He looked back and saw her looking out the front of the wagon. He grinned at her amazed expression. "Ma," he called, "reach up and pick me off a cloud."

They did get to Pacific Springs for nooning, though it was a late one. The children hopped around from spot to spot on the marshy turf and had great fun trying to "make the ground shake."

Mary let them enjoy the novelty for a few minutes and then put them to work getting water from the springs which bubbled up through the middle of it. As Charles pointed out, the place had been almost completely grazed off and they had best not linger, because no one seemed to know how far they would have to travel before they found a camp for the night.

"Don't we follow Pacific Creek?" John Henry asked.

"Yes, for about three miles, and grass grows beside water, but there's been too much grazing before us," Charles gave him a bleak look.

Seeing that he had worried the boy, he added, "It just means that the folks ahead of us have got the pick of things. We will just have to look farther and travel longer for camps. We ought to be at Green River in three days, even if we have to go out of our way a little. There'll be fine grass there, I'm told."

The old carrot trick, thought Mary, only this carrot is a Green River.

Charles was talking directly to John Henry, now, "We aim to cut across to the Little Sandy River, which should be about thirteen to fifteen miles, before we stop to camp."

It would be a long day.

Millie held the baby while Mary buttered their bread and poured buttermilk for all of them. The odds and ends of meat had kept nicely, wrapped in a moist cloth. She called the girls and let the family pick up the pieces of meat with their fingers. She hoped it was all right as long as their fingers were clean; it was easier to wash fingers in cold water than dishes and silver.

Charles leaned against a near wheel and slowly tipped his cup back and forth, studying the cup or the buttermilk. "If we can keep the cattle we'll pull through."

Mary's heart jumped fit to choke her.

The children did not get the full impact of what he was saying. Except, maybe, John Henry, who wanted it spelled out. "You mean 'Keep them out of the alkali spots'?" he asked.

"Yes mostly that, I guess," Charles agreed, evidently with some private reservations. "We are in for poor grass and hard pulling — and, yes, alkali. I hear we'll be seeing some dead cattle, and I just hope we can keep from having any of them our own."

"First, people — now, cattle," Mary blurted out.

Charles gave her a straight look. "God willing," was all he said.

The children stared at their father in worried silence, not knowing exactly what he meant, but certain that it was some kind of pious reproof.

Gradually the weight of the grim silence lifted as they finished their brief meal and were promised the tarts for dessert at "tea time."

While the girls were off "squishing" the turf one last time, Charles spoke again to John Henry. "You understand," he said directly to the boy, "our lives may depend on keeping our animals out of the alkali. If you think you can't handle them any time, be

142

sure to call me."

Mary felt the cold deep in her bones. Even in the bright sun she felt it. She wished she hadn't slept so long. The wind was coming up, too.

When they were finally able to stop for the night, the wind that had made them uncomfortable all the long day, made cooking even more miserable than it would have been anyway, with nothing for a fire but willow and sage. It was all Mary could do to get the sidemeat and mush fried.

The milk seemed to have a queer taste. She watched the rest of the family to see whether they detected it. If they did, they said nothing about it, and she did not want to start anything by suggesting it. Maybe it was just the dust and grit in everything.

As soon as the sun was down, they had begun to feel the cold, and the fire had done little to take the chill off them.

That night they wasted no ceremony getting into bed and piling all the covers they could find over themselves.

As they lay listening to the sounds of the wind and the cattle, Mary heard little Mamie muttering to Pauline, "I'm glad I'm not poor old Orth — out in the cold."

"Be quiet and let me sleep," Millie snapped, with what was for her an unusual display of temper.

Mary reached across the intervening aisle to quiet the child with a love pat. She wished she didn't have to put so much on Millie. It was not right for an eleven-year-old to carry as much of a woman's work as she did. But I don't have any choice in the matter, she thought, and added another loving pat to the only one she could reach there in the dark. Mamie reached out from beneath the bundle of covers and caught her mother's hand with a reassuring squeeze, as if to say that her feelings weren't irreparably damaged and not to worry.

As usual, Charles had sighed almost the minute his head hit the pillow and that was it. Before long, the children's regular breathing assured Mary that they, too, were asleep. Having slept during the day, she was more wakeful. She lay listening to the night wind, the cattle, and the promises she was making to herself.

Every day we get more uncouth, she worried. By the time we

get to Oregon City the children will have forgotten what it is like to sit down to a well-set table. I'm not sure I'd know how to act myself. If there is any way to do it, I've got to get the girls into that seminary as soon as we get there. It will take more than I can do to smooth off these rough edges. Having thus formulated a carrot of her own, she settled down to sleep and gain strength for the next day, the evil of which might well be sufficient unto itself.

Certainly the beginning of the next day was gray and chilly enough to make them all look wan and cold. Breakfast was almost as bad as supper had been the night before. It was a relief to be hitched up and on their way along the southwesterly flow of the Big Sandy River.

About mid-morning, while John Henry was ahead with the team and Charles was taking a turn with the cows, John Henry called out, "Well, here is the first one."

Mary didn't need to look, but she did.

Somebody's cow, left right where it fell. Her breakfast flipped over in her stomach. She hastily sat down at the end of the bed where she could reach the chamberpot if she needed it in a hurry. She put her hands over her eyes to help blot out the pathetic, frightening sight, but the picture burned in her mind. Nothing she could do or think about would erase it from her consciousness for long. It haunted her.

At nooning she blurted out to Charles, "How could they do a thing like that?" thinking that it dominated his thoughts, too.

"Who'd do a thing like what?"

"Not even bury their cow?"

He looked at her in unbelief at her inability to grasp the realities of the road they were on. "How would you go about it" he asked, with a meaningful glance to the hard, barren ground. "If we stopped the train and every man and boy chipped at the ground for all they were worth, how long would it take, do you suppose, for them to get a cow buried?"

Although he had put it as a question, Charles had intended it as an answer, and Mary got the message two-fold: those who had left the cow were sensible, practical people; Mary was an impractical romantic.

Mary was properly abashed for having made so hasty a judg-

144

ment. In judging, she, too, had been weighed and found wanting.

That night they heard a wolf howling.

What kind of land would ever be worth dragging a family along a road strewn with dead cattle and wolves howling through the night?

By the time they had finally reached the Sandy, Mary knew she had the ague, or mountain fever, or something. The "something" she would not even try to name to herself. If Charles noticed, he didn't give any sign. Maybe he didn't, really. All the women were complaining about the effects of the altitude, effects for which they had not been prepared. Everything took a most unreasonable time cooking, and they all had sore backs from being so long at it.

At least there was some grass and water. But being over the hump could not give them very much satisfaction when each day's travel took its toll on the cattle. Every day they saw that the sores rubbed by the yokes were growing bigger and bigger.

As Orthodoxology were being unyoked the three little girls stood soberly by to see how their sores were. The sight of dead cattle along the road had horrified them, and Mary could think of little to lighten their mood.

At first they had all been fairly loud in voicing their disapproval of folks who drove their oxen too hard or allowed them to drink alkali water, but, as the count had now got past twenty, the situation became less easily disclaimed. Their righteous indignation had turned to a holy dread.

That is why, weary and worried as they were there at Green River, they were glad for a Sabbath. There had been enough of a rain to settle the dust somewhat. Perhaps their cracked lips and sore eyes would heal a little during the Sabbath lay-over.

Mary looked up at the rushing water and then across where they would make camp. Nature, cold and remorseless, encompassed the weary, disheveled, gaunt voyagers of The Trail and here offered man solace and insult.

So this is Green River, she thought, and rightly named.

She had walked down to the bank of the stream with the others, and she stood shielding the baby's eyes from the sunlight on the water, when Charles came up. They stood watching the ferry approach the far shore.

"There are no two ways about it", he said. "We'll just have to pay their price."

She was almost afraid to ask how much that was, but she did.

"Three dollars a wagon — but that is cheap beside what we stand to lose, if we look for a place and try to ford it. That water is ten feet deep."

Mary did not comment. She knew he was merely allowing her to hear him thinking aloud, and she knew she was supposed to be properly impressed. She was, at least happily impressed that he was inclined to take the ferry, expensive as it was. She was half glad he was so tired if that was the reason for the extravagance.

She watched the ferryboats working their way in reverse across the deep water by means of the suspended ropes. Crossing in them would be hazardous enough, enough to stop her — if there were such a thing as stopping. She caught herself shivering in the afternoon sun. I must have been more nervous about this river than I realized, she guessed, as she went back to the wagon to await their turn.

When they had finally crossed, Charles offered to look after the cattle by himself if John Henry would get a fire going quickly to speed up supper.

John Henry tried to get the fire started. "Where there's smoke, there's fire," he growled, backing away and rubbing his eyes, "But I'd like more fire and less smoke."

"Let's hope the smoke is harder on the mosquitoes than it is on us," Mary answered as cheerfully as she could. And what I'd give for a basket of buffalo chips, she thought, wryly remembering how loathsome the practice of using them had at first seemed to her.

The next morning after they had tried to sing "Safely Through Another Week" and "Sweet Hour of Prayer" she had to admit it was a pretty poor excuse for a Sunday morning service the second Sunday in August. None of them felt like singing. They were just too cold and tired, for one thing, and besides their lips were too cracked. The gritty feeling of the alkali dust in their clothing and hair did not exactly add any joyousness, either.

146

In the afternoon, despite its being the Sabbath, the men began working on some of the gear. Especially the yokes. They said they were smoothing them. A drastic job of "smoothing," Mary thought, as she watched John Henry working away on one. Then she heard him say, triumphantly, "I've taken off a good pound from this one, Pa."

Margaret, with her hands behind her back, stood watching. "What good does making it smaller do?" she asked.

"Not smaller, silly, just lighter and easier on their necks. We're on the last half of Sublette's Cut-off. Know what that means?"

"What?"

"Rough going, that's what."

Charles looked at his son sharply. "We wouldn't be taking it if we were not equal to it. Don't overdo it, Son." Then he changed the subject so deliberately that Mary, listening, couldn't tell whether he was being intentionally obvious or not. The tone changed, too, from stern admonishment to genial conversation. "We will be going through some very interesting country in the next few days. We'll see lots of Snake Indians, probably."

Pauline had been edging in closer as Charles had been talking. Now she, with a flurry of importance, got in a question. "Why do they call them Snake Indians?"

Before Pauline had completed her question, Millie was ready with a possible answer, "Because they snake dance?"

Charles straightened his back and reset his hat to relieve the crease it was making across the top of his forehead, meanwhile giving the question the benefit of thoughtful consideration. "For a fact," he said, "I don't know as I ever heard why."

"Probably some connection with the Snake River," John Henry sagely offered.

"You could be right," Charles agreed, in the man-to-man tone that never failed to make John Henry flush with pleasure.

Millie apparently felt that some leveling was in order. Sauntering casually along behind him, she hissed, "Smarty!"

During the next two days they were so busy with the rough terrain, avoiding dead cattle, and trying not to attract Indians that they were in a continuous state of high tension. Because little

Mamie's blonde curls never failed to attract the Indians, Mary kept her in the wagon whenever they were about, but so many Indians brandished guns as they galloped by that Mary realized too well that the wagons would not begin to have adequate defenses, should the Indians turn hostile from caprice or plan.

As the grass got better, the mosquitoes got worse. Millie sighed over the state of things as she helped Mary change the baby, "I guess God has to find a way to keep us humble."

I wonder what the child thinks we have to be proud about, Mary thought to herself, struggling against tears of self-pity and weariness.

But that was the week that John Henry caught fish on two different fishing attempts, and the change in diet did wonders for their spirits. However, frying them made Mary sick. Only by walking away on a pretext, once in a while, was she ever able to finish frying them for a meal. She knew she wasn't getting any better. "If I can just hold my own, that is all I ask," she prayed, hardly realizing she was praying.

The days were warm enough now that getting her hands in cold water to wash made her feel a little better. However, before the next Sunday she would have welcomed some more cold. Friday and Saturday were hot and dusty.

Pauline was the first to cry, "I see it. I see the quaking aspen. Ooh, it makes me shiver to see them quiver!"

When they finally got to the Aspen Grove, Charles almost spoiled it for her. When they pulled up for the night, worn and shaken from the long dry stretch and the rough road, he waved his hand and said in class meeting tones. "Good grass and fine water."

Just as if he'd created if, Mary sniffed to herself.

The children were off and exploring as soon as the pails were full and the fire started. Suddenly Mary realized that she had forgotten to warn them to stay near by. She had felt ashamed of her demeaning thoughts about Charles. It would be a judgment on me if anything happened to them, she thought, while dropping the dough into the bubbling pot. When a bit of the hot liquid splattered and burned her hand, she felt that perhaps the children were in a mite less danger! Still, she could not call them in to supper fast enough and did not draw a full breath until they were all back and safe around the fire. Somehow the fears and frights of crossing rushing water, of passing dead or dying animals, of sojourning among the arrogant Snakes — all had left her unnerved. Then she had relaxed her vigilance. She was trembling.

It was Mrs. Baker who said, "Are you sure you don't have a fever?"

Charles looked at her sharply, and suddenly she couldn't stand being looked at. She knew she would cry if she weren't careful. She smoothed her hair back from her forehead with the back of her hand. "Oh, I've been leaning over the fire too long," she answered as briskly as she could.

That satisfied Charles, but Mrs. Baker looked at her pretty straight as if to say, "I have my doubts," but she said nothing aloud about her obvious reservations, to Mary's relief.

The day had been sultry, but now it was turning cold. They all went to bed early and piled on everything they could think of to keep warm, but Mary had been chilled through before she got the supper things put away. Nothing could warm her, evidently. She slept fitfully, and every time she awakened, she found herself shivering.

By Sunday morning the storm broke loose with everything. Hail whitened the ground, thunder crashed and rolled ominously around them while lightning bolts streaked and jabbed as if some malicious god, perhaps blinded by his own strokes were trying to find them. The storm was frightening enough but its effect upon the cattle was an even greater threat. If the cattle should stampede ..., but Charles was not going to let that happen, not if he were trampled in the effort.

"John Henry," he said sternly, "you are to stay in the wagon with your mother and the girls. Under no circumstances are you to leave them alone while I am out." Then he disappeared out the back of the wagon into the wild mountain storm.

Baby Charles had begun a storm of his own, so there they sat huddled in the wagon, listening and waiting while the storm raged on, while Mary rocked the baby in her arms and talked mother-comfort to him.

Charles did not come back until the storm had nearly spent

itself, and when he did come back, he reported that they would be better off to stay in the wagon and keep dry. Some of the men would try to get a fire going and have some coffee and tea ready whenever they could, Since he was already wet, he would milk the cows as soon as they calmed down.

Millie sat wiggling her toes in her scuffed and battered shoes. She turned them this way and that, as if to see which cracks were the deepest. Finally, she spoke with the resignation of a little old lady. "At any rate, we are not losing any traveling time today!" And that summed up about the best that could be said for the whole day.

Monday morning dawned clear and bright. When Mary saw the sunshine she was sure she was going to feel better.

Mrs. Baker nodded approval as soon as she saw Mary's face. "You do look better," she said. "The storm cleared the air and we'll all feel better."

Every adult in the camp seemed impelled to say the same thing. Mary had the thought for a minute that she wished something else could come along to provide another topic of conversation. In the next minute, she was afraid she had just asked for trouble. That seemed to be the order of the day, as far as the terrain was concerned.

The storm *had* cleared the air. As the day grew pleasant, their damp clothes dried. That would be one day they wouldn't be bothered with dust.

Then they met the packers coming from Oregon. These packers were more talkative than some of the rough, taciturn characters who had passed before, evidently not wanting to waste their time answering questions and waiting for letters to carry with them. These men seemed glad to give encouraging news. They told of meeting emigrants nearly through to Oregon City.

"It seems as if Oregon is just over the hill, now," Millie confided to her mother.

XIII

Amiss at Matchmaking

MILLIE'S REMARK ABOUT OREGON'S being just over the hill had a sage quality as Mary remembered it through that week. Almost every day some event reminded them of civilization and journey's end. Two bridges, new roads, wood for fuel, good water, mountain berries, and maybe best of all, a man selling groceries! Charles splurged and bought enough potatoes for three good meals, even though they cost twelve and a half cents a pound.

The day they came to an Indian village, the Indians were ready for them with moccasins that would eke out their shoe supply. Charles got every one of the children a pair. Mary, who had done little walking, refused before Charles offered to get any for her. "I really won't need them," she suggested, and he did not insist. She would have liked to have them just for the fun of having them, but she knew she could not justify the extravagance of paying a dollar for them.

Sister Carter got some for herself and the children, but she really needed them as badly as the children, because she was walking much of the time.

"I don't see how you do it," Mary had said of her walking.

"If you had had the fright I had in the wagon, you'd be afraid *not* to walk," she had replied.

Mary was sure it wasn't that simple, but she wasn't going to argue about relative frights and let it go at that. But she did wish she had some moccasins, too. Sometimes she watched Sister Carter swinging along with a twin on her hip, walking with the same freedom the Indian squaws had, and she wondered whether she wouldn't enjoy walking more if she were wearing moccasins. It serves me right for being self-effacing, she thought.

By Friday night Mary had almost forgotten how miserable she had felt the week before. When they were moving, the rugged terrain did not encourage introspection — except in those eternal moments of suspense when the wagon teetered or lurched down a rough hill or went over a boulder that threatened the wheel. When they stopped, there was the cooking and washing — and the baby, though Millie was taking over much of his care.

This is one family that is learning to count its blessings, Mary thought. When Charles asked the blessing before a meal, he never missed an opportunity to be as specific as possible.

Friday night it was "Let us be thankful for the berries and the fish."

Saturday night Mary found herself concocting her own blessing. It would go something like "Let us be thankful we *didn't* get a mouthful of the grasshoppers today." She felt awfully silly, probably from a light touch of fever, she seemed to be developing. She would drink an extra hot cup of tea. Tomorrow she would try some of the soda water from the Soda Springs. Perhaps she was still a little giddy from the effects of the grasshoppers on her eyes.

She had been riding up front when the storm of grasshoppers started. It had been just like riding into a snow storm. She had ridden it out on the seat rather than chance lifting the curtain and letting the dirty things get into the inside of the wagon.

Thank goodness tomorrow was "Oh Day of Rest and Gladness" day.

Sunday was such a lovely day it seemed unbelievable that only the week before they had been miserable. Mrs. Baker bustled about chirping snatches of hymns while she was getting breakfast and set the mood for everyone within hearing distance.

Charles announced that no one of his children was to visit the Soda Springs until after Sunday services, and they were not to drink any of the soda water until after dinner. Mary was secretly proud of the discipline Charles maintained. She knew a number of children in their wagon train who could not be depended upon to follow instructions like that without some supervision to enforce the law. She would have been very much surprised to find that Charles had been disobeyed.

That morning their service was unusually short, because wagons were rolling in and out all the time and there was a great deal of running back and forth with cups and sweetening for the drinks they were all bound to have before they left the place. Charles was not one to capitulate, but he was not one to let a service become ridiculous. Brevity effected the dignified compromise.

Charles had discovered a Mr. Davis, who had come from Illinois, around Lockport, but he had originally come from Ohio. Charles thought he might have known some of the Carters' relatives or friends and immediately took him over to the Carter wagon. Mary could hear the peculiar tempo of their three-cornered conversation, with starts, spurts, and slowed conclusions as they essayed to link connection with the past to the present.

Hmm, Mary thought, he seems like a nice, single man. Wouldn't it be nice if he took a shine to Sister Carter. She will need a husband, and she would be a good wife.

Mary soon had herself practically convinced that the match was inevitable and was so busy with her own thoughts that she was quite surprised to see the two men walking off together, evidently to look at the stock. Well, she thought, be stubborn if you will, Mr. Davis, but you are missing a good bet, and the lady won't be single very long, I'll warrant.

The children had made many trips to the springs before their parents got around to going, and they were excited with the idea of conducting a guided tour of the various springs. They danced tangents to Mary's and Charles's paths recounting what they had heard others say after their first taste of the water or how they looked. Millie was even able to repeat a recipe for the proportions of acid and sugar some woman had told her.

Mary had planned to try some of it, but the odor repelled her and she finally had to admit she couldn't possibly drink any of it. The children were disappointed, but Charles made up for her by showing great eagerness for some by their recipe. Pauline was all for letting the baby try some of it.

Pauline, who had been the baby for so long that she sometimes had showed a reluctance to move over for the new baby, looked quite pleased with her seniority when Mary explained that the baby would not be old enough to enjoy the privilege of drinking soda water and "lemondy" for a long time.

Although Mary was not feeling well, she was not feeling ill

enough to let it spoil their very pleasant day.

Towards evening, who should drive in but the McMillens, and it was difficult to tell who was the happiest to see them — the adults or the children.

As tired as they were, they let the children take them on a tour of the springs almost immediately. The two young women brought a gaiety and sparkle into camp with them. Later on in the evening Cecelia brought out her accordion. For almost an hour the valley rang with music and laughter, while the evening breeze fanned the fire and stirred the cedar and pine branches just enough to scent the air with their clean fragrance.

The touch of fever that had been nagging Mary seemed quite inconsequential as she relaxed in the pleasant atmosphere and joined in the singing. She felt a hand on her shoulder and looked up to see Mrs. Baker settling herself on the ground beside her.

The firelight revealed Mrs. Baker's beaming approval. "I could hear you singing along with the rest of them," she whispered. "It did my soul good."

Mary giggled like a schoolgirl, "It might do your soul good, but I'm thinking it couldn't have done much for your ears."

"Now, now," Mrs. Baker scolded, chuckling.

As she scanned the faces, rosy in the glow of the firelight, Mary saw that they all were having every bit as good a time as she. No picnic back home had ever been gayer than this. Maybe Oregon would be good to them. Somehow, just seeing Mrs. Baker gave Mary a sense of the goodness of God, but she had not always felt that way about it.

There had been a time — the first time she saw her — that she had actually disliked this big, raw-boned woman who then appeared to be so crude and coarse. Just one of the many who threaded in and out in the shifting companionship of the Trail. Mrs. Baker's outward manner and speech seemed less and less important to Mary as she became more and more aware of her hearty goodness.

Evidently the hard life of the Trail was not much more grueling than the life to which she had always been accustomed. Her only family seemed to be two sons whose obvious differences she never mentioned. The casualness with which she accepted her hardships, together with her compassion for those whose lives had not prepared them for rough times, gave Mary a new measure for her own values. To Mary, this earthy, good-natured woman's presence represented unaffected strength and goodness.

More than she realized, Mary was going to need strength and goodness in the days ahead. What she did realize was that she was very glad to see the good woman's face shining in the friendly circle around the campfire.

In the morning the train moved out on the momentum of good fellowship from the evening before. Almost every prospect was bound to please. Steamboat Spring was just a mile on their way, but the whole train stopped, and no one mentioned that it was a waste of valuable time. Finding another trading station there increased the feeling that they were indeed arriving at the threshold of their new country, which was full of strange and wonderful works of nature.

Great crevices in the rocky slope inspired their awe. John Henry, having tied the cows to the back of the wagon for their safety from some of the water that was said to be poisonous, was free to explore and found great sport in peering into them and announcing their depth as measured by his eyes. One, he announced, had no bottom, as far as he could see, "and I have pretty good eyes." He had a great time looking over the great masses of volcanic rock that had once been spewed out of the earth and discussing with the awed little sisters how the earth must have "jiggled" to have caused the great cracks and eruptions.

"That boy has a good head on him," his father announced to Mary.

Then all afternoon they rolled along good roads or splashed gaily through lovely mountain streams. At night, they came to rest beside a gay little creek.

Mr. Davis had traveled with them all day, but the matchmaker could see that Mr. Davis was hardly fair game. He was only about twenty-seven years old. No doubt he thought of a thirty-five-year-old woman only as a reminder of his mother, she thought with gleeful malice.

After that, he did not exactly travel with them, but they did see him off and on until Friday. Whenever their paths crossed, Mary waved to him. Two or three times she thought she discerned a puzzled look on his face, as if he were wondering why she was disposed to be so friendly to him. Once, Charles saw her wave and his face mirrored the same look of puzzlement. Mary laughed aloud. "I'm reminding him of his mother," she said.

Charles looked as if he couldn't believe his ears, and then he remembered. Slowly an almost impish grin spread across his face.

"Hail Mary," he said, just barely loud enough for her to hear. He evidently had said it before he thought. As he looked away a dull red suffused the little part of his face that she could see.

So somebody else sometimes speaks before he thinks, she gloated. She might have known that he could not forgive her for his mistakes, however. He made a special point of keeping her in her place afterward.

By Tuesday afternoon the train was struggling along the ridge between the Bear and the Snake rivers, straining up and inching down such steep inclines that they all got out and walked most of the time. Progress was so slow that they had plenty of opportunity to pick an abundance of berries — enough for meals ahead, even for seven. Mary discovered that she could tuck the baby against her left shoulder and pick with her right hand, dropping the berries into Margaret's basket without disturbing the baby. Mamie and Pauline were picking together. She could hear their voices as they gabbled companionably nearby, and she could tell from occasional words and silences that they were sampling generously as they picked. Margaret, too, was eating more than she was putting into the basket, and she welcomed her mother's contributions against the time she would have to compare her basket with Millie's. Millie was picking ahead with the older girls and was taking herself quite seriously as a commissary aide.

Since she could be of no help with the wagon, it was easier for Mary to busy herself with the children and the berries than to watch the agonizing struggle with the oxen. The best she could do would be to have a good supper for the workers that night. She knew that John Henry and Charles would relish the berries and cream.

156

When the train drove into a lovely little valley for their camp that night, she was reminded of the one near Devil's Gate.

As Charles was unhitching the oxen, she teased, "Are you sure we aren't traveling in circles? Here we are in Paradise again."

"Pretty steep circles," he answered, too weary to enjoy her pleasantry.

Wednesday they continued their tortuous descent down to the Snake River. An abundance of berries, along the way, lured all who were not needed with the train to berry-picking forays. Mary went along with the rest of them, the baby against her shoulder, but she had walked only a little distance before she realized that something was wrong. Her knees threatened to buckle under her. At first, she thought that she might have "overdone" the day before, but she began to feel worse rapidly. She knew she was ill. Could it be that she was getting "mountain fever?" Suddenly giddy, she dropped to her knees and sat down, rather than to take a chance of falling with the baby in her arms.

Mrs. Baker came along and eased herself to the ground beside her. "I thought you looked as if you had a touch of fever again last night, but I didn't want to suggest it to you," she said, in her brusque, kind way. "Can you walk a part of the way back to the train?"

Mary tried to get up.

"Huh" snorted the good woman, "I've seen newborn colts do better than that," and she immediately took charge. She sent one child for Charles and another for Millie, who got there first. To Millie, Mrs. Baker handed the baby.

The whole train was stopping, and Mary was as ill of embarrassment as of fever. When Charles came to them, Mrs. Baker said, "Sister Adams would drop in her tracks before she'd admit she was sick."

"Well," said Charles, as if he were considering moving an awkward piece of furniture, "I think it would be easier for two of us to carry her on a hand-seat than it would be to swing the wagon over here.

One of the other men came along and offered to help, and so with the whole train watching, it seemed, she rode on the seat improvised by hands clasped to wrists between the two men.

Mrs. Baker helped her to bed in the wagon, and the train moved on.

"Oh, what shall I do?" Mary moaned, as tears of weakness, frustration, and humiliation dampened her cheeks and soaked the pillow.

"Just stop feeling sorry for yourself and let the rest of us help you get well," Mrs. Baker answered briskly. "You don't have much choice, as nearly as I can tell, except in the way you take it."

Her matter-of-fact tone was exactly what Mary needed. She laughed weakly through her tears. "Go on, scold me," she said.

"I will when I think you need it," Mrs. Baker answered briskly, as she hung up Mary's clothes and lifted the canvas a little way, to catch a breeze. She bustled about as best she could in the moving wagon and restored order.

Finally, she draped a damp washcloth across Mary's hot forehead and swollen eyes and slipped a handkerchief into her hand, chuckling as she did so, "Use this — if you're going to snivel any more."

Mary caught a whiff of it and sighed, "Lavender is nicer than sage."

"My initials are in the corner of it," Mrs. Baker added. "I don't know what possessed me to carry it today, but I hadn't used it yet. It'll smell better than oxen." Then she climbed out of the wagon and left Mary to lie and wonder how the family would manage — with the baby and all — until she could get back on her feet. She tried to think of the things Millie could do. Then she realized that Millie couldn't be expected to take over the "housekeeping" and care of the baby, too.

Perhaps she had lain there an hour when she heard the baby crying. Then she heard Charles stopping the team, and Millie climbed in with the baby.

"Come to Mother," Mary said, and at the sound of her voice, he stopped crying.

While her mother arranged herself and the baby for his feeding, Millie stretched and rubbed her arms. "I thought they'd break," she admitted.

"He'll be all right with me now. He'll sleep after he has been fed."

"Should I stay by to help change him?"

"I think I can manage the baby if you will see that the girls stay fairly close."

Millie's face showed her relief. She started to drop out the back and then remembered, "Mrs. Carter says she will fix something for our lunch and for you not to worry about the family. She'll take care of us, Mother."

All the rest of the day, as they jolted down the valley of the Snake, Mary felt a sense of having been shelved. Life flowed around the wagon and the wagon moved along on its way. Inside, under the undulating brown of the weathered canvas top, she and the baby lay in a kind of social suspension.

At nooning, Mrs. Baker brought her tea, which felt healing to her throat. Millie came in and changed the baby. Then Mrs. Baker carried out the diaper pail. In a few minutes she brought it back, fresh and clean, with a little water in which the next batch of soiled diapers could soak. In no time at all, Mary and the baby had the wagon all to themselves again. That was the way it was all afternoon, with both of them sleeping fitfully despite, or perhaps because of, the restless motion and the heat.

Eventually there were the shouted orders, strange voices, and all the other sounds of coming into camp. As soon as the wagon stopped and the sounds of unhitching began, Millie and Sister Carter appeared.

"I've tried to give you some peace and quiet this afternoon," Sister Carter announced with some pride. "Mrs. Baker said you might be able to sleep off the fever if you had a chance to rest, and we thought you'd rest better if you had the baby where you could see he was all right — as long as he didn't bother you."

"You do look better, Mother," Millie said, scanning her mother's face anxiously.

"I'll be fine by morning," Mary promised her. "Do you think you can manage for me this evening?"

"Oh," Sister Carter laughed, "Millie and I have everything planned already, haven't we?"

Millie nodded soberly, her eyes fixed on her mother's face.

Mary had felt a sharp twinge of jealousy at Sister Carter's

easy announcement of their plans and she had a peculiar feeling that Millie had read her mind. "Just this once," Mary said, "and then I am sure I'll be able to do my own work, as I should." In her heart, she knew she was promising herself as much as them.

For one thing especially she was grateful — that she had been isolated on orders and not from her family's choice. But she couldn't understand why neither John Henry nor Charles had been in to see her yet.

It was almost time for them to eat before they got back to the wagon, but they did slip in for a minute. They both gave evidence of a little extra grooming, Mary noted.

"We're going to have some more good company for a while," Charles said. "Our good fortune is Providential. Just when we should be joining forces to form a larger train going through this part of the territory, we meet a train captained by a fellow Methodist, and not only that but a Methodist preacher."

His enthusiasm was infectious. Mary quite forgot her irritation at his comment on good fortune as he went on in genuine pleasure about their new traveling companions.

"Ma," John Henry grinned, "you'll have to get well so you can meet Captain Hyland. Say, Pa, which do you call him — Reverend or Captain?"

"We'll call him Captain on week days and Reverend on Sunday, I guess."

"He's from back home, Ma."

"Iowa?"

"No, Illinois — Plainfield."

Seeing her menfolk had perked Mary up considerably. She indicated fixing her hair, "Does our new preacher make sick calls?"

"Only on Sunday," Charles answered with a perfectly straight face. Indeed, neither he nor John Henry looked at all amused. Mary decided maybe it wasn't funny, either.

They had not been gone more than a few minutes before Millie brought her some soup and some tea, both in cups so that she could handle them more easily. The soup was rich with flecks of meat and the tea was hot and strong. As she suspected that Millie had not had her supper, she made it evident that she could manage quite well and then sent Millie on her way to eat with the rest. When Millie showed dutiful reluctance, Mary said, "Hurry along, dear, and don't keep Sister Carter waiting supper for you. Afterwards, you will feel refreshed and you can come back and help me with the baby.

Having her conflicting duties resolved for her, she went merrily on her way, and, Mary, left alone with the baby, steadied herself on an elbow and thoughtfully sipped the tea. The soup did not go down so easily. For that she took longer.

Outside, she could hear the sounds of the camp life flowing around the wagon as if she were not there at all. How different it all was from the birthing, she thought drearily. Then, she had been the center of attention; now, she was more like a pebble that the stream flows by. She smiled to herself at herself for the distress of the morning when she had assumed that her illness would be catastrophic.

Before she had finished her soup, she had philosophized full circle and assessed her reactions for what they were worth — the grousing of one getting well enough to begin thinking irritably instead of desperately. How well she had learned to recognize the symptoms in her children! They were always getting better when they became cross and fretful! Mrs. Baker had said, all she had to do was to get well, and that was what they were allowing her to do in the relative peace and quiet of the wagon.

Soon the children, well fed and sleepy, clambered aboard, the two little girls to get the night clothes. Mrs. Baker was making up a bed for them in her wagon. Charles and John Henry would take turns sleeping in John Henry's lean-to by the wagon by taking different shifts of guard duty during the night.

"Guard duty?"

"Captain Hyland wants four men on duty at all times from now on," Margaret parroted what she had heard.

Mary wanted to know what the emergency was, but she didn't want to take a chance of making a mountain of a molehill. She waited until Charles came and tried not to fret herself in the meanwhile.

"Just a precaution against the Diggers," he said offhand.

"Are they dangerous?" she had to ask.

"More thieving than anything else. If they know we have a

guard — and we'll make that evident — they probably won't bother us at all."

Mary had heard of the Digger Indians before, of course, and she had noticed that they were never mentioned with respect, the way the Sioux were.

True to Charles's prediction, evidence of a guard was sufficient, and the night passed without incident.

Thursday was hot before it began. It wilted Mary's firm intention of getting up and about. The burned and desolate land lay in a torpor, and Mary wasn't able to do much more.

They all rolled the sides of their wagons up and looked out between the wagon ribs across the miles of almost completely arid basin in which they were traveling and watched the heat waves. The glare in the wagon was only slightly less intense than that outside.

"I don't know how a body would know whether he had a fever on a day like this," Mrs. Baker said vexedly, as she changed the damp cloth on Mary's forehead.

Sometime during the day — Mary never could remember whether it was before they reached Fort Hall or afterward — she heard the children call, "Hello Mr. Davis." This time Mary did not wave.

XIV
All Kinds of Help

A S MRS. BAKER SAID, when she climbed into the wagon
"to tidy up," (which was her way of saying she would
empty the chamber pot and clean up the diaper pail)
"Well, I declare, some people have a soft life. All you have to do
is turn your head to see all this beautiful scenery."

"Yes," Mary answered dryly, "with the sides up I can see the
mosquitoes circling over me like buzzards, and once in a while I
can see an aspen tree."

"You'll be seeing one sight for sore eyes pretty soon now. We
are getting close to Fort Hall. I can see an old adobe house a little
way ahead, and about a mile beyond it, unless I am seeing a
mirage, is Fort Hall. Doesn't that news perk you up a bit?"

"Yes, it does," Mary answered. "If you could push me up
with another pillow and lay my shawl around my shoulder's to
make me more fit to be seen, maybe I could sit up a while. I've
just got to get my strength back, and I might as well be at it."

The good woman beamed approval, "Now that's the spirit. I
do believe that heat is good for something — it's baked the fever
right out of you. Somehow I just dreaded to have them bleed you
for it."

Sitting up was not as easy as Mary had expected it to be. Her
head seemed to be light and heavy at the same time and her eyes
seemed to be undependable. However, she tried not to let Mrs.
Baker know how difficult the right-angled position was, and that
pleased friend returned to her own wagon secure in the impression that "Mis' Adams is getting well fast."

Mary, by shifting every few minutes, did manage comparative uprightness until they reached Fort Hall. When she finally
saw it, she decided it was hardly worth sitting up for.

The McMillens' married daughter, coming by the wagon and
seeing her sitting up, stopped to pass the time of day, putting

Mary's own thoughts about its impressiveness into words, "Not much bigger than a good-sized barn!" she commented.

"Are you going in to the fort?" Mary asked.

She laughed gaily, "I gather that the last thing in the world those soldiers want is a swarm of emigrants buzzing around in there. Father says they aren't eager to sell, either, and only a few of the men are going to try to buy provisions."

"I see you have a good helper," she added, as Millie, hot and disheveled came along with the baby. She had evidently fallen behind while the teams had been making better time along the level road to the fort, and had carried the baby for over an hour. That was longer than Mary would have wished.

"Oh, Mother, you're sitting up," she cried, pleased as could be.

"Yes, but if you'll help straighten me out again, I'll take the baby," Mary offered.

"Here, let me take him and hand him in for you," the young lady suggested.

Millie sighed gustily, "Just don't make me move my arms too fast. They're absolutely numb clear up to my shoulders."

"Here," the young lady called to her sister, who was then catching up with her. "you rub this little girl's arms while I hand the baby to its mother."

Millie willingly handed over the baby, but she backed away, embarrassed, not being sure whether she was being teased or being taken too seriously. "Thank you just the same," she called over her shoulder and clambered aboard at the back of the wagon.

"Now, if your team will oblige us by holding still another minute, we'll return this little nugget to the mother lode through the side of the shaft," the young Mrs. Adams teased. She handed the baby in between two wagon ribs.

Mary was holding her breath for fear the team might jerk the wagon during the transaction, but the young lady's easy assurance was boundless, it seemed — and justified.

"Sister," the other hissed, "the soldiers are looking at us."

Let them look fast," the other laughed, "we'll be gone in the twinkling of an eye."

164

Oh you happy girls, Mary thought, was it a million years ago that Nancy and I were talking like that to each other. The thought, however, was not one of self-pity, but more of wonder, for their light chatter had lifted her own spirits. She would have liked to share their banter, even though they probably thought of her as a poor old, sick woman with a lot of children.

What a lot of difference thirteen years makes — and six children, she added to herself as the baby commanded her attention with a well placed foot.

"Here, Number Six, take this she said, arranging him and herself as well as she could as she reached back to let down the side, now that the girls had moved on and would not feel that she was being rude to shut them out. No one outside would have known that she was nursing her baby, but she felt better with it down when she was, if people were about.

"What did you call the baby? Millie asked.

Mary laughed softly, "Number Six."

Millie considered. Then she said, half whimsically, half testingly, "That makes me second rate, doesn't it?"

Mary might still be sick, but she was ready for that one in the time it took to draw a deep breath, "No, it makes you my Number One Girl," she smiled above the busy little man.

Such an ado at the back of the wagon! Even the baby stopped nursing and listened. In their haste, the three little girls were falling into the wagon like three little kittens, Mary thought.

"Millie, how many wagons do you say there are?" They were all talking at once in their eagerness.

"Fourteen, Sillies."

"No, No, Not ours — theirs."

"Whose?" Millie evidently didn't feel like playing their guessing game.

"The Fort's. Didn't you even SEE them? All those big wagons with U. S. on them?"

"Oh, them!" Millie stretched out her legs and wiggled her toes in identical arcs. "I was busy carrying the baby." Having thus established her mature responsibilities, she was now ready to play their game, "So how many are there?"

Margaret, too, was ready with her own kind of maturity —

she was ready to let the little one show off. "Tell her, Pauline."

Pauline said, "I counted clear up to fifty, but I think there are more than I counted."

"They're not standing in a straight line" Mary explained.

Suddenly Mary realized she had forgotten her other responsibilities. "Are we nooning here?"

Margaret was abashed. "I forgot to tell you, Father said we could eat what was ready if we wanted to while we were waiting here, but we are going to stop early today. I'm sorry I forgot to tell you."

"I'm surprised you weren't hungry enough to remember."

"Mrs. Carter fixed us buttered biscuits in her wagon. We were supposed to ask you if you wouldn't like her to fix you some."

"What about your father and John Henry?"

"They're over there now."

Mary said it before she thought to hold it back, "This wagon seems to have a fifth wheel."

She need not have worried about the children's reactions to the remark, however. They only laughed at Mother's joke. It was Charles just coming in, who caught it.

"What's that?" he asked.

Mary decided to chance sailing right over the situation. "I'm glad someone is ready with your meals," she said.

"Yes, we are very lucky to have a good friend like Sister Carter," he allowed, just in time for Sister Carter to hear, for she, too, was at the back of the wagon, but when she looked in and saw how full of family it was, she merely called, "What good little helper wants to take this bit of lunch to Sister Adams?"

"I do," John Henry's voice broke into laughter outside the wagon. He jumped in easily and turned around to get the large plate which she handed to him.

Bringing it to her, he said, "If you eat all of this, you may be able to sit up again all the way to the place we are going to camp."

"Oh, you're not ready for it yet. Where can I put it so you can reach it when you are?"

"I'll hold it for her," Millie offered.

"Good girl, Millie," said Charles. "I think it is about time we will be moving out. You stay here and look after your mother."

The little girls sitting along the bedside, pulled their feet back under them, and the two men of the family climbed out importantly.

Mary kept the baby beside her and they both dozed through the heat and increasing dust until the train stopped to make camp on Bannack Creek, about two miles beyond the fort, where grass and water combined to make as agreeable a camp site as the parched country could afford.

Evidently Mrs. Baker had established a conspiracy with Sister Carter to divide what would have been Mary's duties between them, the one looking out for Mary and the baby, the other providing the meals. Mrs. Baker, in assuming the responsibility for Mary's physical wellbeing, seemed to have included general morale as well. It was she who insisted that Mary be bundled up and got out of the wagon to eat with the rest of her family around the fire. She bustled about the wagon, deciding on a generous coverlet and over-riding all Mary's remonstrances about "too much bother." Before Mary knew it, almost, two of the men whom Mrs. Baker had evidently alerted in advance, lifted her down and carried her to a yoke by the fire. That was where she was when Charles returned from caring for the team. He could not conceal his surprise, but if he was displeased, as she had feared he might be, she could see no evidence of it.

She stayed up longer than she should have, partly because she was a little timid about asking to be helped back to the wagon and partly because she was having a good time.

Mr. Hyland was telling them how the Diggers make their winter's supply of bread, relating the process with considerable dramatic skill.

One of the children had brought a big black cricket to show him.

"Yes," he said, "that is the kind." Then he turned so that the rest of those around the fire could hear. Holding the cricket up so everyone could see it, he commented that probably everyone of them had seen at least a few of the critters along the way.

A general moaning of rueful acknowledgement greeted that remark.

"They are pretty thick around here, in the right places. When the Diggers find a place where they are plentiful, they build pits in the sand — oh, say two feet down and maybe three feet across the top — big enough to fill with enough sagebrush and willow to make a 'heap hot fire.' Then the old men, the women, and the children form a big circle away from the fire and beat the bushes as they converge on it, driving the crickets before them." (Here Mr. Hyland imitated the beating action with one hand as he pointed to the fire in approaching it. All eyes were on the dramatic presentation.)

"Now," he said, pointing to the ground between himself and the fire, "the crickets fall into the fiery pit, where they SIZZZZLE, swelllll, and finally POP, POP, POP — just like roasted chestnuts.

"Now the squaws really go to work. They grind those cooked crickets (here he picked up an imaginary mortar and pestle and made a determined grinding motion) and grind them and mash them with roots and herbs. When they are all mashed and ground together into a kind of mealy stuff — (here he paused while he let them watch his hands rolling something between the palms) they roll it into little flat cakes, which they set out to bake in the sun like bricks.

"And that is what the Diggers eat in the winter," he laughed.

Mary didn't know whether the story had spoiled her dinner or whether she had got a little chilly — or maybe just over tired — but she was shivering again before she got back to bed in the wagon.

The first thing they did the next morning was to ford the creek where they had camped. That offered no problems, but two miles on, Mary nearly died of embarrassment. They were going to ford Port Neuf river, but it was too deep to go across without raising the wagon beds first. Mary could hear them discussing it. She looked out and wished she hadn't. There, splashing and rushing by, was an expanse of almost sixty feet of water between steep banks. She could not guess the depth, but she distinctly heard someone say something about six feet. She felt about as desperate as a woman could feel. Then she heard some man's voice saying something about a ferry costing two dollars and she heard Charles's voice saying, "I don't have any choice. I'll just have to strike out and find it. I am not going to take a needless chance, if I know it."

John Henry rounded up the children and off the Adamses went by themselves, leaving the rest by the river busily raising their wagon beds. "All because of me," Mary bitterly told herself.

Charles must have had good directions, because he seemed to have no trouble locating the ferry. Mary didn't have the courage to look out, but she lay tense, visualizing the process by the sounds: the stop, the palaver, the slow creaking, ominous rumbling onto the restless, angling little ferry, the uneven movements, the slapping of the water, the noncommittal words of the ferryman, the grating, jerking stop, the undulating motion with more slapping sounds, as the team unsteadily began the pull with a jerk and a bumping before the pitch of the ascent up the bank.

The last wagon had forded the stream and was pulling away when Charles and his returned to the train to take its dust.

"Well," thought Mary, "I cost him two dollars, but I saved him all the work of raising the wagon bed."

If it weren't for the dust, it wouldn't have been such a bad bargain at that, except that the train went on and on. The sun was almost down and Mary was beginning to wonder whether they ever would stop, when they finally reached a good camping place with a nice spring and plenty of grass.

That night there were no dramatics by the fire, nor thought of anything much but enough food to appease hunger and then rest as quickly as possible against an equally hard day to come.

The next morning Captain Hyland made it clear that he wanted to keep going that day until they could find a good camp in which to lay by for Sunday, but he did not plan to stop more than briefly at American Falls because there seemed to be doubt how far they would have to go for water and grass.

Mrs. Baker was telling her about it while she "redded up" the wagon for her in the morning.

"Aren't we following the river?" Mary wanted to know.

"Yes, but the Snake flows through a lot of volcanic rock at the bottom of a gorge, they say, and it is as much as a person's life is worth to get down the rock walls to the water and grass," she explained.

"You mean it's dangerous?" Mary struggled up as if determined to get out of bed.

"Now, now, don't you fret yourself," Mrs. Baker plopped herself on the edge of the bed beside her. "I heard Brother Adams giving the children their marching orders as I came by Sister Carter's wagon just now."

Mary dropped back on the pillow.

"Sister Adams, you'll just have to have faith in God and the rest of us to take care of your children. The truth of the matter is, they seem to take good care of each other.

"If you can stand the dust, I'll put the side up a little way so you can keep an eye out"

That is how Mary's fear for her children caused her to see what was going on at American Falls. She heard it long before she saw it, leaping and tumbling down under a rainbow of spray. It was as if the arid desolateness of the country through which they had been plodding, had suddenly and dramatically come alive. The sturdy Snake Indians were at hand to sell the fish they were catching, too.

As Mary lay peering out, the girls saw that she was trying to see. They ran to the side of the wagon to tell her what lay beyond her range of vision. Mary tried desperately to imitate the leaping salmon, Margaret was a Snake, spearing the fish, and Millie just stood there holding her sides and laughing. Pauline looked aggrieved at Millie!

Mary, who had grown rather weary of fish in their diet, was at least grateful for fish to liven the hideous monotony of lying all day in the hot, dusty wagon. She felt fairly well until she tried to sit up now, but she had promised herself that the Sunday lay-over would help her "catch up with herself."

The girls moved away from the wagon toward the falls for a closer view, having promised faithfully not to get any closer than Millie's length. By that time, John Henry had tied the cows to the back of the wagon and came alongside, and Charles had dropped back so that they met right beside Mary.

"Do you see how they're fishing, Pa!" he exclaimed. "Spearing them when they're falling back from the leap. I say they're really smart." He and his father moved a bit closer to follow the

170

work of one stocky young brave who had speared a great fish and was now playing it by the long cord attached to a willow pole gripped in his hands. Then Charles left John Henry watching and returned to Mary, as if eager to speak to her while they could be alone.

He looked at her with an appraising eye and nodded, "You do really feel better, I can see. One thing that bothers me mightily is that I brought you and you didn't want to come. Now you're sick and the next few days are not going to be easy, but just hang on, Old Girl, and I swear I'll get you through. Hang on 'til we get to the Dalles, and then our troubles will be over. I'll sell the stock there or get someone to care for them until I can come back in the spring. (A lot of migrants are doing it that way, they tell me.) We'll take a boat and get you down to Portland in two days from the Dalles, and all your troubles will be over.

"Just trust me; I promise I'll get you there."

She could see that her reluctance, which had given him no concern in the beginning, was now giving him real concern, whereas, she had long since wished for nothing more than to get the trip over with. Her fear had not been for herself except that she was not able to do her share as she should.

Seeing the graves along the way had of course been rather frightening, but she had never thought of herself as a candidate for one of them. That Charles had thought that she might not pull through or even that she thought she might not, was something of a shock. She didn't know whether to be amused or to accept the fact that her condition was more serious than she had realized. One thing she did know — tomorrow she was going to sit on the front seat for a little while, even if she had to prop herself up.

Just making the resolution made her feel equal to carrying it out — tomorrow. Today, the dust was getting worse. Every wagon on the Trail had evidently come to the falls and helped pulverize the road.

As the train pulled away, the dust began to rise in billows. Millie jumped into the wagon and closed it as tight as she could. Even so, dust streamed in almost like water. Mary covered herself and the baby as thoroughly as she dared and was thankful this was not the day she had promised herself to sit up. Lying thus,

171

shut off from all except the baby and the covers, she lost all track of time, except that she had fed and changed the baby a number of times. Finally, she realized that they were stopping, and the girls clambered into the wagon, each one caked with dust from head to foot.

Mary took one look at them. "Oh, girls," she said, "go outside and shake the dust off before you come in."

"Mother," Millie spoke, almost as if she were the adult and Mary the child, "just look around the wagon."

Mary groaned as the girls pointed out layers and drifts of dust everywhere.

"Don't worry, Mother," Margaret offered, "Mrs. Carter says it's clean dirt and will shake out in two shakes of a lamb's tail."

That did it for Mary. "But I don't have a lamb's tail."

"Oh, Mother, you're not contrary, either," Pauline chortled, not only because Mother was joking, but because she was well enough to joke.

By the time Charles and John Henry came back, dusk was almost dark.

"I'm glad tomorrow is Sunday," she said.

Charles dropped down on the other bed for a moment, then wearily pulled himself up. "So are we all," he said.

Suddenly she remembered that tomorrow was the day she had promised herself she would ride on the front seat. She wouldn't have to keep that promise for another day. And she was glad. She had a sneaking feeling that she couldn't have kept that promise no matter how hard she tried.

"Do you know where we are, Ma?" John Henry asked, trying to make some kind of conversation.

She managed a smile up at him, "Another Sunday closer to Oregon City?"

"Well, Yes," he agreed, "but you'd never guess what they call this river — Hell river!"

She rolled her eyes at him. "Wouldn't you know! We've been to Devil's Gate, so this is right enough. But where do we go from here?"

John Henry started to laugh, but his father cleared his throat and John Henry changed his mind about laughing.

But Charles had not really meant the sound as a rebuke. He was merely beginning his own little joke. "Don't you think we should wash somebody's mouth out?" he asked slowly, and then cued them with his own effort at a guffaw.

Instead of eating around the campfire with the rest, as they had been doing, letting Mrs. Baker take care of her, Mary's family brought their plates back to the wagon and ate with her by the light of one precious candle. Dusty and tired as they all were, a sense of solidarity and optimism pervaded the shadowy wagon.

That night Mary went to sleep on Charles's shoulder, lulled by a sense of emotional security she had not felt for what seemed like forever.

The next morning, as Charles put it, Captain Hyland "turned his collar around" and became the Reverend Hyland. At Charles's suggestion, he preached close enough to their wagon for Mary to hear, propped up and "prettied up" by Mrs. Baker. It was really quite nice, Mary thought, the way people dropped by and spoke to her as she sat there with canvas up, for all the world as if she were sitting on her front porch and they were neighbors dropping by. In the glow of sociability she kept forgetting to ask about the McMillens, who were nowhere to be seen.

In the afternoon, after the canvas had been dropped for privacy, she heard cries of "There they come," "Say, look who's coming," and "Thought we'd lost you for sure." The McMillens had caught up, after camping somewhere behind them. Only then did she find out that there had been almost no grass for the stock the night before. By daylight, grass on the hills was revealed. Everyone it seemed, agreed to give the cattle extra rest and grazing time before moving out Monday morning.

Mary had intended to surprise Charles by having Mrs. Baker help her up onto the front seat after they had started, but Sunday evening she confided her intentions to him and he, in a burst of gallantry, insisted on lifting her up onto the seat himself after the team was yoked. It was too dusty, however, and in a very little while, he stopped the oxen and lifted her back to the comparative shelter and comfort of the bed. She did not tell him, but she was sure if he hadn't lifted her off when he did, she might have fallen off by herself!

All in all, it was a dispiriting day. They made only nine miles, and when they got to the Raft creek there was little grazing left for them.

In the night, they were awakened by the howling of wolves. Some time before morning, the howling stopped, but the fear did not.

Though the night had been cool, the day would be another scorcher. Of that they could be sure, and since there was little to be gained by letting the cattle attempt to graze where the grass was all eaten off by the hundreds who had been there before them, it was a grim-faced Charles who staggered out almost before he was awake the next morning in the first gray light. Even Mrs. Baker seemed subdued when she came into the wagon as the teams were being yoked.

"Not much use shaking things out," she grumbled. "We're in for a long, dusty day — that much I can tell."

If dust had been all they were in for, Mary would have welcomed it, if she could have taken it alone. But today they were to plod through Granite Pass. The wagon jolted, pitched, and rocked all day long over boulders that must have been immense. Two or three times Mary was sure they were going to tip over. Either the rocks were too continuous to avoid or they were buried in knee-deep dust — that she couldn't tell, but she was pressed to decide whether she should leave the baby in his basket and take a chance on the wagon's not going over or keep him beside her and take a chance on being thrown so suddenly she could not avoid crushing him. Finally she called Millie.

"Millie, do you think you could carry Baby Charles? I am afraid to keep him in the wagon."

Millie's eyes widened, but she said nothing until she had him in her arms with the shawl over his face. Then she said, "Father is being very careful. I am sure he won't let our wagon tip."

"Of course he won't, Millie," Mary assured her, "but the baby is too little to understand that, and I think you can keep him on a more even keel than I can."

Millie still looked very serious but a little more serene when she climbed out the back with the baby.

After that, Mary felt easier for having to take the jolts for

174

herself alone. All she could do was hope someone else would offer to help Millie with the baby.

Even the thick dust could not soften the sounds that came to her either. The poor weary oxen, as well as the cows, were protesting as they dragged through the rocky dust, and the wagons were creaking and straining with sounds almost as insistent as the animals'. These sounds came to her ears as a kind of cacophony of anguish, punctuated by screams and sharp cries of command every once in awhile, as a wagon tipped or threatened to. It was a long, weary day to spend listening to such sounds in an agony of suspense in the smothering heat of the gloomy wagon. Any attempt to sit up would have been the sheerest folly.

Occasionally, a low-keyed comment would reach her about a wagon part or how long it had been dead, or how it had been left right there, or something about a new total, and she could imagine the scene all too well — a wagon broken and abandoned, cattle left to die on the road, and, worst of all, graves. All were paving the way to Oregon. She couldn't help thinking of Charles's assurance that he would get her through. The more she tried to put it out of her mind, the more it seemed to assert itself, suggesting the very doubt it was supposed to have erased.

When she realized that perhaps she was magnifying the more morbid comments by listening for them, she determined to listen for pleasant ones. Then she became all the more depressed, because there weren't any. Clearly, if they didn't find grass and water for the night, they would be facing desperate straits.

Millie brought the baby for her to nurse. Yes, there were some abandoned wagons and dead cattle. No, there weren't more graves than usual, she said in answer to Mary's attempt at casual conversation.

The child's answers were so matter-of-fact that Mary had a queer feeling that the children were accepting all this as commonplaces of the road. In almost the same breath, Millie relayed the news that there would be a swamp where they were going to camp for the night. She had heard the men saying that the cattle would have some grass, at least.

Mary could tell that the baby was not getting as much milk from her as he should. Perhaps the jostling and fear were to blame — or the heat. She would try a little supplementing with cow's milk that night if she couldn't do better after supper.

After supper, however, she decided not to take a chance on upsetting his stomach with a change. Better for him to have a short supply than a wrong one, especially under the circumstances.

The next day was about the same as Tuesday, except that the road was not so rocky, but they traveled farther and longer. She had heard Charles saying to John Henry that the camp that night would very likely be Goose Creek, and she could tell by their comments when they got there that it was bare of grass. Then she heard a voice say, "Look, here's a sign! How long do you suppose it's been there?"

"Might as well go and see." someone else said.

"Real thoughtful, whoever he was."

"It had better be right."

"All right, everybody on." And the train started up again, and they didn't stop until after sunset.

Some kindly emigrant, there before them, had left a sign telling the next campers about a spot ahead where grass was plentiful. As Mrs. Baker said the next morning, "If wishing a blessing on someone — you don't know who — could do him any good, the man who wrote that sign should be the blessedest man in the Oregon Territory today."

"It's given us a new lease on life," Charles said soberly. "We'll lay by and recruit, and we've got a lot of recruiting to do."

"It just seems we were meant to get through all right, now," Sister Carter suggested when she came in during the morning. Indeed the kindly emigrant was the subject of much conjecture.

Mrs. Baker bustled in and insisted on helping Mary with a "spit bath" for herself and the baby. She even changed the sheets. As she put it, "Seems like Sunday doesn't come around fast enough and when it does come, who knows whether we'll have as good a supply of water!"

She also passed on the word that this was to be a moonlit night and there was some discussion about traveling by moonlight to make up for the weekday they had lost. Mary, thinking of having the sides of the wagon up, rather hoped that it might be so. The men, however, had been looking at the stock — had even treated some for "Hollow horn" — and they voted to let the stock rest through the night.

By the next night Mary began to wonder whether they would ever find grass and water enough to camp, for the night was long since begun before the train finally stopped. For some reason, there were more sounds about the camp than usual. She could hear the men on guard duty talking quietly or giving each other subdued greetings as they came on or went off their shifts. Through it all, came the constant sound of the restless animals.

In the morning, Charles suggested that if she felt like it there would be plenty of time to try sitting up because the train would not be moving on for two more days. Captain Hyland had said the cattle would be better off later if they got what rest and grass they could get here, he explained.

When Mrs. Baker pulled up the side of the wagon and Mary saw the dry, barren landscape, she began to wonder what was ahead of them. She did sit up a few times, but the fever and dust had left her feeling dry and sore. Nothing tasted good to her but tea, and she hesitated to ask for anything that required fuel. The women had nothing to cook with but sage, and even that was not plentiful. No one told her, but from scraps of conversation she had heard, she knew that emigrants here before them had taken to burning some of the wooden parts of their wagons in their desperation for fuel.

Mary had been left alone in the wagon more each day, it seemed. Rather than to be querulous when someone was with her, she had tended to listen to the scraps of conversation which drifted into the wagon from without and to piece them together to get the picture of which she was a hidden part. That she was eavesdropping did not occur to her.

Saturday afternoon she already knew that a company from Chicago was camping nearby. When she heard strange women's voices, she listened, just out of idle curiosity to learn what she could of them from their voices and speech. They were speaking in a sort of undertone, she realized later, but not at the time. As so often happens when people speak *sotto voce*, they speak more distinctly than they ordinarily do and as a consequence, their voices carry farther than they realize.

At first Mary didn't realize what she was hearing.

"That's the wagon the boy was from."

"I'd feel queer about nursing a strange baby, wouldn't you?"

"Jerusha said he was so appealing and so manly about caring for his baby brother, she couldn't turn him down."

"Is she going to do it again?"

"She told him she'd try it twice a day."

"That'll just mean today and tomorrow, won't it?"

"Very likely."

Mary lay staring blankly at the patch of light coming through the back end of the wagon. She wasn't supposed to know. But she knew. She knew.

"Baby Charles," born in a covered wagon on the plains, as a young gallant. (From the author's collection.)

178

– The OREGONIAN

Fort Hall in Idaho was a Hudson's Bay Co. trading post
constructed of clay.

– The OREGONIAN

Fort Boise was near the present city of Parma, Idaho. These
views were drawn by the staff artist of the mounted Cross Rifle
Regiment, commanded by Major Osborne Cross in 1849.

179

XV

Coping With Reality

THE NEXT MORNING Captain Hyland "turned his collar around" and became the Reverend Hyland again, and again he took a stance near the wagon so that Mary could share the service. The text was a strange one to her — something about "We seek a land" or "They sought a land." She couldn't tell which was the text and which was the application after he had warmed to the topic. Besides, she had a hard time keeping her mind on his words. The Illinois people had joined them for the service. They looked nice enough — as nice as anyone else on the Trail looked. There was no indication which women were the ones she had overheard and the mother who had nursed Baby Charles could be any one of three, she decided.

She tried to imagine John Henry's approaching any one of them. She simply could not. Finally, she concluded that perhaps it was best for her not to know which woman was supplementing her dwindling supply of milk. Perhaps it was a case of not letting your right breast know whom your left breast has fed. (Oh, Mary, you'll probably say something impudent to St. Peter and be sent around to the back door of heaven or not get in at all, she told herself.)

One part of the service she did enjoy mightily. That was the singing. Those younglady daughters of the McMillens made the singing something special with their accordion and their nice voices. Mary found herself wiggling her toes in time to the rhythm. She felt better for even so little participation in the service. In my extremity, I am joining in, she told herself.

Then she wondered how it was that she could lie there joking to herself. Because I am feeling better, she answered, and because my baby is being cared for while I am in short supply, and because my husband has promised to get me through — and my husband always keeps his word.

When the service was over, Mary felt as renewed as if she had been conventionally following the service — maybe more!

Sunday night was a rough one. Almost a third of the men were on duty at camp or with the cattle the whole time. Other trains, with horses, had been having trouble with the Indians, but Charles had felt that there was not much to worry about except the cattle, as they were using oxen. However, Captain Hyland had a horse, and that may have been what the Indians were after. Anyway, early in the night, one of the camp guards shot. Immediately there was a squeal and other muffled sounds. The shot had got an Indian dog; the Indian had got away, but he or they had left ample evidence of their call in the night. Somehow, the incident seemed more exciting than frightening, perhaps because of the moonlight.

Mary kept the feeling of improvement all day Monday, despite the fact that she knew that week would be one of the hardest. Even if she had not become accustomed to listening, she could hardly have missed the oft-repeated phrases, "thirty-five miles without grass" and "twenty-two without water." They were going to cross the desert any day now, she realized. Tuesday she heard them say something about "by moonlight," and when the train halted as if nooning, she knew they would be traveling by moonlight that evening.

Sure enough, as soon as the moon came up, they started on again.

As Millie said, "The moonlight seems to settle the dust." But it was still bad enough. Furthermore, the night was cold, bitter cold.

All through the night and much of the next day they dragged on, with only brief stops to look in vain for grass or to get the cattle down to water, for the Snake was mocking them from the bottom of a dangerous canyon and the cliffs were bare of vegetation. Even at Salmon Falls, they found no grass.

Mary couldn't be sure whether she was the reason for the train's splitting or not. For some reason, one wagon was made into a ferry and some of the train went across the river with the cattle for two days.

Each time they stopped, they looked about for another sign

181

from the kindly emigrant ahead. Mary wondered that no one suggested that the sign-leaver might have been Mr. Davis. She tried the idea out on Charles as he sat on the edge of the other bed changing his socks.

He didn't even look up — just snorted, "Probably the ferryman, looking for business."

"What does the ferry have to do with the grass?" she asked, wishing that he would look at her.

But he was getting his boots back on. "The grass is on the other side, and we have to take the ferry to get to it, evidently," he spoke as if to a child.

Mary realized that he did not understand how difficult it was for her to be inert. Or maybe she didn't understand how hard it was for him to relay information unnecessarily. Within herself, she made a bitter resolution not to ask him any questions, if she could help it.

Before the train started up again, Sister Carter brought in milk and cold salmon for her lunch, which Mary managed to get down without gagging. She did manage to get the facts about the sign cleared up.

"I didn't know the sign that told us about the grass last week was advertising a ferry," she suggested timidly.

Sister Carter saw the point right away. "We just now found a new sign," she explained. "We have to go about five miles to a ferry. We may not take it, the way I hear it, but we will decide when we get there."

Well, then, Mary thought, Mr. Davis could have left the other sign, after all.

Mary was alone in the wagon most of the afternoon. A high wind was coming up, alternately tugging and pushing at the canvas top, adding its rushing and flapping sounds to the creaks and grindings of the wagon and the moans of the oxen. These sounds seemed to isolate her from the rest of the train, somehow, for the human voices which usually surrounded her seemed to be gone with the wind. Even the cattle sounds seemed to be farther away.

Poor Millie, she thought drowsily, out there in the wind, trudging along with the baby in her arms, while I lie here no good at all — no good —.

When she awakened, she found a fine film of sand over her face. They had been in a sandstorm, she guessed, and wondered whether the children had stayed out in it rather than awaken her by getting into the wagon.

"Poor little Millie" climbed in at the back of the wagon in a little while. She was laughing and disheveled from walking in the wind, but she showed no signs of weariness. Someone outside handed the baby up to her after she was safely inside.

When Millie laid the baby beside her, Mary automatically felt to see whether he needed changing. He was clean and dry. Someone had fed and changed him.

The train had halted, but the wind was whistling in a higher key. The sound of the wind was even sharper now that the wagons had stopped.

Millie went to the front and looked out. "Here we are at the ferry — if that is what they call it. Just two old wagon boxes tied together for a boat, and a rope across the river to pull it by."

She was quiet for a while as she listened to the conversations outside, and then relayed what she had learned to her mother, "They aren't going to try crossing tonight. The wind is too strong."

The wagons were backing up and turning around.

"We're going to make camp back a way. There was some grass there."

All of a sudden John Henry burst into the wagon. "Ma," he said. "do you care if I trade that old gray shirt for a great big beautiful salmon? There's an Indian out here with one Mrs. Carter says she will bake for us, and I think he wants a shirt for it."

"Just so you don't have to ride bareback into Oregon City," Mary offered.

"If I do, I'll earn a new one right off." he bragged.

"The Promised Land!" How can they count on it so, Mary wondered.

The wind died down some time in the night. Morning dawned clear and beautiful. The mood of the whole train seemed to be that ferrying across was to be more of a pleasure excursion than a trouble.

Charles was somewhat apologetic about "going ahead with it today." If he hadn't said that, Mary would not have realized it was Sunday — their week had been that mixed up for her, at least.

Mrs. Baker had brought her hot tea early and now she was attempting to nurse the baby. She seemed to be able to do the best for him after a night's rest. At least, she thought, I am able to give him a good start each day.

Charles was looking around to see whether anything needed fastening down before they started onto the ferry, but he did not seem especially concerned. "The girls are to ride with you and see to the baby," he said. "I told them at breakfast."

"Charles, don't you think I should try to sit up when we go across?" she asked. As soon as she said it she wondered what had possessed her to say such a stupid thing. Something within her was trying to assert itself, but she wasn't sure whether she was really feeling better and ready to try to get up again or whether she wanted Charles to see that she was still there. It had seemed lately that he acted as if he expected her to stay in bed and accept all the arrangements and care that were being provided.

She had been covertly watching him. He, on the other hand, had spoken to her almost as if she were not there, perhaps to give her the privacy she preferred when she was nursing a baby — she couldn't tell. But now he stopped and looked down at her. "You will do me a favor," he said, "not to try anything foolish."

And that was that. He had spoken to her very much as he would to one of the children. But when he turned to leave his tone was more as she would wish it to be. "There are six wagons to go across ahead of us," he said, his hand on the opening at the back of the wagon behind him, "so there will be plenty of time for your breakfast and cleaning up before we have to go." That made her feel as if she were still mistress of her own wagon.

Mrs. Baker came right after Millie brought her breakfast. Between them, they decided that the side of the wagon should be rolled up for a little while at least, so that Mary could see the river in the sunshine.

Mary suspected that it was Mrs. Baker's idea that the sight of the river crossing arrangements would put her at ease. The roar of the water had indeed sounded furious and ominous to her ears, as she had lain listening to it. Now, watching the ferry in operation in the calm Sabbath sunlight, she could see that the deep rushing water was all the challenge to their safety that she had imagined, but the ferry had evidently been in successful operation for quite some time.

After the wagons ahead of them had gone across as smoothly as one could ask for, Mary relaxed and almost enjoyed their boat ride, though the slaps and shocks of the water caused her to keep a tight grip on the baby every minute of the crossing.

Only when she felt the bump that signaled the other bank did she begin to breathe naturally again, and when the wagon bumped up the incline from the water, she tried to loosen her fingers, only to find them so stiff and numb from the tension that she could hardly flex them.

She had supposed that they would make camp right away for the rest of their Sunday, but they didn't. Over rocks the wagon jostled and pitched at first and then, until noon, ground through deep sand.

The canvas had all been closed down tight since they had prepared to cross on the ferry, but from the sounds she could tell that they were coming into a camp site that was pleasing. She could hear much sound of water, and wondered whether they were coming to another crossing, when Margaret broke into the wagon, proud to be the bearer of news.

"Mother, you should see all the springs 'way up high in the rocks. You should SEE it."

"Maybe I could if you would pull the canvas a little so that I can."

Margaret crawled up from the foot of the bed and along the side where she could push the canvas a little way. "See?" she asked dramatically.

Mary pulled herself over against the hot little body and looked, more to please the child than to appease her own curiosity. The sight was refreshing — as much as she could see. They were in a valley where water tumbled down rock walls from springs above to feed a creek nearby.

"Isn't this worth traveling on Sunday for?" the little rascal

185

asked.

"Did your father say that?" Mary asked her.

That was all the reproof Margaret needed, but she wasn't going to admit it. She looked around hastily to see whether she had been overheard by the master of the house, and then, feeling more secure, muttered doggedly, "Well, isn't it?"

Mary did not have much stamina left for a battle of wills. "The Sabbath was made for man, and I guess this valley was made for us." She gave Margaret a pat and then shut her eyes to let the child know she accepted the bounty of the valley but was too tired to do anything more about it just then.

Margaret leaned over, unexpectedly, and kissed her, before backing down and off the foot of the bed.

The unexpected kiss was too much for Mary. Before she realized it, tears were dribbling down her temples and getting into her ears.

Angry with her own weakness, she opened her eyes wide, batted her eyelids quickly, and said, almost aloud, "Stop that."

Before Millie or any of the others came into the wagon, she had wiped away the evidence and lay there wondering whether she was getting weaker or stronger to break into tears that way.

When Millie did bring the baby to her, she could see that he had been fed and changed at least once since she had had him with her, but if there were a conspiracy to keep her ignorant, it was working at least in part, for she could not bring herself to ask. Since she herself was not adequate, she decided that perhaps she should be grateful that someone was giving him what she could not. Her mind fumbled with the axiom about not looking a gift horse in the mouth, but somehow it seemed wrong side to, or something, she ... couldn't ... quite tell ... how.

The next thing she knew Sister Carter was there beside her apologizing for waking her up, but which would she prefer for supper — rabbit stew or baked salmon?

Mary struggled back to consciousness, trying to remember where she was. Her first impression in the shadows was that she was home in Tennessee in her own little bed and that some neighbor of her mother's was sitting there. Then, she realized that it was Sister Carter. But what was Sister Carter asking her about supper for? Where was Mother? Not until her eyes fixed on the canvas above her did she finally catch up to the present reality.

XVI

Roles Change

S ISTER CARTER SMILED unperturbed, "My goodness, you were in a deep sleep. You had such an innocent look on your face — almost like a child waking up."

"I was a child, waking up a million years ago in Tennessee," Mary said, wonderingly.

Sister Carter looked puzzled and then worried, as she tried to make some sense out of what her sick friend was saying. She evidently decided that the first thing to consider was food to make her well in body and stabilize the wandering mind, for she assumed a firmer tone and repeated the question about the choice of rabbit stew or salmon.

Mary would have liked to say "Neither" and go back to Tennessee, but she wasn't an escapist at heart. Perhaps rabbit stew would be easier to eat and give more strength. She said "Stew."

When Sister Carter looked startled, at the shortness of her answer, no doubt, Mary realized that she had waited too long to say please, so she said, "Thank you."

A smile of relief broke over her friend's face. Mary sounded normal to her again.

As she left, Mary could feel herself drifting back to sleep again, but some quiet or some sound attracted her attention. As Sister Carter climbed down out of the wagon, someone was helping her, but neither of them said a word.

They must know how sleepy I am, Mary thought, letting herself drift back to her own bed back home in Tennessee.

The next thing she knew, they were bringing her some supper and someone was raising the canvas along the side of the wagon. It was Sister Baker, suggesting that she might enjoy seeing the sunshine on the rock now that the hottest part of the day was over. The scent of cooking was heavy in the air and the sounds of scraping dishes and pans gave evidence that most people had finished their early evening meal.

"We are going to have a Sunday Sing tonight," Pauline announced. Sure enough, folks began to gather and Captain-turned-Reverend Hyland announced "Just a simple little vesper service tonight, for in the morning we need to get an early start over a difficult hill."

Somehow the threat of tomorrow's problems deepened the appreciation of the serenity of their Sabbath pause. Mostly they just sang — songs like "Now The Day Is Over; Night is drawing nigh; Shadows of the evening steal across the sky ...," "How Sweet the Hour of Closing Day," "Oh For a Closer Walk," and, finally, "Lord, Dismiss Us With Thy Blessing."

As gently as if someone had smoothed her forehead, the gentle hymns of faith soothed her. The words "And I am Whole Again" came to her mind. Add a little strength to that, she thought, and I'll be as good as new. Why, I can make a rhyme of that.

> If Charles will get me through
> and I'm as good as new
> Very nicely that will do.

About thirty-six hours later, she fussed wearily to Mrs. Baker, "Just as soon as I begin to feel like myself, we hit a stretch that takes the starch right out of me again." They had had a hard day Monday, traveling over the steep hill Captain Hyland had mentioned and then on through the rocks or sand until long after dark, finding themselves, finally camped on the same stream with Indians. Mary felt she could afford to be grumpy now that the feeding prospects looked more prosperous in the light of day.

It was probably good that she did not know then that there would be five more days of the same thing, the only variation being which of the necessities would be in the shortest supply: water, fuel, or grass. The weather was hot and dry, the country unvarying in its arid desolation and the road was either steep and rocky or deep in dust, so that the oxen were either straining and stumbling or suffocating in the brown clouds of dust that enveloped them and everything else that moved with them.

As in an eerie dream the emigrant trains moved slowly through the sun-baked miles, where a few ravens or blacktailed rabbits were the only other signs of life they ever saw except for swarms of nasty, white gnats. The wolves they did not see, but night after night they could be heard, and those howls coming across the barren hills added another dimension of horror to the daily sight of roadside graves which the children had become accustomed to counting.

In the gloomy depths of the wagon, Mary lay day after day looking up at the dirty canvas canopy above her, a canopy that kept the heat in and the air dead as much as it kept the sun and dust out. Much of the time she was alone; Millie carried the baby as much as she could. Mary could hear him crying occasionally, but she never heard the crying for any length of time. Either Millie carried him where she couldn't hear him or someone else appeased his hunger. She still tried to nurse him in the morning or whenever Millie brought him to her and suggested that she should. That he was being reasonably well cared for she could see. As long as that was so and she could do nothing better, she was too timid to ask. The rest of the family evidently thought she was too sick to notice. Whatever the reason, they never once suggested that anyone else was nursing him.

Besides being lonely and sick, she felt dirty most of the time and loathed herself. Mrs. Baker managed to sponge her off twice that week but the feeling of being sweet and clean was pitifully short-lived in the heat and dust. Getting clean was the first thing she thought of when Millie clambered into the wagon late Saturday afternoon and announced that the train was coming to a good camping place to lay-over for Sunday. Her second thought was that perhaps she could sit up a while and begin to get her strength back.

Millie plopped herself down on the side of the other bed, her elbows on her knees and her chin in her cupped hands and watched the baby's waving arms and legs as he lay where she had put him beside her mother.

Mary seized the opportunity to ask, "Have you heard anyone say how far we've come this week?"

Millie's chin went deeper into the palms of her hands, setting the tone for her answer. "Amos says he doubts we've averaged even fifteen miles a day."

190

Mary answered as lightly as she could manage, "I guess that's what is called 'inching' our way."

At that very moment the wagon stopped, and Millie laughed. "What shall I do first?"

"Maybe you and Margaret can shake the dust off the blankets and things as soon as the teams are unhitched."

Millie was rocking back and forth on her toes, "Anything else?"

This child, thought Mary, walking most of the day over rough ground with a baby in her arms, wants only a different activity to rest her, and here I lie wishing I could get up enough strength to sit up a little. Anyway, observing the irony of it made her feel a bit superior to her situation, a feeling for which she was in sore need.

Irony was the tenor of their Sunday lay-over. Even the pious and the dull assumed it for the good of their souls. When one is surrounded by gruesome desperation, the alternatives are few. One can grovel, one can laugh, one can go mad. They laughed about being high and dry above the river, made impious jokes about the Balm of Gilead growing near the wagons, and for the cattle, suggested "Let 'em eat grass."

What passed for a divine service was not exactly hearty, because hardly anyone of the adults felt like singing. When someone suggested the hymn "How Happy Is the Pilgrim's Lot," there were three or four recognizable snickers, making some other wiseacre bold to suggest "Jesus, Thy Wandering Sheep Behold."

Mary, listening from her bed in the wagon, was startled by the mood which the suggestion revealed. She was proud to have Charles counter with the suggestion of "Zion Stands With Hills Surrounded." It got them back on the track. They finished with "Jesus, Where'er Thy People Meet," which was realistic enough to satisfy them all.

"Well, here I go, losing what I gained over Sunday," Mary thought as the rocky road bounced her and the dust suffocated her in the wagon on Monday morning. After nooning the road became smooth and hard. She could even have the side canvas up and look toward the mountains. The deep broad valley through which they were traveling looked like a giant grain field, giving

191

the false impression of fertility. Tuesday's terrain was more hilly and honest and that night there was a trace of rain after a windstorm, but Wednesday was the day!

Mary could tell, even without looking out, that they were making a long, gradual ascent, but she had been lying with her eyes closed for about an hour when she heard the girls screaming. The wagon had paused, and they tumbled in. Thank God, they are here — all of them — was her first thought. Then she could see that their faces were happy ones. They wanted her to look out at the trees. Trees! She had almost forgotten that such things were, not having seen a real tree for a month. No wonder the girls were excited.

Charles had turned the team so that she could look down from the crest of the long hill they had been climbing, down into the Boise River valley, where trees grew along the banks. He now moved back to speak to her, the first time in weeks, it seemed, that he had done so. He was as pleased as could be as he waved his arm toward the river. "We begin making a descent fairly soon," he said, pushing his hat to the back of his head, "but it doesn't look too bad. We'll be right down there by the river before the afternoon is over."

Charles was right on all counts. As they approached the river, Indians, eager to trade, besieged the train.

First thing she knew, John Henry had climbed into the wagon and was looking around for something he could trade. "I could get me a pony — a good one — for my coat," he said. "Look at 'em. They're crazy for clothes and guns."

Just then a buck galloped by, and Mary had to laugh with John Henry, even though it took more strength than she could spare for the effort. The brave had a frock coat on, and very little else.

In a few moments, who should come galloping back by the wagon on the very same pony but one of the men in the Mc-Millen group.

"See," said John Henry, as if someone else were to blame for his having missed the bargain. Mary looked at him quickly and decided that he merely sounded that way in his excitement.

Before the proud new owner of the pony paraded by again,

John Henry was ready and waiting at the back of the wagon. "How much did you have to give for him?" he called.

Mary couldn't hear the answer, but John Henry returned to her with a foolish grin on his face. "Pa wouldn't ever let me give up a gun, I don't suppose."

"It wouldn't hurt to ask him, would it?"

John Henry brightened and bounded out of the wagon in about two leaps.

Almost immediately, he was back with his father, and the two of them got down on their hands and knees by the other bed to pull out a box. From the very bottom Charles withdrew a gun and handed it to the boy. "If you can get a good pony for this," he said, "go ahead. If you can't, put it back where it was, right away."

The effort of the past few minutes had so wearied Mary that she dropped back and closed her eyes. Lying thus, she lost track of time. Two times she thought she heard her boy's voice, but she couldn't be sure. She kept hoping he had not forgotten his father's order about returning the gun to its place under the bed right away.

Then she heard. "Hey, Ma," and she looked out to see him wheeling the pony right beside the wagon. John Henry had got himself a fine pony, and he was the happiest boy she had ever seen.

Mary vowed that she would not give voice to any of her thoughts about why he probably got such a good bargain. Sufficient unto the day would be the evil thereof when some emigrant, whose pony had been stolen, pointed this one out as his own.

Thursday the train traveled in dust again, but somehow it didn't seem quite so hard to bear, now that there was plenty of green grass and water for the cattle and fish for themselves. And jackrabbits — well, they were, as Margaret eloquently expressed it "thick."

All day Mary heard the children counting jackrabbits. Toward sunset, she looked out and was amazed to see one of them merrily bouncing beside the road ahead of the wagon. Its tall pink ears were erect and quite translucent in the slanting rays of the setting sun. As much as she liked rabbit stew, Mary couldn't see how anyone, watching this bouncing fellow with big, beautiful, see-through ears, could raise a gun to shoot him, as many of the train had been doing to his uncles and his cousins by the dozens all that day.

Not wanting to be unfair to the eager hunters, she did a bit of computing. If the exclamations she had heard were fairly accurate, the rabbits weighed from ten to twelve pounds, generally one would be enough for five huge servings. How could they justify shooting more than they could use?

"Bang!"

"Another one. That makes eighteen I've got today," a man's voice in the distance shouted.

I hope he didn't get my joyous friend with the sun shining through his pink ears, she thought.

Another man's voice, evidently a companion of the other one who had just spoken, laughed, "It looks as if they wanted us to get them. One flushes another, and that one flushes out another, and on they go popping up to get popped at, like dominoes — only in reverse — across the fields."

Maybe if I were a hunter with a gun in my hand, they would be an irresistible target she thought, but I don't think so.

When Sister Carter sent her rabbit stew for supper — just as she had expected — she wasn't sure whether she could eat it. When Mary sniffed its fragrance and looked down at the plate, she felt more receptive.

"Millie," she said, "I'm glad rabbit in the stew doesn't look like rabbit on the hop."

Millie, who had already eaten, at first looked quite uncomfortable. Then she quickly recovered as she saw that her mother was spooning up the stew with a good show of appetite. She smiled, as she was reminded of the good news she had been waiting to tell. "Mother, you should see what the teams are eating tonight."

"Rabbit stew?"

"Oh, Mother, you do feel better! There is rye grass taller than a man all along the river. They are having a wonderful time chomping away on it." She imitated the semi-rotary motion of a cow chewing its cud, an imitation she loved to do.

194

Mary couldn't eat all the stew she had been sent, but she drank every drop of the tea.

While her mother was finishing her tea, Millie dropped on the other bed slant-wise so that she had room to stretch out her legs and wiggle her toes. That she was in a happy frame of mind Mary could tell, for she was tracing twin arcs in the air.

Seeing that she was observed, Millie sighed and sought another means of self-expression that would share her feelings with her mother. "I feel as if we are getting close to the Promised Land."

"So do I." Mary agreed, "and I'll get well fast and do the things a mother should."

Suddenly aghast that she had not thought about him sooner, Mary asked, "Where is the Baby?"

Millie flushed, "Oh, one of the ladies in the other company said she'd be happy to borrow him for a little while."

Millie's eyes were anxious.

Mary did not want her to feel guilty. "Just as long as he is well cared for, I'm glad for you to have help. I'll soon be better. I'm sure I will."

Friday morning they were so slow starting Mary began to feel some concern. From the voices she could tell there were strangers on some kind of business in camp. She hoped they were not looking for the pony John Henry had got. She could hear words like *travel, footsore,* and sums of money quoted, as she lay nursing the baby the best she could. Then she heard them evidently herding some animals off.

Presently, Mrs. Baker puffed into the wagon, "Well I declare I hate to see them go, but it's better than leaving them by the road."

"Who go?"

"Didn't they tell you?" She spread her skirts and sat close to Mary. "We've sold off at least half of our cattle to some traders who will take them and get them back into good condition again."

"Not—?" Mary could not bring herself to say their names.

"Oh no. Orthodoxology are doing quite well, considering. They have had the best care a body could give."

195

She helped Mary wash, combed her hair, smoothed the bed, emptied the chamber pot. When she left, Mary felt able to sit up a little while.

In fact, she was sitting up when Charles came in after hitching up. She tried to make a joke. "When you're trading in worn-out cattle, too bad you can't trade in a worn-out wife."

If she had butted him in the stomach with her head, he would not have looked more shocked. There was something besides shock in his expression. Intuitively, she was sure the thought had crossed his mind and he was too surprised and honest to treat the idea as a joke.

She laughed as easily as she could, which was rather weakly, "Don't you count on it. I'm going to be much better soon now, just you see."

"I told you I'd pull you through," he said, with a kind of stubborn honesty, "and I mean to do it." She could see that he was gripping his hands behind his back rather awkwardly.

She felt sorry for him. She looked down at the cover over her lap and carefully smoothed it from side to side. "I always know you will do what you say you will do." she answered softly.

"Well, then, let's not have any more foolish talk," he said shortly, the master again, as he turned and climbed out the back of the wagon.

It was discouraging to travel through dust again on Saturday, but getting to the Boise river fording place before afternoon was over did raise their spirits.

The girls were to ride inside the wagon with their mother and the baby, Charles explained. John Henry would ride his pony across.

As they waited in the wagon, the girls raised the side canvas for Mary to see. The main stream was, as Charles had said, "about a hundred paces across," and hardly more than knee-deep. The girls would have waded across if their father had let them, for what they could see was the gravel bottom of the main channel. Beyond that were two sloughs of the river to be crossed, too, and they were not so clear or certain.

They need not have worried about the sloughs, however. The entire crossing was not only easy, it was downright pleasant. The splashing water threw a million diamonds from every hoof and wheel, and the gravel beneath sounded a playful roar as the wheels ground through.

To herself, Mary formulated a bit of alliteration to celebrate the crossing: A ford without fear is fun for all.

While they were crossing, the canvas had been down tight all around. All Mary had seen then, was out the back when the wagons went up a slope, but once they were across, the girls had the canvas up again in a hurry. They especially wanted to watch John Henry's performance. It was worth seeing, for he and his pony were splashing about in fine style, making a number of trips back and forth.

Finally, he rode up to the wagon to speak to his special audience. "Did you see him?" he called.

"Who?" they chorused back.

"Mr. Davis."

"When?"

"Just a few minutes ago."

Mary knew she was guilty of a silly vanity, but nonetheless, she was glad that Mr. Davis had not seen her. She had no illusions about looking romantically pale, or even "respectable."

That evening they enjoyed a "fine fire," as Pauline called it. Mary did not try to get out of the wagon, but she did watch the splendid flames turn the camp into a rosy scene of sociability. If they lay-over tomorrow she might even try to get out of the wagon for a while, she planned.

But by Sunday afternoon she was ruefully telling herself she might have known better than to count on hatching out of the wagon before the lay-over. She could hardly have expected Charles to go along with the plan to go to Fort Boise on Sunday. She never did know what persuaded him to do it, but he did. She did know that someone said the fort was only about five miles.

Anyway, they started out for Fort Boise on Sunday morning and kept on looking for it the whole day long. It just didn't seem like Sunday at all, and the traveling jolted any thought of sitting up right out of her.

Monday morning they started out early, just as if they had had a real Sabbath the day before. About nooning time, Millie rolled up the canvas so that Mary could see Fort Boise. "Not that it is so much to see," she said, in obvious disappointment. Mary thought the high walls and buildings of sun-baked clay were rather attractive. At least, she thought, they cast a stronger shadow than a covered wagon. The idea of making bricks like mud pies and building as big a house as one wanted struck her as an intriguing idea. If the imminence of a choice as to whether they should try to ford the Snake River there or pay three dollars to ferry across had not driven the project from her mind, she might have built an adobe dream house before lunch. Then again, probably some of the other affairs would have diverted her anyway, because there were Indians about eager to make the children mocassins for twenty-five cents.

Mary was afraid Charles would say that if they all got mocassins, they couldn't afford the ferry, but he didn't. The children had walked in sand so much that they were through nearly everything they had to wear in the way of shoes. The thought of fording made her sick with apprehension. Hearing men talk about the swiftness of the first stretch, the depth of the last one, and how laying everything high on the wagon boxes would probably keep their goods dry — all these remarks made her feel that the three-dollar charge for ferrying was sensible enough.

She heard Charles call to John Henry, "Check the oxen for me while I go to the fort for provisions."

She noticed he was not gone long, and when he came back, he had just one small package. He came right on into the wagon and held the package up with a look of disgust, or dismay, she couldn't tell which until he spoke, "Sugar. Seventy-five cents a pound. That is all the provisions they will sell us.

"Just about all of us are either out or will be out of bread in a week or two."

He slumped dejectedly on the other bed.

Mary pulled herself up on an elbow. "Don't worry, Charles, fish is good for us, and I see there is plenty of that."

He snorted, "Fish doesn't stick to your ribs very long when you're driving oxen — especially in country like this."

"You'll get us through."

"Sometimes I wonder if I didn't bite off more than I knew."

Mary was so surprised to have him admit it, she couldn't think of a thing to say. Finally she broke a straining silence with a bit of teasing. "First, you haven't enough to bite on and, then, you have too much. You're a hard man to please, Charles Adams."

As usual, he didn't care much for her humor, but she had filled the silence and she hadn't given him a false assurance that would be an insult to them both.

He didn't seem in any hurry to be on his way. There was something yet to be said between them, but she couldn't tell what it was. Was it reassurance that he had done the right thing and all would come out well? Or did he have something difficult to tell her? She tried to read his face without making him uncomfortable. He looked almost as if he had something to confess, she thought, as he hesitated to introduce whatever it was.

She decided to help him get it out. "Is something else bothering you, Charles?" she asked, fearful of what she was asking for.

He hunched over, his elbows on his knees and his head between his hands, so making his eyes seem deeper set than usual. "There's a party forming to leave the train and pack into the Dalles. They could make it in ten days and meet the train with provisions. What do you think?"

Mary was aghast at the thought of being left with the children. Mrs. Baker had told her only that morning about the mother and her baby that had been forsaken at Fort Boise just a few weeks before. The horrid story was still fresh in her mind. "You mean you want to leave the children and me with the train and you pack in to the Dalles?"

His face worked convulsively. He was furious. Then he saw the woebegone look on her face, and he began to laugh. "By the Eternal, you don't really think I'd do that — unless it was the only way," he exploded.

Suddenly she was exhausted and cross for having been needlessly worried. Her voice broke. "Then — then what are you talking about?"

For a moment he looked blank. Then he slowly began to realize how unclear he had been. "All I was thinking," he said compassionately, "was do you think it would be all right to let John Henry pack in with them? There'll be Mr. McMillen and others who'd look out for the boy and see that he got safely to the mission. Some good Methodist there will surely make arrangements for us to get you where you can get some better care than you're getting."

The thought of sending John Henry on was almost as frightening to her as the thought of Charles's going. She wondered whether John Henry was really mature enough for such a task or whether their straits were desperate enough to require it.

"Does he want to go?"

"He didn't say one way or the other. He just said one of the men suggested that it would be a good way to get the good out of his new pony. I told him I'd talk it over with you."

"What do you think?" she asked, knowing full well that if he had decided he wouldn't have asked her.

"I'm of two minds," he admitted. "I think he'd be almost as safe with them as he is with us."

"But don't you need him with the cattle?"

"I could sell or butcher one of the cows and keep the other tied to the wagon all the time."

She could see that he wanted her to make a choice — whether it would be the final one or not. "Why don't you let John Henry say whether he wants to do it," she suggested. "I'd hate to send him off on an errand like that unless he really wanted to try it. Maybe he wanted us to decide against it for him."

Charles looked surprised. "You know, that hadn't occurred to me." He pulled himself off the bed and paused, jingling the coins in his pocket for an accompaniment to the action he now saw clearly.

"I'll put it to him," he said, "and find out whether he really wants to try it before I say he can go.

"Whew, maybe he really doesn't want to go," he ejaculated softly. "Why didn't I think of that?" He was chuckling as he went out the back end of the wagon.

If Mary thought John Henry might not want to pack with the men, she soon got the straight of it. Charles had not been gone five minutes before the boy plunged through the same opening his father had left by. He was excited.

"You mean you'll let me?" he exulted. "You don't care?"

"I care very much," Mary scanned his flushed face. He calmed down quickly. "I'll be careful, Ma," he promised.

The enormity of leaving them swept over him. For a moment he looked almost dismayed. He straightened himself as he looked down at his mother. Without warning, he swooped down, kissed her on the cheek, and dashed out of the wagon, as nearly on the run as the quarters would allow.

My poor little man-boy, she thought.

Soon they were lining up for the ferry, which was the usual make-shift affair — wagon beds lashed together and pulled by ropes. Once the train was across, they set up camp nearby for the night.

Mrs. Baker and Sister Carter both came in to help prepare John Henry's pack for the trip while the girls watched in solemn awe.

XVII
Days of Fear and Tension

IN THE MORNING, as soon as he had breakfast, he was
ready to be off and came in to say goodbye. He picked up the
baby and gave him a resounding smack, saying, "Now see
that you are a good boy while I'm gone."

When he put the baby down, he leaned over until Mary
could feel his nose in the hair over her ears. "Take care of yourself, Ma. I'll find a good place to take care of you until you get
well."

He had pulled away so abruptly she didn't get a chance to
kiss him. And he was gone.

As no one had thought to unfasten the canvas, she couldn't
lift it to see him go. She lay there listening to every sound. She
could tell that he was kissing his sisters goodbye, too, and she
thought she could tell when he and his father shook hands. Then,
the thudding of hoofs and the subsiding sounds of all the
farewells as the packs were added and the pilgrims *a la* pack had
set off, eleven altogether, with three ponies among them. They expected to make thirty miles a day and so reach the Dalles in ten
days. That will be the first of October, Mary calculated. She tried
to visualize him among strangers in a strange river town, but she
realized she was thinking of a river town in Indiana. Maybe out
here they would have buildings like Fort Boise. She could not imagine what she and his father had sent him into, and she felt as if
they had dropped him over the edge of the world.

To make matters worse, the cattle had strayed during the
night, there having been no guard, now that the danger of their
being stolen seemed past, and Charles had to do what John Henry
would have done had he remained with them. Charles didn't say
anything about it when he finally came back, but he looked very
tired and serious as he realized how much more of his own
strength would be taxed in the days ahead.

By the time the train was ready to go, it was afternoon and a strong west wind had come up, choking the oxen and making the dust too thick to see where they were going. All in all it seemed an ill-fated day.

When the wind changed enough to drive the dust across the road, rather than into their faces, they started up again, but the day was virtually lost. What was worse, they went into a ravine, expecting to find grass and water, but they found neither. By that time, it was so late they camped anyway. And there they were, without feed or drink for the stock, only sage for fuel to cook what they had with them of food and drink. As the sun set, a bitterly cold night settled down upon the train. Dejected and shivering, they all got into bed as fast as they could.

Mary lay awake, and Charles lay awake. Neither of them said what they both were thinking, "I wonder how John Henry is getting along tonight?"

Everyone in the train seemed to get up the next morning with but one thought in mind — to get out of that ravine as quickly as possible. When they got to the summit of that one, they found themselves going down into another, which eventually brought them to the banks of the Malheur river.

Too many emigrants had been there ahead of them recently for the grass to be plentiful, but there was water, even though it was anything but sparkling, and there were willows for fuel.

Charles did not tell her, but Mrs. Baker did, that there was another long arid stretch ahead of them, and this would have to do before they started on. He did say, however, "As long as there are enough jackrabbits I think I'll keep both cows."

Thursday, the road was so smooth that Mary sat up for quite a while and felt rather encouraged. About noon, she began to smell sulphur. The canvas side was up. When Charles dropped back to check up on the cows, she couldn't resist asking, "Are we coming to another Hell Gate? I smell sulphur."

He looked at her with evident forbearance. "Sulphur Springs," he replied, tolerantly.

Cattle and emigrants were too dry to refuse the water, and it was good for them that they drank, for the train went on and on, up into the hills, long after dark, without finding water. Another gloomy, cold night! Millie was shivering as she brought Mary a bowl of warmed over rabbit stew to eat by candlelight.

"I hope John Henry is camped by some pretty stream with a nice big fire," she almost whispered it. "About all we have to be thankful for tonight is dry grass and sagebrush.

"Things will be getting better soon," Mary suggested. "The country begins to look a little more fertile than it did."

Margaret had followed Millie into the wagon. "It has a long way to go to be decent," she spoke darkly.

Although Mary had voiced the same thought to herself often enough, she couldn't admit it to the girls. "Well," she sighed exaggeratedly, "I don't want to try to go back."

As usual, her absurdity pleased the girls. They laughed appreciatively, even as they shivered.

The next morning, they found water, such as it was, within a mile of their camp. However all-but-stagnant and odorous of sulphur it was, the cattle were glad enough to get it after all the dry grass they had been eating. Four miles later, they came to Farewell Bend and filled up everything they had to carry water, after they had filled themselves. Their precautions, this time, were needless, however. Within another four miles they were camped for the night on the banks of Burnt River, where the water was clear and sparkling. For those four miles they traveled the same canyon as the river. Mary, looking out the side, marveled at their luck, for the river left not more than twenty feet of the canyon for them to travel on, and though the sun reflected sharply on the bare rock walls, there was, sometimes, shade, a cooling breeze, and the refreshing music of the water beside them.

The next day the canyon and the river proved less considerate. When they had had to cross the river three times within five miles, Mary heard someone call out, "Let's just stay in the water." The going would have been rough enough without the crossing, for they were going over the dried out part of the river bed which was very rocky. Every foot of the way the oxen were stumbling on loose rock and the wagon teetered and careened as the wheels were sorely tested. Finally, they pulled away from the river and pulled themselves wearily over the high bluffs to a small creek for their camp where there was almost nothing for fuel.

"There's nothing for it but to travel tomorrow," Charles said as he got into bed that night. "I swear when I get to Oregon City I'll never travel on Sunday except to church."

Mary's heart sank. She had been looking forward to a respite from the terrible jostling of the past day. Whatever her soul needed, she knew her bones needed rest.

The next day she couldn't help wondering whether they weren't getting their just desserts for traveling on Sunday, for they had to cross the river five times in six miles.

The jostling she was taking had made Mary very ill. At least, she thought, the children have learned to get along without my care. And Charles — well, he couldn't get along without a wife. There were plenty of women like Sister Carter. Like Sister Carter! There *was* Sister Carter, she suddenly realized. First, Charles had promised Doc Carter to look out for his family, in his place, and now Sister Carter was looking out for Mary's family for her, in her place. Well, she thought, another day like this one and there'll be a clear field.

Not very long after the fifth river crossing, they came to a green spot where a lovely grove of birches welcomed them to spend the rest of Sunday, but Mary had been braced so hard against the erratic motions of the wagon that even after it had not moved for hours she could still feel it. Feeling the motion when she knew there was none made her wonder whether she was going a little bit crazy.

When Mrs. Baker came in, Mary mentioned the matter, explaining that she had experienced the same sensations other times but not so violently as this.

Mrs. Baker laughed heartily. "Why, bless you, we all feel it, but you feel it more because you're bumping your head. We're just bumping you-know-what."

Mary didn't know how much sense that made, but she felt a little bit reassured by Mrs. Baker's attitude.

The children revived from their fatigue quickly and went dashing off about the camp and back again to tell her what a beautiful spot it was.

"Mother," Margaret insisted, "if you'd just look out you'd feel a lot better."

Mary could hardly lift her head. While the children watched, she tried and gave up.

Before she realized what they were doing, Mamie and Margaret were at the head of the bed. "Now," they said, propping her up with their hands.

Mary looked and agreed with them so that they would let her down again, but she did get a glimpse of evergreen trees and other vegetation more generous than any she had seen for weeks. It *did* make her feel better. "You were right," she told them. "I do feel better already."

Monday the wagons were in the water almost as much as they were out of it. They crossed Burnt River once more and then, climbing all the while, zigzagged back and forth nine times through a little creek as they followed it up the steep ascent, only to follow another ravine down again. There they came to a spring. Mary was hoping they would camp there, but her hopes were in vain. They went up then down and on and on. She could hardly believe her ears when Charles said they had made only fourteen miles.

That evening she heard strange voices in camp. She immediately sensed a tension in the conversation: there was almost a keening in the strange voices, sharp questioning and low, slow answers, or comments. She knew those strange voices were reporting some kind of trouble, but there seemed to be little resolution — more resignation — in the familiar voices that commented. Without being able to distinguish a single word, she lay trying to guess what the trouble was, the girls sound asleep all around her. She felt sure that if the trouble involved John Henry, the whole family would have been told.

She concentrated so hard on listening that she put herself to sleep and didn't awaken when Charles came to bed. She slept right through the night, but not restfully. She heard John Henry calling her and she was trying to answer him. Only she couldn't make a sound. At last a sound broke from her lips as she awoke and realized that she had indeed heard a call, but it was their morning call and Charles was getting up.

Reality never looked better. Then she remembered and caught Charles with her question before he got away.

so that Mary could see what everyone was exclaiming about. There was the Grande Ronde, a perfect little "O" of a valley, about fifteen miles across. Mary could see more than the valley; she could see that the descent into it was going to be a bad one.

Charles saw her look of consternation at the sight of the hill. "It looks as if they have saved the worst for the last," he admitted. "We'll have to use ropes on some parts at least, I guess."

Mary was afraid to try to keep the baby in the wagon while they were making the descent and she was afraid to have Millie carry him. It was quite a relief to have Mrs. Baker say, as she was tucking Mary in "good and tight," that she would be "glad to walk down with him."

Mary almost asked why the woman who had been nursing him didn't help with him. She had thought about it so much that she almost forgot that she wasn't supposed to know. Then she realized that the unknown benefactress would probably be busy taking care of her own child.

Mrs. Baker stood a moment, hesitating. "Brother Adams says he'll come and see that everything is down good and tight before you and the wagon start down the hill. I'll go back and do a few last-minute jobs in our wagon and then come back and get the baby just before you start down."

Mary was afraid. She admitted it to herself, but she couldn't tell anyone. All who were able to walk were to do so to ease the load on the ropes. Besides, it was safer to walk. She could not even ask for a small child to sit beside her on the way down.

Fear must have been written on her face when Charles came in. He sat down beside her. "We are going down first," he said. "The ropes are strong and our team is still in fair condition. Remember, I'll be right beside them every step. I can count on them to do exactly as I say, that you know. Now don't worry."

He looked around the wagon briskly. "Mrs. Baker has done a good job of packing the wagon, I see. Not so much to pack as there was five months ago."

She tried to smile, but she could feel her lips quivering as they stretched over her teeth, so she raised her hand. That trembled, too, but she kept it moving to disguise the trembling and felt like an actress. Then he was gone and Mrs. Baker came in to get the

"They were packers from behind," he said. "Folks s[...] ing are running out of provisions." And he was gone.

Mrs. Baker was a little more informative when she ca[...] breakfast, "They are destitute," she said, "and the men [...] to get through and back in five days if they can."

"Why that's impossible," Mary looked into her eye[...] Henry couldn't be more than halfway there, could he?"

"Maybe they won't have to go all the way to the [...] Mrs. Baker spoke as if she knew it was a forlorn hope.

"Couldn't we spare them something?"

"The chances are we would be endangering ourselv[...] than helping them. "We'll do better by getting ourselves [...] and sending help back."

The next day, when traders from Oregon came along[...] for lame cattle to buy up and the country began to shov[...] fertility occasionally, she thought, "It's always darkes[...] dawn." They must be coming to something better. The fe[...] creased until Thursday night. They were "getting some[...] but they would have to hurry. When they came into a go[...] that night, they found more Oregon traders already there[...] of warnings. Snow, they said, was already on the mount[...] Blue Mountains, which the emigrants had been admiring[...] days. Rains, they said, had set in early in the valley. Imm[...] they said, had better hurry or risk getting caught by[...] weather.

As Mrs. Baker said. "They don't need to tell me it'[...] cold. That rain feels cold enough to be snow right now."

Mrs. Baker had been talking at such a clip Mary had[...] ized it was raining, but now she heard it. The girls came r[...] the wagon for shelter.

All that day and the next, they suffered from the c[...] had almost nothing dry enough to burn. The only good ne[...] had was from one of the packers who passed them on his[...] the relief of his destitute friends. At Grande Ronde he had[...] fifty pounds of flour for thirty dollars. He would surel[...] them in good time.

By Saturday, all the climbing they had been doi[...] rewarded. When they reached the crest, Charles turned th[...]

for an explanation. She felt it was due them — and him.

"Your father is getting very tired," she said softly. "I think he depended on John Henry more than he realized."

They nodded their heads soberly.

"We all do," Margaret said it, clearly implying that *they* weren't stamping *their* feet.

"Will John Henry really be at the Dalles when we get there?" Mamie asked, evidently bringing out something that had been worrying her.

"All eleven of them will be lined up with a brass band, waiting for us at the fort," Mary teased.

After that, they trudged off to breakfast, leaving Mary to her secret doubts.

Before Sunday night, they were well into the mountains, with almost never a level or a straight stretch of road, and never a smooth one.

Tuesday night Charles was "just about played out," he admitted. "Now we have grass, and water, and fuel," he said, "and the going is almost as hard as it was on the desert."

Then he brightened. "It was Providential that I bought that flour at the post. Did Mrs. Baker tell you?"

"About what? How would she know about the flour you took to Sister Carter?" If Mary sounded a little impatient, she didn't care.

If Charles noticed, he did not stoop to acknowledge it. "We have caught up with Company Number One." he said. "We were able to share the flour with Doctor Miller. They are killing off their cows, so we traded flour for meat. You had some of it tonight." He swallowed hard and went on, "The Reverend Delazon Smith got a chance to go on ahead. He's probably down the Columbia by now."

"I heard someone saying something about the cattle being about all worn out. They weren't talking about ours, were they?" There was nothing to be gained by discussing the Reverend Smith.

Even in the flickering shadows of the grease lamp, she could see the surprise on his face as he turned and looked at her. Perhaps for the first time he was aware of how isolated she was from some of the facts of the trail — so obvious to all the rest of them.

"We are over-working them every day, and we don't have any choice in the matter," he said flatly. Some folks are driving cows in place of oxen. It's a matter of getting along the best we can for a few more days."

She hated to ask, but she had to. "Do you think Ortho-Doxology will get us through?"

"Better than most."

She hated to be quizzing him when he was so tired, but she had one more question that she couldn't hold back. "Do you think John Henry might start back to meet us?" Mrs. Baker had suggested it.

"I told him to wait for us at the Dalles."

"Then he'll wait at the Dalles," she said, resigned.

The next morning there was no early call. The train was to recruit their weary beasts, now that they were nearly out of the mountains and they were in an almost ideal spot for a camp.

The children played hide-and-seek among the trees, the lovely pines and spruce and fir, as well as tamarack. The women "washed out a few things." The men worked at repairs and tried to let the cattle graze at will without getting lost.

Charles put both sides of the wagon up about noon, when it was warm enough. The wagon got a good airing out.

Millie helped prop her mother up when the sun filtered through the trees at the right angle to warm her and when a little breeze played across her cheeks, Mary thought it the loveliest of sensations, probably, she admitted to herself, because it carried the scent of all the lovely greenery of the forest.

Margaret flopped onto the other bed late in the afternoon and wiggled her toes the way she had seen Millie do it. "Oh", she exploded, falling backward and bouncing, "this has been the loveliest day!"

Mary was that encouraged about herself and all that she felt almost the same way. "One more day like this and I think I could begin to sit up and get well."

The next day, when the girls found out that they were to remain until noon, Mamie chuckled, "This place is getting to be a habit with us."

Even when they were at last on their way again, it was

almost as good as the camp, for the trail led them through thick timber and rich grass, which the cattle were allowed to enjoy as they went along.

That good feeding had to last them a while thereafter, for the going was rougher down into the Umatilla Valley.

Mary heard Pauline squeal to Millie, "The whole valley's speckled with ponies and cows."

Then Margaret grunted, "Indians, too."

The canvas was loose enough for Mary to look out. The girls were right!

Millie and Margaret had their heads together. They were looking intently, quizzically. Their gaze attracted Mamie and Pauline.

"What are you looking at?"

Suddenly all four of them were jumping up and down, screaming, "It's him. It's him. John Henry's coming!"

– The OREGONIAN

Methodist Mission near The Dalles as drawn by
an army artist in 1849.

XVIII

Providentially

S URE ENOUGH, John Henry was coming. He had disobeyed his father.

Mary dreaded the consequences.

As he approached close enough for her to see his clothes she wondered how they had recognized him at all. He was gaunt and dirty. There was not a single article of clothing that he had on that was distinguishable from the nondescript tatters which most of the boys were wearing, except that his were farther gone than the others.

The girls, who had run to meet and surround him, subsided as they returned. Millie had relieved him of the reins.

Charles said nothing until he had gripped the boy by the shoulders. "Why have you come back, Boy?"

"Pa, I couldn't stay there and wait for you — not after what I saw you were in for."

Mary could see his eyes begging his father to understand.

Then the boy slipped from his father's grasp and hurried over to the wagon. "How are you, Ma? You any better?"

"I'm holding my own. As soon as we get there I'll be all right." She wanted to reach out and touch him, but she didn't dare — he was that close to the breaking point.

Charles had followed him back to the wagon. "Why don't you get up on the front seat and rest a while? Millie and I can take care of your pony for you."

The poor boy stood there as if he was too tired to make up his mind. Then he said, "Pa, everything you gave me is in that pack of provisions. It's mostly flour and corn. From the looks of things at the Dalles, the asking price won't be going down. If we don't need it, you can surely get your money out of it. Maybe make a little profit to boot."

Charles looked shocked. "We have been too close to need

ourselves to make a profit out of our friends' needs," he said.

Instead of looking abashed, as she had expected him to do, John Henry nodded his head approvingly. "I'm glad you feel that way, Pa. I've seen a few who didn't see it that way. The prices are going up something awful."

Charles studied his son for a moment and then turned to the wagon and Mary. When he saw that she had dropped back on the pillow, too tired to hold herself up any longer, he stepped closer. "Why don't we let John Henry rest a while on the girls' bed. He can tell us more later."

That was all the invitation he needed. Almost before his father had finished speaking, the boy pulled himself up over the front wheel, onto the front box, and back into the wagon, where, with a half turn, he landed flat on his back on the bed, without letting his travel-soiled boots touch the bed.

Keeping his feet in the air, he pulled off those boots and dropped them on the flooring beside the bed. "Good night, Ma," he sighed, and let himself go limp.

But he was too tired to sleep. Just as soon as his breathing indicated he was asleep, his body would twitch and he'd try another position.

Finally, he lay on his back with his arms folded under his head. "I just don't see how the cattle can make it all the way to the Dalles," he sighed.

"Why," Mary exclaimed, "I thought we were almost there!"

"We can't make it in less than two weeks' time. We might need longer, and where there's water there's no grass, and where there's grass, there's no water. The country between here and the Dalles is pretty much like before we got into the mountains — one dry, barren hill after another."

Suddenly he gasped and looked almost frightened. "Where's the baby?"

Mary knew in an instant what the fear was that gripped him. "Mrs. Baker was giving him a bath and a nap in her wagon. He's getting along very well."

"We've been pretty lucky, considering."

"I'm not so sure it's luck."

"You may be right, Ma," he said and thereupon went sound

215

asleep.

When he finally awakened, he found himself something of a personage in the train. Everyone was eager to hear about what he had seen and experienced. When he came to bed that night, Charles described how John Henry had been the chief adviser at their pow-wow, and Mary could see how proud Charles had been of the way John Henry acquitted himself with the men.

"That boy estimated travel and described terrain like a scout," he chuckled. "The whole train is acting on his advice and is going to hold up, at least for the morning, to let the cattle get what little they can before we start up. Then, instead of looking for water to camp near, we'll take our water with us and camp where there's grass for the stock.

"We'll tally up the cows that are giving the least milk so that we can set up an order for butchering them as we need them, and we'll share and share alike from here on in to the Dalles.

"We have made a pact to sell enough cows when we get there to make a fair payment. Folks whose cows are left will have been sharing their milk with the rest of us.

"If they want to keep their cows and have someone there winter them over, they can make up what they owe out of their own pockets, if they want to."

"Did he go to the mission?"

"They will try to get a passage for us and have someone ready to meet us at Portland."

"Portland — I thought we were going to Oregon City."

"We get to Portland first. It may be wise to stop there for the time and go to Oregon City later. All the Methodist ministers were meeting in Portland for Conference the first of the month."

"Which month?"

"Will we be that late?"

"We are more than a week into October right now. Add at least two weeks to get to the Dalles; that would make it the twenty-second. Add a day to the Cascades and another day to Portland. That puts it at the twenty-fourth, without counting on any palaver at the Dalles or any delay getting there."

"How did we ever think we could get there by the first of September?"

216

"We lost some time along the Platte, you may remember. The bulk of the emigration ahead of us got the pick of the grass. Besides, some of the streams, that would have served us earlier, were dried up by the time we got there.

"And now tomorrow we lose some more time. You best use it to sit up a little while you can. They have vetoed any more Sunday layovers until we get to the Dalles."

He said it flatly enough to sound casual, but Mary knew more from that than any other thing he said how desperate their situation seemed to him. She must have gasped or given him some indication of what she read from his remark, for he said, almost roughly, "I said I'd get you there, and I will."

I wonder whether it makes any difference to a fifth wheel where it is carried, she wondered.

Charles was saying, "It really seems Providential that when we need to carry water with us it is the time when we have plenty of empty barrels to carry it in."

"Yes, Providential," she answered. "Just so there's some Providential water to fill those Providentially empty barrels."

Charles was yawning and probably hadn't even heard what she said. Providentially, she thought.

In the next four days the train progressed but thirty-five miles, loading up with water when they came to some and stopping for the cattle to graze when they came to grass, the best of which was dry. Everyone who could was walking to save the teams from pulling any more than was necessary, and Mary did not have to look at them to know in what emaciated condition Ortho-Doxology were in, despite the care that Charles and John Henry had lavished on them when they could. The cows, which were now as dry as the hay-like grass they had been eating, were now in the harness with the oxen. One wagon had been abandoned and the load added to the Bakers' wagon, which both teams now pulled.

Mary guessed that whoever the baby's wet nurse had been, she was no longer with the train, because Millie often mentioned the gruel which Sister Carter made for him and how good he was about learning to eat from the spoon.

Mrs. Baker was most considerate about coming over and

propping Mary up enough to look out the side whenever the train halted for any length of time during the day. Then Mary could see that her own were no worse off than other women's children. Their clothes were in disrepair and mostly bleached by the sun or darkened by dust until they were all more the color of the dry landscape than of intended effects of dye bath and loom. They are more like little children of nature with nature's protective coloration, she noticed.

Despite their lack of milk, none of them were suffering too much from their diet. The meal and flour that John Henry had brought back, along with the beef they were using up as they went along, and an occasional prairie chicken, did very well for their hearty food. From the way it was sparingly used, Mary knew their molasses was almost gone. If there was any dried fruit left, she guessed the children were getting it for treats.

Wednesday was as dry and wearing as any other day of jolting in the dust over one rocky hill after another in the pitiless eye of the sun, until she heard a ripple of excitement run along the train. She was sure she heard the word "house" any number of times. She listened as carefully as she could, knowing full well that they might be saying "mouse," except that mice were commonplace of the past few days. No, they must be saying about a house.

"Go tell Mother," she heard Millie call. Millie usually carried the baby far enough away from the wagons to avoid the dust.

In a minute Pauline and Mamie were all but tumbling into the back of the wagon. "We're coming to a house," they were chattering. "Not a mud house — a real house of wood. A real house!"

Soon the train had halted and John Henry was loosening the side so that he could roll up the canvas for her, and the two little girls fixed a pillow to prop her up. Charles had turned the wagon so that she could see the Indian agency house. There was Millie showing Baby Charles the house! Poor baby, she thought, four months old, almost, and never near a civilized house before!

Then Mary saw the traders, and Charles talking to them. Maybe he wasn't trading; maybe he was just getting advice. Others, she could see, were preparing to leave wagons and cattle.

Mary could not tell how much bad news these transactions would indicate, and she wasn't sure that she could count on an unvarnished answer if she asked. So she watched and listened.

The members of their train swarmed over the yard of the agency. They walked up and felt of the house. They looked down the well in the yard. As she watched them pitying them, Mary knew that if she were able she would be going through the same pathetic rite of association.

Gradually, the train pulled away from the frame marvel and on through an afternoon of miserable dry slogging in sand. It was as if the Trail were showing them they weren't through yet, Mary thought.

And they weren't. The next day there was more of the "miserable sand" as Mamie called it. About noon they came to a most unattractive stream, which she heard Charles tell the protesting Margaret "would have to do." Why then, did their voices sound so pleased and happy within a few moments? Had they discovered gold in the stream?

Mrs. Baker was the first one to tell her, as she climbed in smoothing her hair under her sunbonnet. "It's Mr. Torrance, the Indian agent, coming back from Milwaukie with provisions," she explained. "Did you know that an Indian agent is not an Indian?"

Mary looked to see whether that was a joke. The wagon was too dusty and shady for her to see any special indications, so she just laughed and said, "When is an Indian not an Indian? When he is an Indian agent!"

"Precisely," said Mrs. Baker.

At least I didn't say the wrong thing, Mary thought.

Abruptly, Mrs. Baker changed the subject. "Sultry. Rain, maybe."

"What will we do?"

"I guess we'll find out if it does. We can't ride, that is sure, and I don't think we can walk in the rain."

"The McMillens are all chattering with that Indian agent as if he was a long-lost brother."

"It seems rather nice, I think, to feel that some of our train is already acquainted in Oregon."

"That it does," Mrs. Baker agreed. "It makes Oregon City

seem just around the corner."

"Around the mountain," Mary laughed, buoyed by the thought.

The very next day the impression was heightened immeasurably by two events of great import.

When Charles came back from breakfast, he broke the news in a queer way. "Make up your mind not to need a doctor before we get to the Dalles," he advised. "He's going on into the Dalles and wait for his friends there."

"I'm glad he thinks he will not be needed." It was all she could think of to say, but not all she could think of.

That very noon, camped by a sluggish little stream and feeling more derelict than self-reliant, they met Mr. Lot Whitcomb, direct from Oregon, with supplies to help out anyone who was destitute.

Charles laughed ruefully when he was telling her about it. "He won't sell, he says. He was sent to help the needy." Thoughtfully, he jingled some coins in his pocket. "Out here it looks as if a man could starve to death with gold in his pocket."

"We're not in any danger of starving with gold in our pockets, are we?"

"Maybe just with silver," he snorted.

"You don't really mean it? Do you?" She scanned his face trying to see whether the point he was making was academic or not.

When he saw her anxious look, he hastily shrugged his shoulders. "I was not thinking of us.

"I was thinking of that train behind us."

"Did you tell Mr. Whitcomb about them?"

"I didn't need to. I think he is going in response to the plea one of the men who packed in sent down the river."

"What is Mr. Whitcomb like?"

Charles hesitated, "Oh, a pleasant enough sort, fair complexion. Does more to his hair than just brush it. Maybe he rolls it up to save paying a barber." Thus Charles did Lot Whitcomb the damage of faint praise.

By Saturday night they were all bone dry, having traveled all day through deep sand and dust without coming to any water until evening, and that was meager, she could tell, even before the sides of the wagon were raised so that she could see for herself. She was surprised, then, when Charles said that night, "Maybe you'll have a chance to sit up some tomorrow. It's not too bad here, and we've got to rest the teams before we go on.

"Just think, Mary, Old Girl, a week from tomorrow we should be there."

Mary had known there were conjectures about being almost there, but to hear Charles say it like that gave substance. Her heart did a big flip. "Oh, Charles, I can't believe we're there," she said.

"We're not — yet."

"You take the wind out of my sails."

"Better not do any sailing until we get to the Dalles."

"I'm surprised you didn't say, 'If we get there.'"

"I'm not pessimistic. I just happen to think I'm asking for trouble when I start counting my chickens before they hatch," he answered dryly.

"Why, Charles, you're just a little bit superstitious, aren't you?"

"Didn't Jesus say 'Sufficient unto the day is the evil thereof'?" he retorted.

"I never have associated the two ideas."

"They are just different sides of the same idea, it seems to me."

"Oh, Charles, you make me so mad — you're always so right."

He chuckled, and the sound of that chuckle betrayed his wise words: he, too, was already there in his thinking.

Suddenly her optimism knew no obstacle. In another week they would be looking for a new home. In the wonderful climate of the Willamette Valley, she would soon be well and strong, the girls would go to the seminary and all the past months would be as a tale that is told.

That night she dreamed that she stood on a mountain top looking down upon a beautiful river in the midst of a lovely green valley where trees were heavy with fruit of red and gold. She turned to tell Charles "I'm glad I came." But he wasn't there.

Oh, well, she thought, he's probably taking care of the team. That, however, was, on second thought, rather ridiculous. They wouldn't have the team up in a place like that.

As she lay puzzling over that, she realized that she was now awake and that Charles was indeed right beside her.

The dream was a nice one to have right before their last Sunday, however; it left a kind of aura for the day.

Had it been any but their last Sunday on the Trail, the conditions of their camp would have been most depressing, for the water was poor, the grass for the cattle quite some distance away, and very little fuel was to be found anywhere.

Their service was rather informal. They quoted favorite verses from the Bible, said a few prayers in phrases that almost any of them could anticipate, and sang a few songs — "God Is My Strong Salvation," "Jesus Shall Reign where'er the sun doth his successive journeys run," and "O Happy Day that Fix'd My Choice."

Mary was able to sit up quite a while. People, coming by the wagon and seeing her sitting up, stopped to comment that soon she would be well and that she looked better already.

Monday morning the wagon was almost as dark as it had been when the train was going through the deep timber in the Blue Mountains. The gloom Mary felt, however, did not seem to settle on her family. Probably, she told herself, it depressed her because she was alone so much of the time. She lay there wondering how she would ever manage to assume control of her household again, now that the family had managed so well without her. She tried to think about how they would proceed when they finally arrived in Oregon City. Perhaps they would have to live in their wagon for a while, but that would be impossible if they left the wagon and took a boat down the river, as Charles had mentioned doing a time or two.

The mere thought of not being jostled and dragged through dust every day would be heaven, she decided. After that, she must have dozed for a little, for the next thing she knew, she was listening to a tapping sound, not like someone trying to get her attention at the side of the wagon. No, it sounded as if little flicks of sand were being dribbled onto the canvas from above. The tempo increased. Then she heard the shouts and knew. It was raining! Now she could smell it — the peculiar, tangy scent of rain on dust and dry ground after a long drought.

She could not call the children into the wagon to get out of the rain, for that was the only shelter, even if she could muster up enough strength to be heard. No one was riding who could walk. They were allowed into the wagons only when the teams were not pulling. Charles would have to make the decision as to whether to stop the team and tell the children to get into the wagon, or to keep going and let the children walk in the rain.

Evidently they were not going to stop the train. From the sounds of laughter and gay shouts, the little rascals were enjoying a dampening down. She almost smiled to herself to imagine the rivulets that must be furrowing the dust on their faces. She wished someone would tell the girls to take off their sunbonnets and let the rain wash their hair.

Almost as if they had read her thoughts, four sunbonnets came fluttering through the back opening and dropped to the floor.

As soon as the train stopped for noon, Mamie climbed in, woebegone and querulous. "Mamma, will I turn to brick when the sun comes out?"

"Whatever gave you an idea like that?"

"Amos said so. He said we're full of dust — the same kind that they built Fort Hall of — and all it would take to make bricks of us was a little rain and some more baking in the sun."

"You're not full of dust. It's only on the outside. If you wash all the dirt off, it can't harden on you. You tell him only dirty boys turn into bricks."

Mamie's worried grimace dimpled to laughter. Mary could hear her chuckling to herself as she laboriously climbed out to throw the taunt back at Amos.

The rain did not last long enough even to lay the dust for the afternoon. Some of it had sprayed through holes in the canvas, but not enough to leave more than a stain here and there. When the sun came out, Mary had the first change in her view of the canvas top in many a day. The rain had left some new splotch patterns in the dusty cover. Soon they dried, however, and blended into the over-all lines and shades.

The train was dragging through a rocky, dusty, desolate land where even grass and sage grew sparsely. Mary thought Mrs. Baker put it rather well Thursday morning. "You can't even say the contour of this land has variety. It seems as if all we do is go up, or down, or around hills that all look just the same. If I couldn't see the sun coming up and going down every day I might guess we were going in circles."

Friday morning Mary chided her for what she had said the morning before. The country was much more rugged than they had seen for days, as they approached the Columbia River. "The trouble with these people who want variety," she said, "is that they don't always make it clear just what kind of variety they want. Look what kind of variety you've wished on us now!"

Mrs. Baker laughed. "Anyway, the men say we are coming to the Deschutes and maybe close enough to get wet!"

"Is it ford or ferry? Have you heard anyone say?"

"The brave and the poor ford. The rich ferry."

"How rich do you have to be to be cowardly?"

"Two dollars a wagon."

Mary sighed exaggeratedly, "I suppose we'll ford. We aren't rich, and Charles is brave. He's not even a little bit lazy."

Mrs. Baker, her arms akimbo, stood looking down at her, having done the usual chores. She started to laugh as an idea came to her. She picked up her skirts and bobbed out of the wagon, singing in a high falsetto "O Happy Day That Fixed My Choice," — then, realizing that she didn't dare continue with the real words, — she continued humming the melody just loud enough for Mary to hear her as she climbed out the back.

The whole performance was so completely alien to her ordinary behavior that she left Mary more surprised and puzzled than amused or shocked.

Mary's guess as to what Charles would do at the Deschutes was correct, but her analysis of his reasons was off, because she didn't know all that he knew. When he saw her face after he told her they would ford, he explained.

"I may need that two dollars more at the Dalles than I need to ferry here," he said. "I aim to buy out some other emigrants' passage down the river if I can, and that money may help me do it. There are too many *if*'s at the Dalles to count very heavily on any set plan."

She hated to ask but she had to, now that he was talking about it. "We won't get to the Dalles by Sunday after all, will we?"

"No," he admitted, grudgingly, "but I've been thinking about riding in to the Mission to see what arrangements I can make."

Late Friday afternoon, Mary heard the pony's hoof-beats and John Henry's voice beside the wagon. "Ma," she heard him say, "try looking out for a minute." He had loosened the canvas as he leaned from the pony's back. She suspected him of doing it more to show off than to give her a view, but she appreciated the attention.

"The Deschutes," he said. There, tumbling over rocks down an incline and making a great ado over the descent, was the noisy river.

John Henry rode away to get a better look and Charles stepped back to speak to her.

"I've changed my mind about this business," he said "We have to ford the cattle, anyway. That will be hard enough. It will be worth the two dollars to ferry the wagon."

Mary was so relieved she could have cried. Ferrying the boisterous water was bad enough, even when you have no responsibility but to lie there and keep quiet, she thought.

At nooning on Saturday, Margaret climbed into the wagon, determination written all over her. She flounced down on the bed beside Mary and looked directly into her eyes, as if to say: Don't evade me. "What," she said, "is a squaw man? A squaw is a woman Indian, isn't she?"

Mary was almost surprised into laughter, but she managed to hold it down to a broad smile. "You are right," she agreed with the child, "A squaw is an Indian woman. People call a white man who has an Indian wife a 'squaw man' because they couldn't think of a better way to say it.

"What made you ask?"

"One of the Tebbetts girls said we were going to see a squaw man today. She heard her father say so.

"Do squaw men live in teepees or houses?"

"Whichever they like better, I guess," Mary answered. "Maybe we'll find out today."

After a while on the road again, Mary heard her voice, shrill enough to be heard by nearly everyone else, too. "A house, Mamma. He lives in a house."

"All right, all right," Mary called as loud as she could. All she could think of was that she did not want to encourage the child to carry on a conversation with her through the side of the wagon. It was too dangerous for the child to be that near, for the wagon was inching down a very steep hill. They were coming to Olney's creek, she knew, but where was Charles, that he had not made Margaret keep a safe distance? Then she heard him scolding. I never thought I'd be so glad to hear that, she told herself.

But he was not the same. His voice revealed the change. Dependent, as she had become, for much of her information, upon listening, her ears had developed an increasing sensitivity to voices. Now her ears were beginning to note a change in Charles's voice. As they neared their journey's end it grew sharper, more emphatic, but less firm.

Could it be that the end of the trail was more of a worry to him than wolves, or rivers, or steeps? Maybe he was just so tired that the thought of not having to brace himself much longer unnerved him? She could only listen and guess.

He even changed his mind about riding in to the Dalles. Sunday morning he said, "I think we'll all ride in to the Dalles together." Not only did the words not sound like Charles, the way he said them didn't sound like him either. More like an equal than the head of the family, she thought.

Then there was the last time they had to let the wagon down with ropes. He said, "I didn't think you'd have to go through this again."

Maybe it was the scenery, partly, she thought. Could the majestic sweep of the great basalt cliffs carved out by the Columbia have awed him that much?

If the broad sweep of the Columbia awed him, the city of the Dalles did not.

They had camped Sunday night at Five Mile Creek, named

for its distance from the town. Rain had started in the night and kept up for hours. What had been deep dust on Saturday became deep mud on Sunday. When the rain began again on Sunday, some of the mud thinned to mud puddles. Then wheels and hooves had conspired to spatter the muddy water everywhere within striking distance. Sunbonnets which, two days before had been stiff with dust, today were limp, wet, dirty rags.

The sudden change from hot and dry to cold and wet, alone, would have been sufficient to shiver anyone's timbers, but they were oh, so terribly tired.

Mary was propped up in bed with a rug over her and a coat around her shoulders. The children were all bundled up in their coats — except Baby Charles. He was rebelling against Pauline's baby jacket, as he sat propped up on the other bed beside Millie. He hadn't needed a jacket or any heavy clothes during the day since he had graduated from blankets and shawls.

Lot Whitcomb, who came with relief supplies in 1852 to aid the desperate members of the train.

– OREGON HISTORICAL SOCIETY

– OREGON HISTORICAL SOCIETY

The artist wrote that this Columbia River overlook
was at "the Dalles."

– OREGON HISTORICAL SOCIETY

The Cascades of the Columbia — also known as
the Great Falls of the Columbia River.

XIX

Awash at The Dalles

AS THE WAGON approached the town, she could tell how vastly disappointed Charles would be. He probably envisioned walking down the streets of a goodly village. Here was mostly a miserable tent and covered wagon camp, a noisy, messy scramble, with not more than five buildings of timber in all.

John Henry had mentioned the blacksmith shop and the two stores, she remembered. What he had not said was that those were all there were, and they, listening, had filled in a background of buildings in their minds.

The boy, of course was not at all aware of the discrepancy. He rode up, pointing up the hillside to some trees. "There's the mission, and over yonder, beyond, is the army post."

"Ride up and see whether they are expecting us," Charles told him.

John Henry came right back from that errand. "Everybody's gone," he said.

Charles, a bit dashed, wasn't going to admit it. "We'll set up camp for overnight," he said, "and I'll make arrangements for the trip down the river first thing. "I'm afraid a good many of these people are planning to do the same thing; I'd best get my oar in." If he was aware of the odd figure of speech, he gave no outward sign.

The two wagons were soon drawn up side by side in an area recently vacated, and Sister Carter came right over, a shawl over her head. "I told Mrs. Baker that I could handle things now that we aren't on the go. They wanted to stop farther out and not come into town tonight."

Mary felt suddenly bereft. Mrs. Baker had not even had a chance to say Goodbye. Surely that was the reason she hadn't.

Now the rain was coming down hard, and a strong wind was

chilling them to the bone. How could she ever have wished for rain?

When Charles came back from the landing, he was soaked to the bone, weary, and dispirited. "At least, we have ample time to see about the team," he said, trying to shake the dripping clothes out the back of the wagon and yet remain covered himself. He was accomplishing neither with any success, and looked miserable.

Mary could see that it was up to her to think of some kind of solace, although she felt a bit low on solace, herself. "After being on the way all this time, I should think one or two days, one way or the other, would hardly matter. After all," she managed to add lightly, "The first shall be last, and the last shall be first. "

Having once admitted a setback, he was determined to reveal the entire problem. He went doggedly on, "I find it's not a simple matter of booking passage on a steamer down to Portland or Oregon City. We have to take a flatboat, or something like that, down to a place in the river, the Cascades, where we wait to get passage on a steamer. They tell me there's a tent city there right now waiting for turns on the boats.

"But that's not the worst of it," he hastened on. "Folks here seem to think the fall rains have settled in."

Without any warning, Baby Charles began to wail at the top of his voice, as if he had understood every word and was taking appropriate action. It was so appropriate it was funny. The children laughed until tears ran down their cheeks.

Mary was too numb to laugh, but she did spread her lips into the effect of a smile. Charles was startled. His glance went around the wagon as if looking for someone who understood what he had said. They were still laughing when he turned up his collar and left the wagon.

That was the signal that brought them to their senses. They stopped laughing as quickly as they had begun. There was an awkward silence. Then Millie changed the subject.

"Mamma, remember how you used to rock us and sing 'Swing Low, Sweet Chariot'? You haven't ever sung it to Baby Charles, have you?"

"For one thing, we left the rocking chair home," Mary

answered, trying for a light tone. "For another, somehow singing that while we're on our way to Oregon almost seems disloyal," and she smiled to let them see they weren't to take her seriously.

"But Mamma," Millie pursued, "the rest of us were all brought up on it." She leaned over the baby. "Poor baby needs a sweet chariot, doesn't he?" Then she turned back to Mary. "Just because he was born on the way to Oregon doesn't mean he shouldn't have the same advantages, does it?"

She was joking on the surface, but Mary caught the wistful undertone that asked whether they had left their "advantages" behind.

For some reason, perhaps just because she was weak and tired, Mary felt like laughing and crying at the same time, and she could hardly keep her chin from trembling. "I guess, in a way, you might say you all were born on the way to Oregon," she began, "because your father was born in Kentucky, your mother in Tennessee, and we were married in Indiana. That's where you first four were born, you know. But did you ever think that it was while we were moving northward through the state? Then, after we crossed into Iowa, Pauline was born."

Millie looked thoughtful. "I guess God really was moving us to Oregon all the time."

"Well, He hasn't made it any too easy," Margaret came back tartly.

"Maybe He just wants to be sure we appreciate it when we get there," Millie piously responded.

Mary managed to shrug and cover up a shiver. "When I get well and we have another rocking chair, I'll sit in it and rock and sing 'Swing Low' until you all beg me to stop." Even as she said it, she had a peculiar feeling somehow linked to the extravagance of her promise. She always felt uneasy about "boasting of the morrow" as the Scriptures put it.

"Your mother is a silly for funning," she apologized.

"You sound more like yourself when you're funning," John Henry put in.

His tone was downright approving. She could feel herself flush with pleasure. The cramped, damp closeness of the wagon seemed almost cozy.

"Why, I feel better," she thought, and for a few minutes she was free of the feverish chills that had plagued her since the cold, wet weather had set in.

Charles was a long time getting back. He looked even more wet and tired and grim as he sat down across from Mary and put his hands on his knees as if he were trying to warm them. He cleared his throat awkwardly.

"We're going to be here a few days, at least. There are too many as bad off as we are ahead of us. We'll be lucky to get passage down the Columbia before the first of November.

They all sat huddled in the wagon. No one could think of a thing to say. They sat and listened as the rain pelted the canvas and spattered outside and the wind tugged and flapped at the edges of the wagon top. Every bit of equipment that hung from or leaned against the wagon rubbed and creaked. Somewhere a chain moved occasionally with an ominous, clanking sound. Though they had wrapped themselves in everything they could find and their combined body temperatures should have raised the temperature they were all chilling.

"A few days ago we couldn't imagine ever being cold," Millie chattered.

"Now we can't imagine ever being warm," Margaret added.

"Feast or famine," Mary sighed. "All those days crossing the desert I kept saying to myself, 'When I get to the Dalles I'll get up and get my strength back'."

"Once we get on a flatboat, we'll be just one more day from the end," Charles spoke with all his weariness, hope, despair, and awe. "Just one more day, and then you can begin getting your strength back. I promised I'd get us through, and I aim to."

"And Pa's got a pretty good aim," John Henry offered his own brand of awkward jocularity.

"I think this is the time for some Scripture and prayer," Charles continued, not really having heard what the boy said. "We need a powerful lot of help."

The next morning Charles had been gone only a short while before he was back with the word, "We've got passage, but I can't feel very good about it — and we have to hurry."

"How did you manage it?" they all wanted to know.

"Folks had a death and are going to stay to have the burial."

No one said a word until Charles stirred them to action with, "We'll have to hurry. The wind may shift at any time and they don't plan to wait until the wind is right."

"What about the Carters? Will they be going with us?"

"She has a chance to go on a raft at a cheaper rate. She may beat us to the Cascades, at that."

There really was no reason why Charles should not have talked to Mrs. Carter on the way back to his own wagon, Mary reminded herself. She felt irritable and befuddled. She realized that her fever was rising. Perhaps she would get sicker before she got better. The fever would have to run its course. Run its course! Odd — the river and the fever — running their course together. Her mind, dilated with surprise at stumbling onto the gruesome pun, posed her a question: How could her skin be so cold on the outside and so hot on the inside?

– W.R.E. STUDIO PICTURE COURTESY OF THE COLUMBIA RIVER PILOTS ASSN.
The river steamer *S.S. Multnomah* carried the Adams family from the Cascades to Portland. This photo was taken in 1853 when Rush Hoyt, Sr., was Captain.

XX

Down the Columbia

B
UT NOW THINGS WERE happening outside. Not in the general confusion of a whole camp, but just outside the wagon. The oxen were plodding along, blowing and moaning, hardly an arm's length from where she lay. She heard the creak and felt the shudder as John Henry lifted the tongue and snapped, shoved, and pulled the pieces of wood and metal together, his voice low and confident as he spoke to them.

She remembered the shrill enthusiasm the day he had called her to watch him demonstrate how well Ortho-Doxology were learning to step into place on command. She saw again John Henry proudly slipping the bows into place in a very fever of excitement and pride.

Fever! Now she had it — and not with pride! If she had any pride left she didn't know about it. Only the bitter humiliation of being utterly useless. Even in the shadows of the dark wagon she knew she must be a pitiful sight. Under the dirty covers her hands were repulsive claws with dried tissue over the bones for skin. If the air would only warm a little she could maybe sit up and get her strength back.

How she wished she could be strong enough to get out of the wagon when they got to Portland, to put her feet on the ground and stand there even in the rain, to look around her and say, "So that is what we've come for," and hear her family laugh at her funning. Maybe there would be time enough. Charles had said there would be a day or two after they reached the Cascades where they were to portage and camp before going on down. He had said something about driving down from the Cascades if the roads were passable.

If, if, if! If they had got to Oregon in time they might have got down to the Willamette Valley by that new road of the Barlows. But they hadn't come in time. And why hadn't they come in time? Because she had held them back. Now there was snow in the mountains, rain and mud down along the river, and she could well imagine what the wind was doing to the river itself. What the family told her and what she overheard from passersby she pieced together with rueful pricks.

Well, it was too late to do anything but take their chances sailing down a river Millie said looked almost as big as the Mississippi. And the wind that would fill their sails was a cold one right off the nearby mountain.

She dreaded it — oh how she dreaded it. Millie told her how they filled those flatboats with wagons and stock and people, how they jerked out into the main stream, and how swiftly they were out of sight.

Soon everything she had left would be rushing down the surface of that river.

Suddenly she jerked back to reality. She must have dozed off. The girls were back in the wagon with the baby and the wagon was moving down an incline.

From the sounds she could tell that their wagon was one of several — maybe they were passing a line of wagons, she couldn't be sure. She could have asked the girls, but they were chattering among themselves as they went back and forth in the cramped and lurching wagon, now to look ahead, now to look behind, the baby sputtering cheerfully as long as someone was carrying him and he was part of the hubbub.

Once Margaret snorted, "This doesn't look like any garden to me. Hardly any trees, and mostly rock. Just look at those big bare hills over there."

The girls were shivering from excitement as well as from cold, Mary thought.

When the wagon stopped, Mary could hear the hollow sounds that the animals made as they stamped on the wharf. And she could hear the river rushing and sloshing below.

Then Millie, now at the front, called, "What are we stopped for here, Pa?

Charles's controlled voice came back, "They haven't got the word up to us yet."

It was not long after that before Charles came back to explain that they had to remove their canvas tops before they could board the sailboat.

Mary was in panic. It would be like being in bed out in the street!

Charles allayed her dismay. They would just take the canvas off the hoops and lay it flat. He and John Henry would do it so that she would be neither exposed nor smothered.

The rain was still pounding down hard and Mary couldn't see how they could do it without getting everything in the wagon sopping wet, but she couldn't do anything about it herself and she was almost beyond caring.

First, John Henry brought the canvas pieces that had been used for side tents. They extended over the beds quite well and provided good protection while the tops were being taken down. Helping hands soon pulled the loosened tops off the hoops and then forward under them, clear to the back of the front seat. The girls cheerfully suggested that they now had a nice cave with plenty of air space.

Sister Carter looked in to assure her, "It won't be more than a few hours."

Then they were jerking forward again, and with each shift down the incline the sounds of the river came closer and closer. Soon the wagon wheels were echoing hollowly on the boards to the flatboat, and the motion and sound of the water created a frightening obligato to the more familiar ones. Millie stood behind the wagon seat, holding the baby and sharing what she could see with her mother. The other three girls sat in state on the seat.

Charles and John Henry were with the teams.

If Mary could be thankful for anything at the moment it was that she was out of sight, and that no one could read the helpless, frightened state of her mind.

Finally, there were shouted commands, jerks, cries of passengers. For a moment Mary thought they were tipping — but no, they were gathering momentum and adjusting to the current of the river. They were on their way down the Columbia. The wind in the sails above them was mercifully clearing the air, even under the canvas, but that wind was cold and wet.

Exclamations about how narrow the river was getting, how steep the hillsides, how deep the forests — all came through a quivering screen of fevered chill. Beneath were the sickening undulations of the water.

How long it was before they bumped and scraped to a landing she didn't know, but it must have been hours. Getting off the boat took nearly as long as the trip, she guessed, for it was dark when they finally lumbered down the planking onto solid ground once more.

"Not much place to camp here," she heard Charles say. "We'll go on to the edge under the trees." She could hear the girls commenting on wagons they recognized as the shifting flare of one campfire after another reflected on the canvas and hoops. The girls were gratefully noting that there was plenty of wood for a warm fire.

Then Charles shouted "There" and the wagon stopped. He lifted an edge of the canvas, "John Henry will borrow a fire. I think we can buy something to eat. There's a store ahead. Anything to get us through the night. Chances of our getting passage right on down the river in the morning seem pretty good. Folks say an extra steamboat is running now."

"I said I'd get you through, and I will. This cold and wet aren't doing you any good, and we're getting to decent shelter as fast as we can."

All night Mary could hear the wind in the trees overhead. She marveled that it could sound so much like the river. Sometimes during the long darkness she thought she was back on the river. She slept fitfully, dreams emerging from her hopes, fears, and memories with a weird malice that mocked her troubled efforts to sort them out. A few times she thought that she had made some sounds in her sleep, but the children gave no sign of being disturbed. Charles and John Henry had bedded down under the wagon and kept the fire going throughout the night.

Perhaps it was the comparative comfort of the sheltering trees, the fire, and the thought of being near the end of the journey. Whatever it was, Mary felt better in the morning. Charles lifted the canvas at the front to make it more like a lean-to over the wagon bed. Between flurries of rain, an occasional acquaintance of the Trail stopped by to speak to her and wish her well.

Some of them were talking about going on down a way by road and staying on the north side of the river. It was fine land, they said, and was soon to become a new state. They seemed exhilarated by the choices.

From the river came the sounds of bells and toots of steam whistles; all kinds of river craft must have been at the lower landings.

Despite the bleak weather and camp confusion, their camp afforded a sense of refuge, tucked in a sort of six-mile pocket of land where protective tree-covered slopes behind caught the brunt of the wind and provided ample firewood.

One more day on the trail, and then they could look for a place to settle down. Mary's spirits lifted. One more day and then she could begin to get well. One more day and they could put the horror of the past month behind them and begin a new life. She felt so optimistic for a few minutes that she tried to sit up unaided. Then she knew how weak she was. A wave of discouragement engulfed her.

At that moment who should poke her head in but Sister Carter. Even she looked pale and drawn. Her trip down on the raft hadn't done her any good. She vowed that nothing would get her back on that river again. She was going to take the road up to a nearby town and catch her breath, she said. She had been carrying a twin on each hip, but Margaret came by and took one of them, Mary didn't notice which.

Mamie was holding Baby Charles. Margaret carried the twin over and sat down beside her near the campfire. There the two played with their live dolls together, while Millie was cleaning up after breakfast.

Mrs. Baker came along just then, and the women greeted each other as if they had been separated for weeks instead of a day. When Mrs. Baker learned of the Carters' plans, she remonstrated, "The *Multnomah* will have us all down to Portland in about three hours. I just heard some men bragging about how safe and fast that boat is."

Charles was coming up, and she turned to him. "Don't you think Sister Carter should take passage with the rest of us on the

Multnomah?"

"Sister Carter has had a rough time of it," he answered rather abruptly, "and I'll let her make her decisions for her own family." Then, briskly, "We'd best get down to the landing and be ready."

He turned to Sister Carter, "'Til we meet again."

"'Til we meet again," she answered quietly. Then shifting the twin to the other hip, she came close to the wagon beside Mary and spoke low enough for her ear alone. "Good Methodists will be more likely to show you hospitality if we aren't tagging along with you. Goodbye, Sister Adams, we'll soon be better off. Of that we can be sure."

She left hurriedly. The boys, John Henry and the two Carters, prolonged the leave-taking with youthful, joking advice and promises. Margaret walked a way with the twin she had been playing with, finally relinquishing her to Amos.

"I declare, if I've said it once I've said it a thousand times, those children do get along together." Mrs. Baker handed a warm, wet washcloth to Mary, who murmured drowsily from around the edges of its soothing, "Uh-huh."

The feel of it reminded Mary of how wonderful it would be to climb into a tub of warm water by the kitchen fire on Saturday night once again. She hadn't had anything but a lick and a promise for so long that it was hard to believe that the luxury of a Saturday night tubbing in the privacy of their own kitchen might be only days away.

She was chilling again before they set out for the landing where the *Multnomah* would take them the rest of the way.

"I'll leave the top over the seat hoop," Charles offered, "and let the girls ride under cover. The wind is still from the east. I guess you don't feel like seeing out, anyway," he added, as he pulled the canvas down around the edge by Mary.

Soon the wagon was moving again — one among many, judging from the hubbub all around them. The girls were excited and noisy, calling to those they recognized and exclaiming over the portage railway on its wooden bridging, the "dear little donkey" pulling the cart full of luggage and freight between the railings. The closer they came to the landing, the greater the confusion of sound, no longer muted by distance, but harsh and insistent. Among the voices Mary heard a girl asking, "Is that the wagon with the sick woman in it?"

The answer was drowned by a man's exclamation and laugh, "Yep, that's the barrel boat all right."

Mary wondered whether the people out West had taken to putting barrels together for boats.

"I can almost see where she was put together," a companion voice agreed. "How many parts did you say she was shipped out in?"

"Don't know as I could say exactly. She may not be purty — looks like a scow that got converted to a side-wheeler, don't she — but she shore makes time, and that's what we're running out of."

Charles's voice cut across the others as he called to the girls to get into the back of the wagon while they were boarding.

Soon they were rumbling onto the boat. She could distinguish Charles's voice and John Henry's as they "talked the team" into its place.

The girls were looking out from behind the seat. "Look at the cage on the smokestack!" Margaret laughed.

A man's voice answered, "That thing you call a cage is a spark-arrester, little girl. Keeps sparks from flyin' out and settin' fires."

After that, time was a troubled dream. The strident sounds of whistles and gongs, the heavy thudding of wood being loaded to stoke the engine, which was beginning to get up steam, the water "chunking" and swishing around the paddle wheels, the pipe organ sounds of the wind, the staccato insistence of the rain, the pervasive smells of wet wood and wet woolens — all created a kaleidoscope of sensation in which her own sense of discomfort shifted wearily.

Once, in the swirl of sound in motion, Mary heard a voice saying, "The woman is very ill. We must get her to Dr. Wilson as quickly as possible. His hospital is not far from where we tie up in Portland."

"Poor woman," Mary thought. "She must be going to die. I've never known anyone who went to a hospital that didn't die."

Then she heard Charles's voice quite close to her ear, "Mary hang on. We're almost there. I told you I'd get us through and I will."

It must have been about that time that she heard shouts and exclamations about Fort Vancouver. Millie was trying to describe it to her — something about "a real town along the water ... a huge stockade ... big ships at anchor ... a big log house set 'way back ... cannon in front ..."

Then the man's voice came through again. "Little girl, why don't you take the baby out on deck where the air is better. The rain has stopped. Here, let me help you down."

A voice said, "Thank you, Captain Fountleroy."

———

Outside Millie spied a piece of wood, a small section of split log. "Why, Charlie," she exclaimed, "here's a rocking chair!" She settled herself on the split side and, holding him close, began crooning "Swing Low, Sweet Chariot."

———

Inside, Mary was way back home in Tennessee. She must have been playing awfully hard, she was so hot and tired, and she was almost out of breath. Her mother's cool hand felt good on her forehead as she smoothed back her hair. "Oh, Mamma," she whispered, "It's so nice to be back home."

The loving hand went on soothingly as she sang the old song she had always sung to Mary as a lullaby,

> Swing low, sweet chariot
> Comin' for to carry me home.
> Swing low, sweet chariot,
> Comin' for to carry me home.

———

They buried Mary in the cemetery located where the Skidmore Fountain now stands in Old Portland. When the growing city demanded the removal of that cemetery, Charles moved her grave out to a section of the land claim which he and Eleanor had established on February 11, 1853. (They had waited two months after Mary's death to be married, on January 10, 1853.)

241

Today, a short drive south from Portland, between Oregon City and Mollala, one may find the pioneer cemetery at Carus, where Mary's grave remains, marked by a simple stone which reads, "Mary, Wife of Charles Adams. Died Nov. 11, 1852."

Joined by the marriage of Eleanor and Charles, the two families became so thoroughly one that Constance, the daughter of Samantha, did not know that Charles was not her real grandfather until his death, and Kenneth, grandson of Margaret, did not even know of Mary Vowell Adams until her grave was rediscovered.

The baby born on the plains thrived, went to the university, occasionally escorted a young lovely, but never married. To the family's surprise, his will disclosed that he had left his estate to his three unmarried sisters, Pauline, Mamie and Irene. (Irene was actually a half-sister, born to Eleanor and Charles.)

"Baby Charles" had grown up to be, as the Salem Statesman noted at his death, "One of the first W.U. men." Containing eulogies by such pillars as A. N. Moores and E. M. LaFore, the newspaper account concluded, "Tender in his sympathies, true to his friends, never uttering profanities, strictly temperate, standing four-square all the time, Mr. Adams was a man the like of whom makes the real backbone of a nation and gives hope for the perpetuation of genuine civilization."

Whenever Millie was questioned about how soon her father remarried, she was able to say — deceptively, if truthfully — that it was the "next year." Millie kept much from that year deep in her heart and finally was able to confide some of it to her daughter Jennette.

Whether Millie's father ever suffered any sense of guilt is not known, but those still living who remember him certainly saw no sign of it. As for the rest of us who cherish our Northwest heritage — we know that many, like Mary, were destroyed by the westering wave. We accept their sacrifice as necessary to winning the West.

Mary lived in a day when women had no rights and little status. Many a home fire was banked with smoldering resentment. Neither was she the first, nor yet the last, to die for something in which she could not believe — for what someone else had established as duty.

– OREGON HISTORICAL SOCIETY

Skidmore Fountain was erected over the site of the first
cemetery in Portland where the body of Mary Adams was
first buried.

First photo taken of Front Street, Portland, in 1852.

BILL'S SKETCHES were drawn on a small pad cupped in his hand "on location" of the filming of the motion picture "The Way West," based on the novel of the same title written by A.B. Guthrie. Studio technicians had spent more than a little time to produce realistic replicas of the travel equiment used on the Oregon Trail.

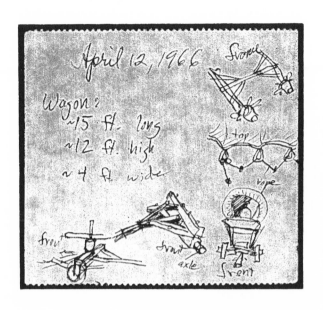

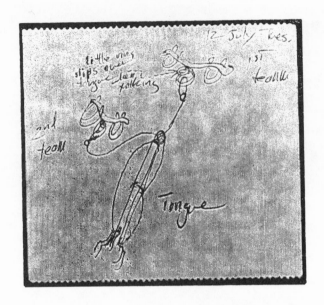

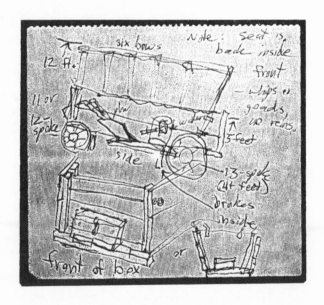

In Lieu of a Bibliography

As early as 1942 some of the notes for this chronicle were assembled. But long before that, anecdotes, family expressions, and general information fluttered into mental pigeonholes, and Jennette Meredith Lockhart (Mrs. E. B.) kept a valuable file of clippings.

Constance French Hodder, the daughter of Samantha Carter French, gave help along with the rest of the family.

Margaret Legge Criffith (Mrs. Wallace) and her brother Kenneth Legge are grandchildren of Margaret Adams Smith.

Jennette Meredith Brown (Mrs. Rodney) and her brother John Phillip Meredith are the grandchildren of Millie Adams Meredith and the children of Frank Meredith, Millie's son.

Two other descendants mentioned in the acknowledgements are Pauline Lockhart McMahon and William Lockhart Bliss, sister and son, respectively, of the author. Each of them went on helpful trips — Pauline, through Idaho and Eastern Oregon, and Bill, to the Way West location out of Bend. There the friendly caretakers answered questions and allowed close inspection of the covered wagons and the oxen in their charge. Bill, using what bits of paper were at hand, made his sketches on the spot.

Of the 1852 diaries written on the Oregon Trail, the most valuable has been that of Cecelia Emily McMillen Adams. Although she taught the first school in Hillsboro, Oregon, no known picture of her survives, according to her descendants. Next in importance, to this work, was that of Alvah Isaiah Davis. Others that should be mentioned were those of E. W. Conyers, John T. Kerns, the Rev. John McAllister (all these through the Oregon Historical Society) and the journal of William Cornell (the property of State Archivist David Duniway.)

Microfilm obtained through the Genealogy Clearing House was valuable for census records of 1820, 1850, and 1860. Microfilm made possible reading all the issues of WESTERN CHRISTIAN ADVOCATE, 1850-54, and all the early copies of the OREGON SPECTATOR, the OREGONIAN, and the STATESMAN.

Copies of the 1851 WESTERN AMERICAN were made by Mrs. M.C. Wheelwright, researcher, Des Moines, Iowa.

— Beatrice Lockhart Bliss

MARY VOWELL ADAMS

The story of Mary Vowell Adams differs only in the details from that of many other girls born along the eastern coast of the United States in the first quarter of the nineteenth century. Born in Tennessee in 1816 and given little, if any schooling, while the family was westering, by 1838, she was living in Greencastle, Indiana. There, on September 13, she was married to Charles Adams. He was born near Louisville, Kentucky, January 18, 1818, and had come to Louisiana with his parents when he was nine years old.

The spelling of her surname may have been a phonetic form of the name Vowle, one found in Kentucky in 1800, or Voyles, the name of nine families in Washington County, Indiana, by 1820.

The idea that "reading and writing" were wasted on girls seems to have had a strong hold on the people of that area at that time, and the results may be scanned in the census records of a little town in Iowa for the year 1850. Cedar Township, with 608 inhabitants by the census record, had a very few local wives who could read or write. Indeed, many of the men, according to that record, suffered the same limitation. At least twenty-nine adults were so listed. Five of them were born in North Carolina; eleven from Kentucky; others from Ohio and Vermont.

A list of occupations, unfamiliar to the modern ear, includes innkeeper, cooper, wagon-maker, blacksmith, miller, saddler, silversmith, tailor, and shoemaker — all were common enough in Washington County, Iowa, in the census of 1850. Farmers, of course, predominated.

Charles Adams married Mary Vowell, who gave her name as "Polly," on September 13, 1838, according to the Putnam County records at Greencastle, Indiana; she, twenty-one, and possibly older; he, not yet twenty.

To that union came first a son, John Henry; then, July 2, 1841, their first daughter, Millie, after they had moved to a place near Crawfordsville. Next came Margaret Jane, November 26, 1842, and Mary Elizabeth in 1844. After they had moved on to Iowa in 1846, came. Pauline.

In 1850 one Charles Baldwin took the government census of

Van Buren County, Iowa. On August 29, in Cedar Township, he dutifully recorded the twelfth family visited as that of Charles Adams, 33; Mary, 35; John Henry, 11; Millie, 10; Margaret, 8; Mary, 6; Pauline, 4.

Just a few houses before that, he had listed the family of Robert Carter, 32; Eleanor, 30. Their children are listed as Amos, 8, and William, 5. The twins he listed by the initials AA and AY. They were actually Miranda Jane and Samantha Ann, born too recently to have been named, perhaps.

Charles Baldwin could not have known as he went from house to house that the future of these two families would be dramatically intertwined in the next few years.

In later life, Charles Adams made much of having been converted when he was twenty-one (after his marriage) and having immediately become a Class Leader in the Methodist Church. The Iowa Annual Conference Journals make no reference to an organized work at Cedar Township, but the Iowa Conference was not organized until 1844, and "much local work in a variety of spots ... did not receive Conference recognition until much later," according to Dr. Louis A. Hazelmayer, of Iowa Wesleyan College. That both families worked together in the church which they considered Methodist is certain.

Charles and Mary Adams sold their 80-acre farm for $594 to William C. Snider, on March 8, 1852, and were soon joining the great migration to Oregon, despite Mary's sense of foreboding.

Also on the road to Oregon were the McMillens, whose daughter, Cecelia, kept an excellent diary of the day-to-day events of the Trail. Some of the McMillen party took passage on the same steamer that Charles and Mary took down the Columbia. A number of the incidents which Cecelia recorded happened to the Adams family. They came down the Columbia in a bitterly cold storm of wind and rain on the second of November, 1852.

The Davis diary of the same year indicates that Mr. Davis's path also coincided, at times, with the others mentioned, but he was traveling lighter and faster, and was well ahead of them at the end of the trail.

Based on these records and substantiated facts in this book — the story of Mary Vowell Adams and her life between

February and November 11, 1852.

The present site of Mary's grave near Carus, Oregon.
(From the author's collection.)